Rupayan Mukherjee and Jaydip Sarkar (eds.)

Popular Literature
Texts, Contexts, Contestations

Rupayan Mukherjee and Jaydip Sarkar (eds.)

POPULAR LITERATURE
Texts, Contexts, Contestations

Bibliografische Information der Deutschen Nationalbibliothek
Die Deutsche Nationalbibliothek verzeichnet diese Publikation in der Deutschen Nationalbibliografie; detaillierte bibliografische Daten sind im Internet über http://dnb.d-nb.de abrufbar.

Bibliographic information published by the Deutsche Nationalbibliothek
Die Deutsche Nationalbibliothek lists this publication in the Deutsche Nationalbibliografie; detailed bibliographic data are available in the Internet at http://dnb.d-nb.de.

ISBN-13: 978-3-8382-1666-9
© *ibidem*-Verlag, Stuttgart 2022
Alle Rechte vorbehalten

Das Werk einschließlich aller seiner Teile ist urheberrechtlich geschützt. Jede Verwertung außerhalb der engen Grenzen des Urheberrechtsgesetzes ist ohne Zustimmung des Verlages unzulässig und strafbar. Dies gilt insbesondere für Vervielfältigungen, Übersetzungen, Mikroverfilmungen und elektronische Speicherformen sowie die Einspeicherung und Verarbeitung in elektronischen Systemen.

All rights reserved. No part of this publication may be reproduced, stored in or introduced into a retrieval system, or transmitted, in any form, or by any means (electronic, mechanical, photocopying, recording or otherwise) without the prior written permission of the publisher. Any person who does any unauthorized act in relation to this publication may be liable to criminal prosecution and civil claims for damages.

Printed in the EU

To Naughty, Titli, Tintin and Rai
The Irreducibles

Preface and Acknowledgements

As we introduce the present volume, the Pandemic has frowned once more. The National newspapers accompany our morning coffee with information of newer breaths becoming air; news channels tirelessly report on the mortality records that are being continuously unmade and remade with each passing hour. It is perhaps impossible to escape a growing sense of nihilism which is slowly adapting to this catastrophe of humanity. An intimidated consciousness, increasingly made aware of the fragility of existence, has often pondered if one can afford to write when the elementary premise of survival has been jeopardised. As we wrecked our brains off and laboured with our mediocrity to produce the book you have in hand, we increasingly realised that we, as the intelligentsia, still live within the ivory towers of indifference. While Rome burnt and is burning still, we lived and are still living warm within our world of reading and writing, contentedly fiddling our thoughts.

Our only apology can be that as scholars and learners of Literature, reading and writing is the only possible mode of response available to us. Armed with no other techne but a nominal ability to read and write, we can only pursue the same, even in the time of exception or emergency. Also, wisdom has so long enlightened us about the need to read, about the possible vitality which reading promotes on the face of adversity. The Bible had helped a shipwrecked and an islanded Crusoe to regain hope; the photograph of an unknown boy seated amidst the ruins of Blitz and reading has become the image of sustenance. For all of us who were quarantined and isolated, either due to the disease in us or due to the disease in us of catching the disease, reading could serve as the only possible mode of dialoguing with the world, of responding to the ailment of the age. We chose to read and deliberately read literatures which are often identified as 'Popular' — an adjective that corresponds to forbidden categories like 'collective', 'mass', 'multitude' which, in these times that are being consistently eclipsed and overshadowed by the fear of contagion, have been heavily controlled, governed, censored and partitioned. Marooned in our secluded islands of solitude, we could not conceive of a better escape from our inferno of isolation. We read and wrote on Popular Literature because it allowed us, even if feebly, to engage with the intimation of the forbidden fruit called mass.

While the Pandemic has possibly been an immediate motive for us, one can also contemplate this volume as a response to the prevalent trends of academic thought that are often guided by, almost unconsciously, hierarchical considerations. In our academic circuits, we often come across high-brow Arnoldian academicians who cherish a firm faith that the term 'Popular Literature' is a fanciful oxymoron. For them, Popular and Literature are an irreconcilable twain which can never meet. One of ourselves had once encountered a superannuated Professor who had expressed his discontent at the incorporation of 'trivial texts' like *Half Girlfriend* and *Sonar Kella* (*The Golden Fortress*) in the recently modified syllabus of English major in Indian academia. Such texts, he observed gravely, lacked 'serious substance'. He had, in that same conversation, also lamented the fact that Shakespeare was now taught by 'anyone and everyone' which, in his erudite opinion, was a heinous act of sacrilege. After all, not everyone could do justice to the genius of the visionary Bard! The listener was tempted but refrained, keeping in mind the reverence that the senior deserved, from asking "But then...he was a Popular playwright on the Elizabethan stage, wasn't he? Then how could he be substantial?"

The present volume has tried to look beyond such reductive tendencies of reading which fail to find substance in Popular Literary works. The chapters have tried to trace serious contentions in Popular literary texts and have tried to interpret canonical literary texts as Popular Literature. In doing so, the book has tried to problematise the idea of Popular Literature and has proposed that, contrary to reigning presuppositions, Popular Literature is not an easily determinable category which can be unproblematically identified with the frivolous. Above all, it has tried to contemplate the possibilities of reading beyond hierarchical presumptions. The volume can claim its success only if it manages to prompt young readers to read, reflect and think non-hierarchically and without presumptuous biases.

The Book would not have been possible without our contributors who have generously provided us their labours. We are grateful to all of them, particularly to Madhuparna Mitra Guha who has managed to provide us her piece within a very short notice. We take this opportunity to thank ibidem press for expressing their interest in the work and extending their whole hearted support to ensure the deliverance of the book.

Finally, we are grateful to our family for providing us the necessary support and comfort by ensuring that no mundane concerns of everyday intervened into our Minerva towers of contemplation.

Rupayan Mukherjee
Jaydip Sarkar
7th April, 2021

Contents

Preface and Acknowledgements 7

Rupayan Mukherjee
Introduction 13

Section I. Juvenile Literature 37

Rupayan Mukherjee
The Proper and the Pure: Biopolitics, Law and Sujectivity in
Rudyard Kipling's *The Jungle Book* 39

Arnab Dasgupta
Making the Chessboard Smooth: Popular as "Nonsense" in
Through the Looking Glass 61

Mitarik Barma
Narrative Function and Identity in Paulo Coelho's
The Alchemist 73

Section II. Science Fiction 99

Shirsendu Mondal
Hail the Monster and Fie the Man: The Construction of
Monstrosity in *Frankenstein* 101

Rajadipta Roy
Rethinking Sciences, Situations and Bamboo-groves in Ray's
Science Fictions: *Guessing Who Speaks What* 117

Jaydip Sarkar
Utopia as Dystopia: Subjectivity at the Limits of Subjection in
Ray Bradbury's *Fahrenheit 451* 139

Section III. Crime and Detective Fiction 159

Pinaki Roy
Reclaiming the Elementaries of Context: Ponderings on
Doyle's *The Hound of the Baskervilles* 161

Mandika Sinha
"Our mysterious neighbour, Mr. Poirot": Locating the 'Other'
Detective in *The Murder of Roger Ackroyd* 179

Shubham Dey and Rupayan Mukherjee
"What Shall I see in my dreams tonight?": Reading the
Repressed in Wilkie Collins's *The Woman in White* 193

Section IV. Romance 207

Puja Chakraborty
Trauma as Calamity or Capital?: The Aporia of Representation
and the Ethics of Reading in Anne Frank's *The Diary of a Young
Girl* 209

Jaya Sarkar and *Goutam Karmakar*
Phantasmagoria of the Hegemonic Cultural Structure:
Interrogating the Indian Urban Facade in Chetan Bhagat's
Half Girlfriend 223

Madhuparna Mitra Guha and Rupayan Mukherjee
Relocating the Classic as Popular: Reading *Jane
Eyre* as a Romance. 239

Post Script 257

Anisha Ghosh
Why my Children Love Cinderella and I Don't: Negotiations
with a Classic-Popular Fairy Tale 259

About the Contributors 273

Introduction

Rupayan Mukherjee

> Artists are the antennae of the race, but the bullet-headed
> many will never learn to trust their great artists.
> Ezra Pound

> You are the majority — in number and intelligence,
> therefore you are the power — which is justice.
> Charles Baudelaire

In the world's largest democracy, where the contagion of post-truth is increasingly saturating the political climate, the word 'Popular' has started to evoke an unpleasant stench. The stench is swiftly identifiable, almost equable, with a headless mass that gather wisdom from WhatsApp universities, uncritically ruminate the ideologies that are propagated by the system and are deeply convinced by the predictable tendencies of Populist politics. As diverse governments introduce innovative policies which are directed only at their target vote-banks (determined on the principle of majority), as celebrities (mostly 'stars' from mainstream entertainment industry) participate in musical chairs to contest in impending elections and deliver popular dialogues in their electoral campaigns to acquire political credibility among the gathered swarming flock, as gross numbers are written, sung and played at political meetings to please the accumulated public, the stench grows an olf more. *All the perfumes of Arabia* fail to sweeten the stench that intensifies with each report of mob-lynching and *khaap-panchayat* where the overwhelming mass subjects the singular, who is often an already disenfranchised subject, to the brutalities of collective violence. Ironically though, the same stenching people who populate the signifier 'Popular' ought to be "solemnly resolved to constitute India into a Sovereign Socialist Secular Democratic Republic" and must possess a rudimentary political consciousness and wisdom to preserve and perpetuate the Spirit of the Nation. The irony around the people and popular, like gravity, is so founded and encompassing that it is barely noticed. Only a contemplative Hamlet or an unkempt but unconforming Berenger[1] who has not yet turned into a rhinoceros is able to notice that *Something is rotten in the State (pun intended) of the World's largest democracy.*

These Hamlets and Berengers are critical of the evolving populist tendencies of governance which relies on the strategic use of the "empty signifier" (Chatterjee 2020, 91) called 'people' to manufacture a climate of political antagonism between "...the people and their enemy". (Ibid., 100) The polarised categories of 'the people' and its 'enemy' are often floating in nature and is often conceptualised on "...existing solidarities such as ethnic, linguistic or religious identity" as well as "...new solidarities...such as distinctions between the wealthy few and the exploited many, or domiciles and immigrants, or a party long entrenched in power and those excluded." (Ibid.) Populist politics is thus relational in nature, for its validation and sustenance, it has to imagine and invent an Other.

This Other-oriented essence of the Popular is not exclusive to the domain of the political. It is also equally relevant and fundamental to an evaluation of Popular Literature. Defining and determining Popular Literature is impossible without considering its arch-other category called Literature. Ken Gelder's thoughtful observations on Popular Fiction elucidate that although Popular Fiction and Literature are "...mutually antagonistic, but they need each other for their self-definition." (Gelder 2004, 13) This relational need of the Other to act as a Foil, and thereby determine, fashion and validate the self, suggests the formulation of an identity in difference.

Gelder identifies a host of contexts, characteristics and aspects on whose premises the *identity in difference* of Popular Fiction is established: artistic intention, craftsmanship and readership being fundamental among them. In other words, he argues that the field of Popular Fiction characteristically departs from Literature in their intention "to reach a large number of readers" (Ibid., 20), in their preference for simplicity and an ingenuous and unproblematic repulsion towards "tangled plots" and "intense formal artistry" (Ibid., 19), and in promoting and catering to a readership that is unthinking and does not read "seriously" (Ibid., 23) but "uncritically" (Ibid., 38), solely for leisure and entertainment.

Jacques Derrida's ponderings on the idea of Literature exposit the nuances that are often inextricably associated with the discourse of literature and the literary. Derrida, unlike Gelder, does not necessarily consort to an essentialist understanding of Literature as "the kind of writing...produced by...Jane Austen, George Elliot, Henry James, James Joyce, William Faulkner..." (Ibid. 11) which "...deploys a set of logics and practices that are different in kind to those deployed in the field of popular fiction". (Ibid. 12) For Derrida, literature is not an exclusive category that is hierarchically distinguished from its other — Popular fiction. Instead, Derrida understands literature as a "strange institution" (Derrida 1992 (b), 36) marked by a characteristic paradox. Derrida explains this paradox as follows:

> ""What is literature?"; literature as historical institution with its conventions, rules, etc., but also this institution of fiction which gives in principle the power to say everything, to break free of the rules, to displace them...The institution of Literature in the West, in its relatively modern form, is linked to an authorization to say everything..." (Ibid., 37)

In what follows, Derrida argues that the "institution of literature in the West in its relatively modern form..." shares a correspondence with the "modern idea of democracy". (Ibid.) However, that is not our concern for the time being. Instead, we are interested in Derrida's forked understanding of "The space of literature" as "...not only that of an instituted fiction but also a fictive institution which in principle allows one to say everything." (Ibid., 36) Literature, as Derrida argues, is suggestive of an ambiguity and holds together contrary tendencies. On the one hand, literature for Derrida is overarchingly accommodative/ absorptive as it "allows one to say everything, in every way" (Ibid.) and thus "is an institution which tends to overflow the institution." (Ibid.) Simultaneously, Derrida observes, answering the epistemological question "What is literature" seems 'unserious' without "an analysis of my time at school...and of the family in which I was born, of its relation or nonrelation with books, etc." (Ibid.) Hence, Literature seems to be suggestive of a characteristic paradox. It is, on the one hand, essentially (almost irreducibly) free and non-hierarchical that absorbs all that is written. Simultaneously, its essence is determined and construed by the intricate considerations of the cultural-ideological. Derrida also observes that "...there is no text which is literary *in itself.*" (Ibid., 44). Instead, the essence of the literary, which Derrida calls "literarity", "is the correlative of an intentional relation to the text, an intentional relation which integrates in itself, as a component or an intentional layer, the more or less implicit consciousness of rules which are conventional or institutional—social, in any case." (Ibid.) For Derrida, literature is often influenced by the poetics of reading which is fundamental to the intentional relation that the reader has with the text. Intention, in its phenomenological connotation, holds the reader as much responsible as the author in determining the nature and essence of the literary. Terry Eagleton observes that "All literary works...are 'rewritten', if only unconsciously, by the societies which read them; indeed there is no reading of a work which is not also a 're-writing'". (Eagleton 1996 (a), 11) Of course, Derrida is quick to mention that he does not interpret or understand literarity as "...merely projective or subjective—in the sense of empirical subjectivity or caprice of each reader". (Derrida 1992(b), 44) Instead, Derrida claims, "The essence of literature, if we hold to this word essence, is produced as a set of objective rules in an original history of the "acts" of inscription and reading". (Ibid., 45) For Derrida, "the literary character of the text is inscribed on the side of the intentional object, in its noematic structure...and not only on the subjective side of the noetic act." (Ibid., 44) The obtuse expressions 'noetic' and 'noematic' have phenomenological references and J Hillis Miller observes that "Noetic means "apprehended by the intellect alone", while noematic refers to "...features in what is to be known that makes them knowable, subject to noesis". (Miller 2002, 62) The noematic in a literary text, as Derrida opines, is constituted by ""in" the text features which call for the literary reading and recall the convention, institution, or history of literature". (Derrida 1992(b), 44) Reading, for Derrida, is very much in concordance with this noematic structure and the positionality of the reader is a subjectivity that 'includes' and recognises "the noematic structure" (Ibid.). The reader is thus "linked to an intersubjective and transcendental community" (Ibid.) and reading as an act is an always-already institutionalised and ideologised enterprise.

Interrogating the Canon

Terry Eagleton introspects into the indisputable pertinence of ideology in determining the literary worth (or what we might, contrary to Eagleton's claim, dare to call literary essence) of a text and in categorising Literature as a discipline. Rather clairvoyantly, Eagleton asserts that "Literature, in the meaning of the word we have inherited, is an ideology". (Eagleton 1996, 19) Eagleton's socialist commitment haunts his genealogical interrogations on the origin of the institute called Literature and he finds in the promotion of the ideology of literature an organised endeavor to sugar-coat typical middle-class sensibilities. He further argues that the canonisation of 'English Literature' in England had happened in the early twentieth century, in the aftermath of World War I and with the inauguration of English Departments in the ancient Universities like Oxford and Cambridge. Reflecting on the influential role that the Cambridge based journal *Scrutiny* played in determining the trajectory of English Literature and developing the canon, Eagleton observes:

"*Scrutiny* redrew the map of English literature in ways from which criticism has not yet recovered. The main thoroughfares on this map ran through Chaucer, Shakespeare, Jonson, the Jacobeans and Metaphysicals, Bunyan, Pope, Samuel Johnson, Blake, Wordsworth, Keats, Austen, George Eliot, Hopkins, Henry James, Joseph Conrad, T.S. Eliot and D.H. Lawrence. This was 'English literature': Spencer, Dryden, Restoration drama, Defoe, Fielding, Richardson, Sterne, Shelley, Byron, Tennyson, Browning, most of the Victorian novelists, Joyce, Woolf and most writers after D.H. Lawrence constituted a network of 'B' roads interspersed with a good few cul-de-sacs. Dickens was first out and then in; 'English' included two and a half women, counting Emily Brontë as a marginal case; almost all of its authors were conservatives." (Ibid., 28)

The map of English Literature, redrawn by *Scrutiny* and elucidated by Eagleton, holds a position of undisputed authority for any individual who inhabits the imagined community of English Studies. While Eagleton argues that the Leavisite current, substantially preached by the *Scrutiny*, "…has entered the bloodstream of English studies in England…has become a form of spontaneous critical wisdom as deep-seated as our conviction that the earth moves round the sun" (Ibid., 27), one can arguably erase the geo-political limit of 'England' stated in the aphorism. Indeed, barring a few exceptional departures, the worldwide canon of English literature has considerably conformed to the 'map' stated above. The academic programme of English major at various Universities across the world, even after the recent interventions of Culture Studies and New Literatures, can be unproblematically accommodated within the standardised map of English Literature. Ngugi wa Thiong'o, the African novelist and intellectual, living geographically far away from Eagleton's England, remarks that the charm of the "Leavisite selected 'Great Tradition of English Literature'" (wa Thiong'o 1987, 90) had cast its spell in Universities which were territorially located in Africa. "The syllabus of the English Department…" as wa Thiong'o remonstrates "…meant a study of the history of English Literature from Shakespeare, Spenser and Milton to James Joyce and T.S. Eliot, I.A. Richards and the inevitable F.R. Leavis." (Ibid.) wa Thiong'o observes, that the formation, sustenance and the reception of the English literary canon in Africa had (and still has) a deep rooted association with imperialism whereby "…the content of the syllabi, the approach to and presentation of the literature, the persons and the machinery for the determining the choice of the texts and their interpretation, were an integral part of imperialism in its classical colonial phase, and they are today an integral part of the same imperialism…in its neo-colonial phase." (wa Thiong'o 1981, 5)

In her magnum opus *The Masks of Conquests*, Gauri Viswanathan observes that the institutionalisation, and thus the canonisation, of English in the colonies had happened "long before it was institutionalized in the home country". (Viswanathan 2015, 27) Viswanathan is critical of Eagleton's "token acknowledgement"

(Ibid.) of the correspondence between the institutionalisation of English as a discipline and the birth of the Empire. Echoing Wa Thiongo, Viswanathan claims that the canonisation of English literature is so intimately associated with the politico-historical event of Imperialism that it is problematic to place the two within a cause-effect design. One is often at a loss to determine if the institutionalisation of English is a cause or an effect of imperialism. Viswanathan opines that English literature acquired "surrogate functions" (Ibid., 33) in the backdrop of imperialism, all of which cannot be listed in the limited scope of an Introduction. To state in a nutshell, it is Viswanathan's contention that the initiation of English in the academic circuit of colonised India and the formulation of the English canon played a significant role in the consolidation of the Empire. The mimic man, "a class of persons Indian in blood and colour, but English in tastes, in opinions, in morals and in intellect" (Macaulay 1835, 8), was the imperfect, but desired, outcome of the Anglo-cultural pedagogic model and the perfect embodiment and exemplar of a colonised subject who was dominated with consent. The holistic description of the private life of the Bengali babu by Deborah Baker is incomplete without a mention of the "Family libraries of...calf-bound copies of Tennyson, Wordsworth, Coleridge, Shelley, illustrated folios of Shakespeare, and the entire run of Sir Walter Scott's Waverley novels..." (Baker 2018, 52)

What thus stands out is the intimate relationship of the literary canon with power and its typically political disposition. The political essence that is revealed is considerably dependent on the position of the revelator, i.e., the nature of the introspective gaze which considers the canon. For a feminist intellectual like Virginia Woolf, the canon is a patriarchal construct which systematically denies recognition to deserving women writers like Shakespeare's imagined sister Judith. Differently, for the avant-garde Bengali novelist and intellectual Nabarun Bhattacharya, the canon is the repository of petty bourgeoisie sensibilities promoting a spirit of conformism, which must be unmade by imagined poets and intellectuals like Purandar Bhaat who write profane and unrefined verses in a crude language that is largely obscene and often sexist. What is thus revealed is the transitive nature of the canon, a face that is revised and re-invented with every intervention of interpretation. Charles Altieri observes that "...what I claim to be canonical (or to be criterion for determining canons) does depend on norms that I establish, or at least, on institutional norms that I certify". (Altieri 1983, 40) Terry Eagleton is of the opinion that the parameter of value, on which the constricted category of the canon rests, is "...a transitive term: it means whatever is valued by certain people in specific situations, according to particular criteria and in the light of given purposes". (Eagleton 1996, 10) One can extend Eagleton's argument further to suggest that it is not just the value of the canon but also the nature of the canon which is transitive. Or else, it is also possible to interpret Eagleton's 'value' as not necessarily a valorised 'worth' but an implied significance that is unfolded through critical evaluation and interpretation and whose nature and essence is dependent on the position and perspective of the critical gaze. Frank Kermode argues that the canonisation of the literary text is considerably dependent on the continuity of attention and interpretation that the text motivates. (Kermode 1979, 78) The evaluation of the text, which can either be an appraisal or a critique (Frank Kermode claims that the literary canon is actually defined "by attacks upon it" (Ibid., 81)), significantly determines its canonicity.

Hence, one can argue that canons are hauntological in nature. In their pervasiveness and consistent recognition (a recognition that happens even in denial) they resemble the historic. The critique of the canon through denial only foregrounds its relevance, just as the wistful urge to live unhistorically only implies the inescapability of history and historicised existence. The canon breathes when it is accepted, it thrives when it is denied. Reverence and denial are distinct means which eventually accomplishes the same end, the validation of the canon. Like the Eliotian tradition, the canon is diffusedly related to the artist through an inescapable trope of measurability, "in which two things are measured by each other" (Eliot 1932, 15).

The problematic relationship of modern Bengali poetry with the aesthetic model typified as *Rabindrik* can aptly illustrate the paradoxical position of the canon with relation to art. *Rabindrik*, a prevalent and overused word in the Bengali language, connotes a "distinctive style" (Chatterjee 2001, 304) of, chiefly aesthetic, expression that is often identified with the 1913 Nobel laureate Rabindranath Tagore. It is a matter of little contention that Tagore occupies a formidable presence in the Bengali cultural field and is a "canon in himself" (Ibid.). In an interview, the celebrated Hindi and Urdu poet Gulzar, rather unambiguously, and to an extent reductively, observes that in the cultural life of Bengal "...that one man (Tagore) is the culture of the entire community...the children begin their learning from him...there is perhaps no other instance where a single man becomes the culture of the entire community." (Live, 5:48-6:23) Apparently, there are generalising strains in Gulzar's comments. Yet, like most other generalisations, the assertion is partially true. The various modernist literary movements in Bengal, which aspired to *make it new*, believed that an unconditional rejection (annihilation in some cases) of *Rabindrik* sensibilities and consciousness was a fundamental requirement for the arrival of modernity in literature. These heterogeneous movements, with each departing from the other in their outlook, historicity and praxis, can be branded together on the basis of their anti-*Rabindrikata*/cism. The poets of Kallol, Krittibaash and Hungry generation unanimously agreed that modernity and rabindrikata were mutually antagonistic and for the first to arrive it was essential to reject the second.

However, the rejection of Rabindrikata and Tagore never meant an absolute autonomy from their sublime shadow. On the contrary, as the renowned modern Bengali poet Buddhadeva Bose notes in an interview, the post-Tagore modernists like Bishnu Dey, Sudhindranath Datta and Bose himself "showed a serious involvement in Tagore. This involvement took many forms: parody, imitation, submission, rejection, revolt." (Bose 1966, 43) Bose's comment emphasises the eternal truth that revolt or rejection is an-other way of involvement and establishes an-other relationship that is founded on the premises of non-relation. In his Memoir *Awrdhek Jiban* (*Half-a-Life*) Sunil Ganguly remarks that the readers of Bengali literature have often failed to comprehend the actual essence of Rabindra-birodh, i.e., the intentional antagonisation of Rabindranath, among the modern Bengali poets and litterateurs.

For him, the true essence of Rabindra-birodh was not to discard or unrecognise the bard's creative authority. It was more an attack on the systemic tendency of Purists who believed that nothing 'literary' has been produced in the post-Tagore era of Bengali literature. (*Awrdhek Jiban* 204) Elsewhere, Ganguly remarks that the "people's obsession with Rabindranath, that mindset they carried where he was the only 'poet' who existed..." (Ganguly 2010) significantly motivated him to adopt an Anti-Rabindranath stance.

What we hence have is the classic case of the canon evolving as a referential point, which must be considered or alluded to even when the contemporaneous seeks to depart from it. The Canon is, to quote Charles Altieri, "...a permanent theater helping us shape and judge personal and social values" (Altieri 1983, 40) Altieri argues that Canons serve "as dialectical resources" (Ibid., 47) whereby it both serves as a model and a challenge for the aspiring artist. He asserts that "Canons make us *want* to struggle..." (Ibid., 48) and in its dichotomous relevance as both a model and a Foil, canons are inescapably relevant to the artists and their art.

Reflections on the canon also point to its contingent and non-singular and non-exclusive nature. It is often problematic to determine a pure canon in a literary-cultural field for there is often not one but many canons. To complicate the possibilities of an inference further, multiple canons often exist simultaneously. Graham Holderness explores this curious but rather recurrent condition of 'many canons in simultaneity' (emphasis mine) in form of a personal reminiscence. Holderness claims that although his "first encounter" (Holderness 2014, 74) with the canon of English Literature had happened in the 1960s when he was a student of English, he had been introduced to "...another canon, a more popular one..." (Ibid., 75) before his formal studies in English began. This "another canon" was a Christmas gift to him from his parents and it was "...a set of ten books called the 'Presentation Library'" (Ibid.). Holderness remonstrates that "the ten books represented a mixture of different canons". (Ibid.)

Holderness's reminiscences clearly exemplify the pluralistic disposition of the category called Canon. Furthermore, it also considers the canon outside the institutional limits of academia. In asserting the existence of "another canon, a more popular one", Holderness problematises the binarised distinction between the Canon and the Popular. Instead, his assertion implies that it is perhaps necessary to revise our (fore)understanding of the Canon as a sacrosanct category that is hierarchically superior to its *baser Other* (i.e., Popular) and far removed from the profanities that is usually associated and identified with the latter. Does Popular as a category hold its claim to the canon? If so, what are the founding parameters and classificatory principles on which such an alternative canon can be constructed and maintained? Is such a canon non-striated in nature or is it governed by more intricate considerations of readership? Can such an alternative canon support the possibilities of free reading or does it eventually commodify the literary? Such questions are perhaps not irrelevant to ponder upon.

In his Presidential address of the Modern Humanities Research Association, later titled as "The Popular Canon", Jean Francois Botrel observes that "Nothing seems further from potentially canonical literature than our subject (Popular Literature)" (Botrel 2002, xxx). Botrel is critical of the canonised categories of "'popular', 'infra' or 'para literature', 'minor literature'" and finds in such "disqualifying epithets" (Ibid., xxix), the unnecessary intervention of the intelligentsia (Botrel calls them "the guardians and supporters of the canon"). For Botrel, such categories barely refer to the literature of the people. Rather, in absence of a genuine intent to "…provide a basis for the de facto development of a popular canon" (Ibid. xxxi) the "literature of the voice" (Ibid.) is often unacknowledged and hence remains perpetually uncanonised. Botrel's thought-provoking essay ends with his assertion that "The popular canon seems…to be the canon that is established notwithstanding the apparent submission to legitimate learning tastes…it is not an explicit, decreed canon, but an implicit, *de facto* one, having no official status, but tacitly and stubbornly opposed to the Canon of the Other…" (Ibid. xxxviii)

Identifying Popular Literature

Contrary to Botrel's assertion, what is often conceived as Popular Literature is an "explicit, decreed canon" which, if otherwise difficult to define, is easy to identify. One possible and immediate strategy of identifying Popular literature is clearly tautological; it is that which is popular among the readers. Hence, depending on its popularity among the readers, a literary work can be accorded or denied the status of Popular. Having said so, it is perhaps wrong to arrive at the easy inference that all Bestsellers are exemplars of Popular Literature and they comprehensively constitute the 'Popular' Canon. Ken Gelder is sharp to remind us that "…a bestseller can mean sales of anything from around 20,000 copies to several million…and some works of Literature, whether it happens over an extended period of time or immediately after publication, can indeed do well in the marketplace." (Gelder 2004, 11) If Readership remains the only criteria for defining and identifying Popular Literature, the long-standing rift between Classics and Bestsellers is likely to dissolve and the great debate around the two will possibly sound absurd. That there is a prevalent presumption that the two are mutually exclusive categories (which they are and occasionally they are not, we will in due course take up this contention) clearly signify that Classics, even when they (arguably) acquire their credibility as Classic by being popular among readership across the limits of space, time and culture, cannot be unproblematically equated with Bestsellers. Salability can barely be the primary criteria for identifying and defining Popular Literature. The plays by Shakespeare, the novels of Dickens or the poems of the Romantics are read worldwide and are arguably popular among a trans-temporal and trans-cultural readership who often, paradoxically, read them as Literary classics. Political pamphlets like The *Communist Manifesto* or autobiographies like *My Experiments with Truth* only problematise the idea of defining Popular Literature in terms of readership.

Gelder further contends that the law of the genre is a significant criterion for the classification and identification of Popular Literature. He argues that "…with popular fiction, generic identities are always visible" and that "Popular fiction announces those identities loudly and unambiguously; you know and immediately need to know that this is romance, or a work of crime fiction (and/or spy fiction), or fantasy, or horror, or a western, or an historical popular novel or an adventure novel." (Ibid., 42) There seems to be a considerable substance in Gelder's claim, for Literary works which conform to these generic types are often recognised (or dismissed? the choice, dear reader, is yours) as Popular Literature. The constituent imperatives and parameters of a genre and its thematic tropes are often formulaically repeated in works which are canonised as Popular Literature. Satyajit Ray, the eminent Indian filmmaker, once observed that Popular Indian cinema has become a manufactured product of Bombay (Bollywood) which "...has devised a perfect formula to entice and amuse the illiterate multitude that forms the bulk of our film audiences". (Ray 2011, 8) This 'formula of amusement', as Ray observes elsewhere, tries desperately to feed the public appetite for entertainment, "...the craving for spectacle, for romance, for a funny turn or two, for singing and dancing..." (Ray 1994, 73) In his classic tongue in cheek humor, Ray elaborates the formula thus:

> "...colour (Eastman preferred); songs (six or seven?) in voices one knows and trusts; dance—solo and ensemble—the more frenzied the better; bad girl, good girl, bad guy, good guy, romance (but no kisses); tears, guffaws, fights, chases, melodrama; characters who exist in a social vacuum; dwellings which do not exist outside the studio floor; locations in Kulu, Manali, Ooty, Kashmir, London, Paris, Hong Kong, Tokyo...who needs to be told? See any three Hindi films, and two will have all the ingredients listed above..." (Ibid., 90-91)

For Ray, the enlisted integral components of Indian (Hindi) cinema are not just empirically identifiable characteristics whose recurrence is only incidental or accidental. Instead, owing to their recurrence through repetitions, these components have acquired the hermeneutic status of being the 'rules of the game' (emphasis is mine). They are formulas for not just procuring success at the box office but also for making the materialisation of the craft possible. For Ray, it is never quite possible to create a Hindi cinema without succumbing to the formula.

Ray's understanding of the formula as a hermeneutic category holds true for not just Popular Cinema but also Popular Literature. Gelder observes that for writers of Popular fiction, the autonomy of creativity is largely compromised for a methodological pursuance of labour. For him, an epistemological and theoretical distinction exists between the categories of author and writer in the sense that while the former "subsumes and transcends the thing he creates" (Gelder 2004, 14), the latter is identified by his/ her "industry", i.e., "production and sheer hard work" (Ibid., 15). One need not necessarily agree with Gelder's contention that the author is the creator of Literature while the writer is the producer of Popular fiction (Gelder's proposed distinction between Literature and Popular fiction is in anyway problematic) but there is substantial validity in his understanding of the writer/ author of Popular Literature as a craftsman labouring within the discursive design of a prevalent mode of production with little aspiration to problematise, question or critique the design. The conformism of the writer is not merely an ideological conformism, it is also a self-subjection to the normative praxis of aesthetic production. Virginia Woolf's critique of the writer who "...seems constrained, not by his own free will but by some powerful and unscrupulous tyrant who has him in thrall, to provide a plot, to provide comedy, tragedy, love interest..." (Woolf 1984, 160) is a precise and fitting, if only a little anachronistic, definition of the Popular writer. Woolf's subsequent praise of James Joyce and the 'spiritualists' (who in her opinion are the embodiments of modernity) are serious symptoms of her own ideological position. Yet, what stands out again is the relevant presumption that the writer of Popular Literature possesses a customised and compromised creative spirit that is continuously tamed by some unperceived and incomprehensible tyrant.

The tyrant is possibly the Market and we will consider the effectiveness of the same as the distinctive criteria on the basis of which Popular Literature can be identified, categorised or defined. However, before that, we must consider the problems that underlie our proposition that Popular Literature can be exclusively identified on the basis of their genre-dependency. While it is true that a Popular work prefers not to mingle genres and usually bears distinct marks of genre-specificity, the tyranny of genres is not exclusive to Popular Literature. Jacques Derrida finds in the pronouncement of the word genre the establishment of "a limit" which is immediately followed by "norms and interdictions…" (Derrida 1992(a), 224) For Derrida, the principle behind this limit is an unavoidable trait "…which one could rely in order to decide that a given textual event, a given "work", corresponds to a given class". (Ibid. 228-229) Derrida further asserts that "…there is no genreless text, there is always a genre and genres…" (Ibid., 230). In similar lights, Tzvetan Todorov and Richard Berrong observe that any avant-garde and unprecedented/ novel work of art "…as soon as it is recognised in its exceptional status, becomes in its turn, thanks to successful sales and critical attention, a rule." (Todorov and Berrong 1976, 160) Such a rule inspires other artists who, driven by the motive of "critical attention" (Ibid.) more than successful sales (or both), seek to replicate the rule. Todorov and Berrong's rhetorical question "Have not Joyce's exceptional puns become the rule for a certain kind of modern literature?" (Ibid.) elucidates that genre-dependency is not an exclusive tendency of writers of Popular Literature. Instead, it is also observable in practitioners of elite literature (if such a distinction still exists in our mind) who often aspire to replicate an unconventional generic model with the urge of being recognised as avant-garde artists (in this case the modernists). In other words, they consciously imitate a genre with the motive of recognition. Such conscious imitations have two-fold implications: not only do they qualify the imitators as the practitioner of a genre, they also end up canonising an unconventional exception as the generic rule. Todorov and Berrong provides us the classic example of Prose poem which "seemed like an exception in the time of Aloysius Betrand and Baudelaire" (Ibid.) but, owing to its repeated practice, has now acquired the status of norm.

Hence, considering genre-dependency as a distinct trait of Popular Literature, although reasonable, can be problematic. Elite literature is also genre-dependent in its own way, all it takes is to reinterpret and reconsider our own understanding of the term genre. The recent trends in genre studies propose to evaluate genre as a contingent category which is regularly revised and modulated.

Todorov and Berrong opine that genres are born from other genres and "a new genre is always the transformation of one or several old genres: by inversion, by displacement, by combination" (Ibid., 161). Furthermore, the codified characteristics which constitute the nature of the genre have a problematic origin. They are sole results of perspective (which Todorov and Berrong calls "point of view" (Ibid.)) or ideology.

The motif of ideology is often considered to be an effective basis for determining Popular Literature. Popular texts are regarded as a vital medium for the propagation of ideologies and as effective safeguards of existing ideological structures like Patriarchy, class and Nation State. The morals of compulsory heterosexuality, class-caste consciousness, nationalism, technocracy etc. are often believed to be systematically disseminated by diverse popular texts which are carriers of dominant ideological tendencies. Hence, Romance fictions are considered to be "...primary sites for the ideological construction of individuals as gendered subjects..." (Ebert 19); Popular plot-centred novels are regarded as a potent means of dissemination of bourgeoisie sensibilities; children's literature is frequently comprehended as an effective literary mode to procure 'good conduct' (emphasis mine) and morality in children and thereby ensure the production of docile conforming subjects who, in future, are conditioned to obey rather than refute the socio-political status quo.

While such conceptual readings of the various segments of Popular Literature is not unreasonable, similar allegations of ideological conformism are often raised against high literature. For Marxist intellectuals, the dispassionate retreat of the early twentieth century artist into the ivory tower of *art for art's* sake has been a clear symptom of ideological conformism. A classic case at hand is Karl Radek's critique of the avant-garde novelist James Joyce and what is often believed to be his literary masterpiece, *Ulysses*. The novel is often regarded as an authentic testimony of the Irish, or to be more specific, Dublin, everyday and Joyce himself had once remarked that he had attempted "to give a picture of Dublin so complete that if the city one day suddenly disappeared from the earth it could be reconstructed out of my book." (Joyce qtd. in Adams

2003, 84) However, contrary to Joyce's claim, the Marxist critic Karl Radek finds in the novelist's depiction an ideologically determined choice whereby "he (Joyce) has selected a piece of life and depicted that" (Radek 1934). This life, as Radek argues, is founded on Joyce's own position and ideological inclination and hence is limited to "…a cupboardful of medieval books, a brothel and a pothouse." The bourgeoisie does not figure as agents of revolution in the novel because for its creator i.e., Joyce, "…the national revolutionary movement of the Irish petty bourgeoisie does not exist…" (Ibid.) Radek's reading of Joyce's *Ulysses* implies that the re-presented unhappening ordinary world of Dublin, lulled by the monotony of a predicated and ritualised everyday existence, is a clear reflection of Joyce's ideological position of self-withdrawal from Irish politics and the Irish nationalist movement and his complacence with status-quo. Likewise, the leftist intellectual and playwright Augusto Boal finds in classical Aristotelian tragedy a "…very powerful purgative system, the objective of which is to eliminate all that is not commonly accepted, including the revolution, before it takes place" (Boal 2008, 41). Tragedy, as Boal interprets it, is an effective literary medium through which the ideology of the ruling class is propagated and ideologically conditioned subjects, who are inclined to conform to and not contradict the existing order, are produced. Hence, it is perhaps incorrect and, as Gelder observes, perhaps ideological (Gelder 2004, 35) to unproblematically consider only Popular literature as ideologically charged. Rather, the ideological is an inseparable component of the aesthetic.

Popular Literature is also often identified and defined as market-oriented. Indeed, this is perhaps the most rudimentary definition that one can imagine of Popular Literature. A practitioner of Popular Literature is expected to serve the market and write for a pre-conceived readership who have an ordinary and predictable literary taste. Such an understanding of Popular literature is miserably flawed for it tends to assume the market as a static and constant category. Hence, the fact that there are markets enfolded within the umbrella-signifier 'Market' is a reality which is often ignored and overlooked. Adorno and Anson's reconsideration of culture-industry proposes to understand the transformation of culture into commodity in the historic period when "...these cultural forms first began to earn a living for their creators as commodities in the marketplace..." (Adorno and Anson 1975, 13) Adorno observes that the "culture industry has its ontology...from the commercial English novels of the late 17th and early 18th centuries" (Ibid.,14). The commodification of culture is thus historically simultaneous with the birth of the author as an 'autonomous' (emphasis is mine) category, free from the constraints and conditions of patronage. It is simultaneously necessary to clarify that the single quoted autonomy is not equable to absolute liberty. Rather, it suggests "...the laws of the marketplace" (Watt 1957, 53) to which the author was, is and will be constantly subjected, often through the meticulous procedures of print culture that are associated with publication. The market is a pre-consideration for any author, it is only that their target readership is different. Ezra Pound, announcing the long-desired publication of James Joyce's *A Portrait of the Artist as a Young Man* in the book form, famously observed that "Members of the "Fly-Fishers" and "Royal Automobile Clubs", and of the "Isthmian" may not read him" (Pound 1970, 82). Nevertheless, Pound was optimistic that "...intelligent readers gathering few by few will read it, and it will remain a permanent part of English literature..." (Ibid. 83). Pound never implied that Joyce's masterpiece was outside the ambit of market and readership. Rather, he realised that it was meant for a different category of readers and would in due course develop its own market.

Popular and the Ethics of Reading

Can we then suggest a better set of parameters on the basis of which we can identify what we presume, if not understand, as Popular Literature? What then can be the undisputed distinguishing mark on the basis of which a text can be identified as a piece of Popular Literature? Is it at all possible to unproblematically define Popular Literature? Considering the nuances which we have discussed at length, the chances of an affirmative response seem less likely.

Yet, response is an important aspect to be considered. Texts demand response, it is the ethical act of the reader to respond to a text through the praxis or act of reading. Reading is the vital act that orients the afterlife of the text, through reading the text is re-born in continuum. Reading as a cultural act often determines the essence of the textual. However, with a few happy exceptions, the act of reading mostly occurs within institutionalised models of interpretation which pre-exist and pre-date the reader. These models are problematic categories not only because they appropriate the reader within patterned reading tendencies but also because they are often the litmus which distinguish between good reading-bad reading, authentic reading-misreading, valid reading-invalid reading. The reader is disallowed the possibility of approaching the literary non-hermeneutically and un-historically. For such an ideologically conditioned reader, the canon and its ramifications are so overpoweringly real that s/he barely stands the possibility of evading the same. It is virtually impossible for the third-world reader to read Robinson Crusoe as a popular novel (Watt 1957, 92) and to appreciate William Shakespeare as a playwright of the masses. The former is introduced to the young reader as an exemplary Classic of world literature, the latter is the visionary bard who is the unchallenged face of culture, serving forever the cause of humanity. Ian Watt or Stephen Greenblatt or Robert Weimann cannot erase the lingering traces of symbolic capital which, due to the history of British imperialism and the subsequent formation and evolution of the culturally colonised Anglo-cultural bourgeois as the dominant class, such literatures and litterateurs embody in the reading circles of postcolonial Nation like India. The liberal humanist reading practices which chant the names of Shakespeare, Byron, Shelley, Keats, Eliot like pious hymns constantly inspire the reader to develop a discrete and fine literary taste and read by the canon.

  One can unproblematically define the Literature of the Popular if one is in possession of such a conditioned reading sensibility. Popular Literature is all that the canonical reading tendencies designate as Popular. It is that which is believed to be readable unthinkingly. It is that which can be read at leisure, it is that which does not deserve the serious and sombre appreciative mode of reading which must be accorded to the canon. In other words, it is all that can be read un-methodically and informally. Until recently, they were excluded by the academic canon in India and even today, they lack the symbolic capital that is intrinsic to a *Paradise Lost* or a *Great Expectations*. Gelder's critical take on the idea of reading Popular Literature explicates that there is often a pre-dominant sociocultural presumption that Popular Literature is a non-readable genre which can be consumed but not read. That is to say, Reading as a sophisticated engagement with the literary, by a critical individual or class, is not possible in the context or case of Popular Literature. (Gelder 2004, 35-36) Hence, Popular Literature is all that which does not deserve the critical gaze of the canonical reader.

J. Hillis Miller has argued that for the mattering of Literature at both an institutional and intimate level, it is not enough to read by the canon. Instead, good reading is equally essential. Miller claims that good reading "…means noncanonical reading, that is, a willingness to recognize the unexpected, perhaps even the shocking or scandalous, present even in canonical works, perhaps especially in canonical works…" (Miller 2002, 189). Miller further claims (and this serves our design) that good reading "is more likely to lead to disconfirmation…of a theory than to offer a firm support to it" (Ibid., 190). Although Miller is principally concerned with an alternative model of reading the canon, his idea of disconfirmation can be significant when considered in the context of reading (if that is possible) Popular Literature.

In all possibilities, a good reading of Popular Literature begins with the assertion that it is indeed possible to read Popular Literature. It is not a rejection of the same as unreadable in the classical highbrow reader-esque manner. Neither is it a systemic exuberant flattery of the genre. Rather, it is the honest intent to engage critically with these texts which the canon has dismissed as non-literature. It is the willingness to accept a blatant disconfirmation of the theoretical presumption that Popular literature is unworthy, unserious, unimportant, trivial, lay.

The present volume is an attempt to (good)read texts which belong to the undefinable genre of Popular Literature. Keeping in tune with the nuances that the present chapter has explored in its attempt to identify and define the genre of Popular Literature, the determined texts are equally problematic. One can validly contend that *Frankenstein* or *Fahrenheit 451* are classics. However, as we have already discussed, Classics and Popular Bestsellers are not exclusive categories and there are ample texts which co-habit both these domains. In fact, their status in the latter compartment often allows them an entry into the former. Further, relevant questions can be raised about the sectional divisions. For instance, one can rightly ask if *Frankenstein* unproblematically belongs to the genre of science fiction and how correct is it to ignore the strains of the Gothic in the novel. We can evade such pressing questions with the disclaimer that the subsections have been created to real-ise the conceived 'design of the book' (emphasis is mine) — which is always an irreducibly subjective and non-formulaic affair. Yet, we have other justifications to offer. We have not intended to be precise and immaculate in designing the subsections for our main motive in the book is not to establish genres but to problematise them. Our readings are typically inclined to explore other possible readings that are possible outside the generically patterned models of reading. Hence, the generic categorisation has been strategic, so as to ensure the possibilities of uncategorised reading of the texts. Of course, the categorisation has not been arbitrary and texts with nominal, if not absolute, signs of a generic tendency have been clustered together. That is to say, we have not considered *Frankenstein* as a Romance because that would be ludicrous. Simultaneously, we have also strategically turned deaf to the dominant strains of Gothic in the novel. This is precisely because we have not attempted to determine genre authenticity. The generic identity has only served as a scaffolding which can host other possible readings that extend beyond the limits of the genre and at times end up problematising the notion of a distinct generic identity of the text.

  Our book is not free from the allegations of epistemic violence that holds true for any designed work which appears to be (at times claim to be, not this time though) complete and exhaustive but is never really so. Design is always already political and we do not contend that we have been accommodative enough to have been able to design the perfect and complete design. Self-criticism makes us ponder if we have not unproblematically accepted a derived categorical notion of Popular Literature which is typically Anglooriented and is utterly disconnected from the more organic non-English speaking mass. Where is the 'People' in our understanding of the Popular? Are the literatures written about in the pages that follow 'literature of the people'? (emphasis is mine) Are they not popular only among the sophisticated metropolitan readership heavily conditioned by the Anglocentric mode of education? Have we, like many other predecessors, conceptualised a design of Popular Literature that has, yet again, systematically excluded the literature of the People?

Perhaps we have lost miserably to the Politics of position.

Notes:

1. In Eugene Ionesco's play *Rhinoceros*, inhabitants of an unnamed provincial French town start metamorphosing into Rhinoceroses. The dramatic action ends with Berenger resolving to cling to his individuality while the rest of the residents in the town have happily capitulated into Rhinoceroses. The play is often considered as a response to the rise of Fascism and a latent but vital critique of mob mentality which often prefer to obey than question, conform rather than confront.

Bibliography:

Adams, David. 2003. *Colonial Odysseys: Empire and Epic in the Modernist Novel*. Ithaca: Cornell University Press

Adorno, Theodor W. and Anson G. Rabinbach. 1975. "Culture Industry Reconsidered". *New German Critique*, No.6 (Autumn): 12-19. JSTOR http://www.jstor.org/stable/487650. Accessed on 31st January, 2021.

Altieri, Charles. 1983. "An Idea and Ideal of a Literary Canon". *Critical Inquiry: Canons*, Vol. 10, no. 1 (September): 37-60.

Baker, Deborah. 2018. *The Last Englishmen: Love, War and the End of Empire*. Minneapolis: Graywolf Press.

Boal, Augusto. 2008. *Theatre of the Oppressed*. Translated by Charles A., Maria-Odilia Leal McBride and Emily Fryer. London: Pluto Press.

Bose, Buddhadeva. 1966. "Perspectives on Bengali Poetry: An Interview with Buddhadeva Bose". Interview by Anonymous. *Mahfil*, Vol. 3, no. 4: 43-48.

Botrel, Jean-François. 2002. "The Popular Canon". *The Modern Language Review*, Vol. 97, no. 4 (October): xxix-xxxix. JSTOR. https://www.jstor.org/stable/3738743. Accessed on 14th February, 2021.

Chatterjee, Partha. 2020. *I am the People: Reflections on Popular Sovereignty Today*. New York: Columbia University Press.

Chatterjee, Rimi B. 2001. "Canon without Consensus: Rabindranath Tagore and "The Oxford Book of Bengali Verse". *Book History*, Vol. 4: 303-333

Derrida, Jacques. 1992. "Law of the Genre". In *Acts of Literature*, edited by Derek Atridge, 221-252. New York: Routledge. (a)

..."The Strange Institution called Literature". In *Acts of Literature*, edited by Derek Atridge, 33-75. New York: Routledge. (b)

Eagleton, Terry. 1996. *Literary Theory: An Introduction*. Minneapolis: University of Minnesota Press.

Ebert, Teresa L. 1988. "The Romance of Patriarchy: Ideology, Subjectivity, and Postmodern Feminist Cultural Theory". *Cultural Critique: Popular Narrative, Popular Images*, no. 10 (Autumn): 19-57

Eliot, T. S. 1932. "Tradition and the Individual Talent". In *Selected Essays* by T. S. Eliot, 13-22. London: Faber and Faber Limited.

Ganguly, Sunil. 2002. *Awrdhek Jiban* translated by me as *Half-a-Life*. Kolkata: Ananda Publishers.

...2010. "I was once anti-Rabindrath Tagore". Interview by Kareena N. Gianani. DNA, December 19. https://www.dnaindia.com/lifestyle/report-i-was-once-anti-rabindrath-tagore-1483038. Accessed on 19th February, 2021.

Gelder, Ken. 2004. *Popular Fiction: The Logics and Practices of a Literary Field*. London: Routledge.

Holderness, Graham. 2014. "'An Arabian in My Room': Shakespeare and the Canon". *Critical Survey*, Vol. 26, no. 2: 73-89

Kermode, Frank. 1979. "Institutional Control of Interpretation". *Salmagundi*, no. 43 (Winter): 72-86

Live, Loksatta. "How Gulzar Met Ghalib and Rabindranath Tagor". YouTube Video, 6:25. Jan 18, 2015. https://www.youtube.com/watch?v=5KROeB_MrX0&t=315s. Accessed on 22nd February, 2021.

Macaulay, T.B. 1835. "Minutes on Education". Retrieved from http://home.iitk.ac.in/~hcverma/Article/Macaulay-Minutes.pdf. Accessed on 21st February, 2021.

Miller, J. Hillis. 1987. "The Ethics of Reading". *Style: Deconstruction*, Vol. 21, no. 2 (Summer): 181-191. JSTOR. https://www.jstor.org/stable/42946145. Accessed on 4th March, 2021.

...2002. "Derrida and Literature." In *Jacques Derrida and the Humanities: A Critical Reader*, edited by Tom Cohen, 58-81. Cambridge: Cambridge University Press.

Pound, Ezra. 1970. "At last the Novel Appears". In *James Joyce Vol. 1, 1907-27: The Critical Heritage*, edited by Robert H. Deming, 82-84. London: Routledge.

Ray, Satyajit. 1994. *Our Films Their Films*. New York: Hyperion.

...2011. "National Styles in Cinema". In *Satyajit Ray on Cinema*, edited by Sandip Ray, 3-8. New York: Columbia University Press.

Rodek, Karl. 1934. "Contemporary World Literature and the Tasks of Proletarian Art". *Soviet Writers Congress 1934*. Retrieved from Marxists Internet Archive https://www.marxists.org/archive/radek/1934/sovietwritercongress.htm. Accessed on 31st December, 2020.

Todorov, Tzvetan and Richard M. Berrong. 1976. "The Origin of Genres". *New Literary History: Readers and Spectators Some Views and Reviews*, Vol. 8, no. 1 (Autumn): 159-170. JSTOR. http://www.jstor.com/stable/468619. Accessed on 15th January, 2021.

Vishwanathan, Gauri. 2015. *Masks of Conquest: Literary Study and British Rule in India*. New York: Columbia University Press.

wa Thiong'o, Ngugi. 1981. *Writers in Politics: Essays*. London: Heinemann Educational Books Ltd.

...1987. *Decolonising the Mind: The Politics of Language in African Literature*. Harare: Zimbabwe Publishing House.

Watt, Ian. 1957. *The Rise of the Novel: Studies in Defoe, Richardson and Fielding*. Berkeley: University of California Press.

Woolf, Virginia. 1984. "The Modern Fiction". In *The Essays of Virginia Woolf. Volume 4: 1925 to 1928*, edited by Andrew McNeille. London: The Hogarth Press.

Section I
Juvenile Literature

The Proper and the Pure: Biopolitics, Law and Sujectivity in Rudyard Kipling's *The Jungle Book*

Rupayan Mukherjee

> "I met a hundred men on the road to Delhi
> and they were all my brothers."
> Epigraph to Rudyard Kipling's *Life's Handicap*

> "He has eaten our food. He has slept with us...
> He has broken no word of the *Law* of the Jungle."
> *The Jungle Book*
> Rudyard Kipling

Rudyard Kipling, who in the words of Edward Said "…saw only the politics of Empire" (Said 1994, 39), is ambiguously received by the academic canon of postcolonial studies. While Edward Said has deciphered the strains of orientalism in Kipling's literary oeuvre and have argued that Empire is "a crucial setting" to his works (Ibid., 63), recent studies have been critical of Said's critique of Kipling[1]. Zohren Sullivan observes that "The problem in reading Kipling…is understanding the complexity of his attitude towards imperialism and the unified subject as agent." (Sullivan 1993, 52) However, what is undeniable is Kipling's unfeigned interest in the excess or the other called Orient and his constant literary and imaginative endeavours to engage, impersonate and at times become the other. Kipling claims that such consistent and genuine urge to engage with the other was necessary to understand the hetero-cultural milieu of India in completeness (Ibid., 50-51). His opinion of the oriental-other is difficult to compartmentalise, it is marked by inconsistencies, disparities and fluctuations. The sense of a fraternity consciousness that is hinted in the epigraph can be juxtaposed against chronic aphorisms like "If there is one thing that the Oriental detests more than another, it is the damnable Western vice of accuracy" (cited in Scott 2011, 306) or "Destruction—the one thing the Oriental understands." (Ibid.) Yet, Kipling is unquestionably preoccupied with the Orient and proposes "wandering through it like Haroun-al-Raschid in search of strange things..." (Sullivan 1993, 51)

The present chapter explores Kipling's problematic engagement with the heterogeneity of the Empire and his consciousness and conceptualisation of the Orientalised other through an allegorical reading of his Popular literary work *The Jungle Books*. The possibility of locating imperialistic strains in *The Jungle Books* is not a novel approach. Among others, Don Randall observes that *The Jungle Books* "presents an allegorical, empire-affirming restaging of the history of British India..." (Randall 1998, 98) with the Mutiny of 1857 serving as its "absent text" (Ibid.). The present reading of *The Jungle Books* is a part of this greater tradition of unearthing imperialism in the allegorical and proposes to reconsider the contentions of purity, identity and law in the stories. In doing so, the chapter reconsiders the liberal face of the Empire and the biopolitical strains that are contained in the assumption that sovereign subjecthood is not a matter of birth-right but is rather correlational with legal conformism. For this purpose, the chapter first attempts a genealogical enquiry into the libertarian influences on the English juridico-legal system which sought to make it more flexible and accommodative in nature. Hence, the chapter briefly refers to the modulations of/ in law that were proposed by social philosophers like Jeremy Bentham and were materialised by the likes of T.B. Macaulay to naturalise the condition of imperialism as a sovereign mode of governance. Besides contributing to the supposed myth of justice that was often self-advocated by the Empire, these libertarian interventions tried to promote the notion of the Empire as an inclusive governing authority that ruled by law and recognised the condition of legal conformism as the only necessary criterion for determining and according subjecthood. Of course, the hidden agenda was to naturalise the colonial condition and consolidate the Empire as a sovereign and not a despotic authority. However, the present chapter does not propose to engage with the question of intent and the "sly civility" (Bhaba 1985, 73) of imperialism. Rather, it tries to explore the biopolitical tendencies that are intrinsic to such a mode of governance that prioritises the juridico-legal 'proper' (emphasis is mine) over the racial 'pure' (emphasis is mine) and attempts to trace such tendencies in Rudyard Kipling's *The Jungle Books*. The chapter argues that the tales allegorically trace the contention between the proper and the pure—a contention which is fundamental to the Empire and its ideal of governance.

The founding epistemic essence of the British Empire is marked by its vision of a homogeneous politicos that would suspend geographical and cultural differences and would instead abide by the juridico-legal imperatives of the Buckingham, singing "Lord save the queen" with reverence, if not pride. What was hence necessary was not just the promotion of a cultural practice in form of Anglocentric Western education and English as the official language of transmission of "useful knowledge" (Macaulay 1835, 7) that could produce "a class of persons Indian in blood and colour, but English in tastes, in morals and in intellect." (Ibid. 8) It was also necessary, simultaneously, to formulate a moral position of superiority for the colonial master that would be validated in a "purity of the administration." (cited in Chatterjee 2012 (a), 165) This 'purity' would not be attained by a ruthless exploitation of the native, which T.B. Macaulay is seemingly critical of in his "An Essay on Clive". Instead, it would be marked by a "business of government" where "...the establishment of good government in India" would acquire "a matter of far greater significance than the providential acquisition of territories." (Ibid., 166)

The question of 'good governance', as validated and sustained by the epistemes of European political philosophy, is often associated with the question of law. Quentin Skinner's rigorous and exhaustive historical evaluation of the origins (foundations) of modern political philosophy exposes the necessity of law for the formulation and origination of political sovereignty. Referring to the conflicting political ambience of twelfth century Italy where city States strived for self-governance and autonomy from the Holy Roman Empire, Skinner observes that the sovereignty and liberty of the city States were often short lived for "the cities had no means of investing" their claim to liberty "with any legal force." (Skinner 1978, 7) On the contrary, the prevalence of the Justinian Code "assured...the strongest possible legal support" to the Holy Roman Emperor (mentioned as the princep in the Code) "in their campaign to subjugate the cities." (Ibid., 8) In absence of the law, the de facto state of liberty was absolutely unrecognised by the political philosophers that consisted of the "Glossators...employed in the interpretation of the Roman law." (Ibid.) Skinner subsequently refers to the climactic emergence of Bartolus of Saxoferrato, "perhaps the most original jurist" (Ibid., 9), in the political arena of Italy. Skinner claims that through the intervention of Bartolus, a significant *revolutionary* (emphasis is mine) "methodological contribution" (Ibid.) was accomplished. This 'methodological contribution' will be essential to our discussion on Macaulay. Before that, let us comprehend the contribution. Here is Skinner:

> "Bartolus's primary contribution was thus a methodological one. He abandoned the cardinal assumption of the Glossators to the effect that, when the law appears to be out of line with the legal facts, the facts must be adjusted to meet a literal interpretation of the law. He instead made it his basic precept that, where the law and the facts collide, it is the law which must be brought into conformity with the facts." (Ibid.)

The revolution referred seems obvious, it concerns the epistemic and theoretical autonomy to make the law conform to the facts. This conformation hints at the possibility of t(a/e)mpering the law. The law is not an apriori ascription of divine providence that is characteristic of a gospel like sanctity. Instead, it is t(a/e)mperable, often fitting the more pragmatic concerns of the material, the immediate and the contingent face of the politico-social.

Macaulay, one of the advocates (both in the literal and figurative sense) and epistemic assets of the British Empire, believed in a "reform of the legal institutions in India." (Chatterjee 2012 (a), 167) His concern was law and the inclusive nature of law that considerably relied on the myth of justice. The stability of Empire would lie in legal reformations that were necessary in order to materialise an inclusive political sovereignty where cultural differences would be approximated by the universality of law. Macaulay, much like his predecessor Jeremy Bentham, believed that the design of a Universal law was directly correlational to its topicality. Hence, to quote Partha Chatterjee, "...Macaulay devoted his energies to the rational reorganization of the clumsy, expensive judicial system and the codification of the law." (Ibid.)

Macaulay's rigorous endeavour to revise and reform the juridico-legal apparatus for a better governance of an Empire that was marked by topical cultural differences was considerably shaped by his intimate experience of the colonised's everyday. As a commissioned officer of the East India Company, Macaulay's field encounters with the social reality of India convinced him that there was not "...a single circumstance from which you could have inferred that this was a heathen country." (Macaulay 1976, 70) In a letter addressed to John Tytler (who taught literature and mathematics at the Hindu College and was in favour of Sanskrit and Arabic as the medium of instruction) Macaulay observed that "the native population if left to itself would prefer our mode of education (the Anglophonic Utilitarian model based on scientific rationalism) to yours." (Ibid., 123) What was only required was a well-oiled ideological apparatus that would produce the category of the brown sahib, who would be subsequently protected and procured by an inclusive legal apparatus and recognised as one like and amidst us, if not one of us. In a letter written in response to the appeal against the Regulation of the Press, Macaulay observed that the establishment of "a system" that could give "legal security to every person engaged in the fair discussion of public measures" while also "effectually secure the government against sedition" was the need of the hour. (Ibid., 124) His subsequent support of the Black Act and its benevolent intent "...to weed out privilege and to introduce uniformity in the dispensation of justice" (Macaulay 1946, 47) only highlight Macaulay's desire to formulate and promote an ideal of law that would cater to his vision of a "single-seated justice" (Macaulay 1976, 146) and would not discriminate between its subjects on any other basis but transgression. Sovereign subjectivity to the native would be accorded and recognised as long as (s)he would abide by the legal decrees of the Empire. In his 1836 Minutes on the Legislative, Macaulay ascribed his vision of Legal reforms thus:

> "The Principle...on which we proceeded was that the system ought, as far as possible, to be uniform, that no distinction ought to be made between one

class of people and another, except in cases where it could be necessarily made out that such a distinction was necessary to the pure and efficient administration of justice" (Macaulay 1946, 176-177)

Macaulay's flamboyant support of The Black Act of 1836[2] exhibits his profound faith in the need to necessitate a legal design that would assure the native equal hope and possibility of procuring for himself/herself the rightful status of the legal subject in match with the colonial white skinned masters. The purity and authenticity of a sovereign political identity of the self was no longer a consideration of race and such other non-juridical considerations. It was more a matter of an immaculate performance of the self that faithfully adhered to the ideological and the juridico-legal imperatives of Empire. The native, through his excellence in performance, could earn for him/her-self the rightful status of the political subject.

This myth of an inclusive ideal of the juridical and ideological is the uncanny fruit of Macaulay's poison tree[3] which enabled the sustenance of Imperialism in India through an unchallenged condition of domination with consent. It had longstanding implications in the native's consciousness pertaining to the legitimacy of the colonial condition and the Master (the coloniser) was recognised by the native as the prudent benefactor and custodian of justice. Ranajit Guha's evaluation of Dinabandhu Mitra's acclaimed play *Neeldarpan* exhibits the latent faith of the colonised in the judicial benevolence and altruism of the Master, even within the explicit and material conditions of exploitation. Guha points out that while the play is critical of the atrocities of Nilkar sahibs (the British Indigo plantation owners) and earned reputation for fictionalising resistance of colonial power, it refuses to exhibit an unconditional criticism of the colonial rule and the law of Empire. Instead, to quote Partha Chatterjee, "...there was in the author an abiding faith in the rationality and impartiality of English law and in the good intentions of the colonial administration as a whole." (Chatterjee 2012(b), 97) Chatterjee, referring to Guha's essay, observes:

"Never did it occur to these newly enlightened gentlemen, despite their fondness for justice and liberty, that the legitimacy of British rule in India might be called in question. In fact, it was the very existence of British power in India that was regarded as the final and most secure guarantee against lawlessness, superstition, and despotism." (Ibid.)

This foreunderstanding of the Empire as the authentic and legitimate governing authority, which was considerably born out of Macaulay's endeavours to devise an inclusive order of the juridical that would extend (at least in theory) the question of sovereignty beyond the constrained contours of colonial power and the colonial subject of hierarchical superiority, marks the transformation of imperialism into Empire. Antonio Negri and Michael Hardt observe that the Empire, unlike imperialism, is not obsessed with "hierarchical social boundaries" that attempt to "police the purity of its own identity and to exclude all that was other." (Hardt and Negri 2000, xii) Instead, the "Empire manages hybrid identities, flexible hierarchies and plural exchanges through modulating networks of command." (Ibid. xii-xiii) The incorporation of the plural and the heterogeneous within the sovereign framework through a moderation of the principles of governmentality suggests a liberal turn and Partha Chatterjee describes this practice of governance as "liberal imperialism" (Chatterjee 2012 (a), 176). The curious infusion of liberalism with governance marks the birth of biopolitics.

In his lectures on the Birth of Biopolitics, Michel Foucault identifies the liberal ideology of governance as the historical antecedent of the modern biopolitical State. For Foucault, the origin of the liberal mode of governance is historically situated in the eighteenth century and is distinguished from other modes of governance in its "…organization of numerous and complex internal mechanisms whose function…is not so much to ensure the growth of the state's forces, wealth and strength…as to limit the exercise of government power internally." (Foucault 2008, 27) Liberal governance, as Foucault evaluates, is "not a form of governmentality which would leave more white spaces of freedom". Rather, it produces and organises freedom under the imperative "I am going to produce what you need to be free. I am going to see to it that you are free to be free." (Ibid., 63) Hence, in the liberal mode of governance, "freedom of behavior is entailed, called for, needed, and serves as a regulator, but it also has to be produced and organized." (Ibid.,

65) The production of freedom is suggestive of a controlled ideal of freedom which finds its roots in the Benthamian notion of the Panopticon. All that is regulated is lawful to be free. The Biopolitical, as Foucault reflects elsewhere, is characterised by a "power bent on generating forces, making them grow, and ordering them, rather than one dedicated to impeding them, making them submit, or destroying them." (Foucault 1984, 259) As such, the "function of administering life" (Ibid., 260) becomes the primary consideration of a biopolitical mode of governance. Bio-politics for Foucault is fundamentally associated with the idea of discipline where docile bodies that do not transgress but obey are recognised as political subjects.

The curious category of the Empire is, as Michael Hardt and Antonio Negri points out, the "new form" of sovereignty "composed of a series of national and supranational organisms united under a single logic of rule". (Hardt and Negri 2000, xii) This *unity in diversity* (emphasis is mine), as Hardt and Negri observes, is substantially acquired, at least theoretically, at a juridical paradigm where "...there is the guarantee of justice for all peoples." (Ibid., 10) Hence, the contentions of law and justice acquires a fundamental significance in context of Empire and the dissemination of a myth of justice becomes simultaneous with the promotion, propagation and procurement of a consolidated ideal of Empire. Of course, Hardt and Negri's proposition of the Empire is not restrained to the colonial condition. Instead, they prefer to consider the Empire in the global context of post-imperialism. More importantly, as mentioned before in this essay, they propose to understand imperialism and Empire as distinct categories where the "sovereignty of the nation-state" serve-s/ed as the cornerstone of the former while the latter "establishes no territorial center of power and does not rely on fixed boundaries or barriers." (Ibid., xii)

While one cannot deny the theoretical justification behind such claims of distinction, yet it does not necessarily suggest that Imperialism and Empire are mutually exclusive watershed categories. On the contrary, there are transitions and overlaps and one such obvious instance of transition of imperialism into Empire is observable in the colonial history of India. The transformation of the Indies from a market for the East India Company to the jewel in the crown of Queen Victoria extensively traces and testifies this transition. It is beyond the scope of the present chapter to comment on the underlying ploys, reforms and policies that made such a transformation possible. Yet, what stands out is an increasing interest in governmentalisation of the colony (i.e., India) and a transposition of acquisition by governance. In this prioritisation of governance over acquisition and administration over exploitation, the bio-political tendencies of British colonialism in India are specified. The introduction of social reforms, the civilising mission of the native, the promotion of industrial capitalism and most importantly, the attempt to incorporate a multitudinous milieu within a singular sovereign order of jurisprudence are substantial instances of this bio-political mode of governance.

Rudyard Kipling, with his profound faith in the benevolent face of the Empire, "…preserved and petrified the "legend of empire" as the eternally responsible parent who could be relied on to provide permanent support to the rest of the world". (Sullivan 1993, 10) Hence, the parental mode of governance practised by an "idealized paternal imperialism" (Ibid., 11), that would protect the disciplined and regulated docile subjects, irrespective of their natural-biological origin and racial disposition, was fundamental to Kipling's understanding of the Empire. Sullivan observes that the ambiguities in Kipling's engagement with Imperialism was marked by the "dominant preoccupation of…how to parent India". (Ibid., 15) As such, the "positive imperial idea" (Islam 1975, 48) which "raises a vision of utopia justifying power as well as the possibility of a solution for the woes of mankind" (Ibid.) is an essential preoccupation in Kipling's literary oeuvre, with *The Jungle Books* being no exception. For Kipling, the Empire signified "a positive force that imposes a pattern of order on chaos" (Ibid., 48-49) and thereby ensure a consolidation of universal model of governance, which Sullivan has described as the "mythology of Empire" (Sullivan 1993, 14).

As such, not the "enlargement of frontiers" (Islam 1975, 71) but the dissemination of "law, literacy, communications, medical facilities and useful arts" (Ibid.) among the chaotic climate of India was for Kipling, the need of the hour. In his poem 'A Song to the English' Kipling advices the Englishman to "Keep ye the law — be swift in all obedience — / ...Make ye sure to each his own/ That he reap where he hath sown". (Kipling A Song) Thus, the contention of law becomes a principal concern for Kipling. In his short non-fictional piece "Across a Continent" Kipling observes that "In a heathen land the three things that are supposed to be pillars of moderately decent government are regard for human life, justice criminal and civil, as far as it lies in a man to do justice, and good roads." (cited in Islam 1975, 72) What is interesting is Kipling's constant emphasis on law and justice that must complement the bio-political model of a developmental mode of governance that is principally preoccupied with questions of transport, health and literacy. Hence, the contention of rule by law must be as fundamental a consideration to the Empire as the initiatives to improve and better the quotients of literacy, communication, transportation and health. Shamsul Islam observes that Kipling sees law as inclusive in essence where "There is room for all within the Law, which sees no breed that has accepted it as greater or lesser than another". (Ibid., 78) Of course, Islam considers the law as a "fluid concept, denoting the code of life projected by Kipling in his writings" (Ibid., 5) and distinguishes between "man-made law" which "can be modified, changed, disregarded and disobeyed in deference to a higher law, which remains permanent and which must be kept at all costs in all circumstances." (Ibid., 9) Yet, he also opines that the higher law for Kipling "is a necessity for the progress of civilization and the progress of man". (Ibid.) Thus, the underlying spirit of the Empire and Imperialism is never in dissociation from Kipling's understanding of law. For what else is Empire but a self-validated Eurocentric narrative of progress and civilisation where the white man is perpetually burdened with the responsibility of spreading light among the "...new-caught, sullen peoples, / Half-devil and half-child"? (Kipling n.d., White Man)

The rule of/by law is fundamental to Kipling's celebrated story of Mowgli in *The Jungle Books*. The very opening song titled "Night-Song in the Jungle" emphasises the centrality of law as it selectively wishes "Good hunting" to only "all That keep the Jungle

Law!" (Kipling 2005, 3) This discrete discrimination between the legally bound and the lawless is not merely the manifestation of an authorly/ writerly prejudice. It also serves to portray the Jungle as a bios politikos, containing not a "...simple natural life but rather a qualified life, a particular way of life" (Agamben 1998, 1). The politicisation of bare life and the natural order of existence by inviting the moderation of law is instrumental in allocating the allegorical strains in the anthropomorphic world of Mowgli. The governance of the jungle by law is likeable to the governance of the Empire. Hence, while John McBratney finds in the jungle of *The Jungle Books* a "felicitous space" of "magical enclaves" where "species who are normally antagonistic, live in brotherhood with one another" (McBratney 1992, 284), it is also not far-fetched to interpret the jungle as an allegorical manifestation of the Kipling-ean notion of the Empire where pluralities co-exist under the governance of a singular law.

Within this rule of law, considerations of purity are substituted for the proper and the latter is prioritised over the former. Sher Khan's pursuit of Mowgli, a "man's cub" and hence not an animal by birth, is firmly resisted by the mother wolf Raksha who envisages the possibility of a future when "He (the man's cub) shall live to run with the Pack and to hunt with the Pack; and in the end, look you, hunter of little naked cubs—frog eater—fish-killer-he shall hunt thee!" (Kipling 2005, 7) It is interesting that Raksha is not just content to imagine an idealistic and inclusive tomorrow whenwhere the distinct (the man's cub) is accommodated within the registered-regular model of existence. She is also optimistic about the possibility of that distinct to materialise into a self-competent and self-sufficient agency who can, if necessary, retribute and eliminate the transgressive that disorients the harmonious design of the collective order of existence. Sher Khan, the "hunter of little naked cubs—frog eater—fish killer" (Ibid.), is an exemplary transgressive agent in the narrative. Disobeying the Law of the Jungle, he changes "his quarters without due warning" (Ibid., 4) and tempts a faction of the Free People, i.e., the wolves, to disobey the law and "snatch children from the villager's door step." (Ibid., 19) More importantly, he is a "man eater" by nature; a trait that makes him a perpetual transgressor of "The Law of the Jungle...which forbids every beast to eat Man except when he is killing to show his children how to kill." (Ibid., 5) Sher Khan is an animal by birth and hence a pure subject of the jungle in terms of origin. Yet, he is not the subject proper.

On the other hand, the Man-cub Mowgli evolves as the proper subject of the Jungle. While Mowgli's survival instincts in the forest are shaped by the Father wolf who teaches him "business, and meaning of things in the jungle" (Ibid., 12); Baloo, "the sleepy brown bear" (Ibid., 10) who is also "the Teacher of the Law", teaches him "*all* the Law of the Jungle" (Ibid., 25). Mowgli learns "the Wood and Water Laws", "the Stranger's Hunting Call" and "the Master Words of the Jungle" (Ibid.) which eventually lead him to infer that he is an origin-al member of the "free people" i.e., the wolf-fraternity and assert "I was born in the jungle. I have obeyed the Law of the Jungle, and there is no wolf of ours from whose paws I have not pulled a thorn. Surely they are my brothers!" (Ibid., 14) The question of being-belonging is not undisputedly a question of birth or origin and is hence not unconditionally associated to the inimical question of purity. Instead, by being the subject proper, i.e., by accustoming and mastering oneself with the prevalent culture of existence (learning business) and more importantly, by obeying the law, one can surpass the considerations of purity and rightfully belong to an apparently alien order of existence.

Kipling, a Western sahib born in the native infested East, was critical of the notion of purity that staunchly relied on the imperatives of origin and lineage. McBratney observes that "...both in his personal life and his work, Kipling quietly rebelled against the particularist and hierarchical premises of racial typology." (McBratney 1992, 281) For Kipling, the white man is not necessarily defined within a purist trope of origin and race. In a letter dated to George F. Beans, dated 15th August, 1897, Kipling observes that by "white men" he means "...races speaking the English tongue, with a high birth rate and a low murder-rate, living quietly under Laws which are neither bought nor sold." (Kipling 1990, 309) Kipling's white man is not necessarily a racially superior subject of European origin. Rather, as Shamsul Islam suggests, for Kipling and his times, the signifier 'white man' has a "secondary symbolic meaning: 'a man with the moral standards of the civilized world'" (Islam 1975, 75). Most importantly, he, i.e., the white man, is marked by an unconditional loyalty towards the Empire, so much so, that "there is no need to talk of "loyalty" among white men". (Kipling 1990, 309) Thus, for Kipling, the Macaulian "native gentleman" who is "Indian in blood and colour, but English in tastes, in opinions, in morals and in intellect" (Macaulay 1835, 8) i.e., native in blood yet English in spirit, does hold the possibility of becoming the white man and hence the recognised subject of the Empire. Such a case is clearly made by Purun Bhagat in the short story "The Miracle of Puran Bhagat", also anthologised in *The Jungle Books*. Purun Dass, a high-caste Brahmin whose "father has been an important official in the gay-colored tag-rag and bob-tail of an old-fashioned Hindu Court", realises the profound truth of the Empire: "that if anyone wished to get on he must stand well with the English, and imitate all the English believed to be good." (Kipling 2005, 169) Thus, "helped by a good English education at a Bombay University" (Ibid.), Purun Dass rises "step by step, to be the Prime Minister of the Kingdom". (Ibid., 170) Along with the Prince who succeeded the deceased King and who had been "tutored by an Englishman" (Ibid.), Purun Dass accomplishes an all-round development of the native State, so much so that he soon becomes "the honored friend of Viceroys, and Governors, and Lieutenant-Governors, and medical missionaries, and common missionaries, and hard-riding English officers..." (Ibid.). He goes to London and the capital of the Empire acknowledges him as the ""...most fascinating man we have ever met at dinner since cloths were first laid!'" (Ibid.) Although Kipling's story does not end at the apex of Purun Dass's achievements and goes on to narrate his transformation into Purun Bhagat, a "sunnyasi or holy man" (Ibid., 171) who goes on to save a mountain village from a natural catastrophe at the cost of his own life, yet one can barely fail to notice that Purun Dass *aka* Purun Bhagat is, or has been, a Macaulayan man. Lest his readers forget Purun Dass in the posthumous glory of Purun Bhagat, Kipling strategically restates the once achicved imperial fame of 'Sir' Purun Dass in the epitaph like denouement of the story:

"They built the temple before a year was ended, a little stone and earth shrine, and they called the hill the Bhagat's Hill, and they worship there with lights and flowers and offerings to this day. But they do not know that the saint of their worship is the late Sir Purun Dass, K.C.I.E., D.C.L., Ph.D., etc., once Prime Minister of the progressive and enlightened State of Mohiniwala, and honorary or corresponding member of more learned and scientific societies than will ever do any good in this world or the next." (Ibid.,183)

Purun Das's story, although seemingly irrelevant to the context of our discussion, provides us a substantial account of Kipling's supposed faith in the justice of the Empire. For him, the Empire is that unbiased domain where considerations of origin do not hinder the possibility of being recognised and appreciated by the governing authorities. All that is required on behalf of the distinct is an undisputed faith in the jurisprudence of the governing and a genuine intent to abide and act by the propagated ideals of governance. The origin-ally distinct native must exhibit an unconditional urge to become the docile biopolitical subject. Subjecthood will follow in due course.

Subjecthood follows for Mowgli as he abides by the law of the jungle and is accepted by the forest fraternity. Akela, the leader of the wolves, stands up in Mowgli's defence when Sher Khan accuses the latter of "troubling the jungle for ten seasons" (Kipling 2005, 19) and once again the defence relies on Mowgli's reverence for the law and livelihood of the jungle. Akela's defence, quoted as the epigraph to this chapter, emphasises Mowgli's conformism to the status quo of the jungle and his unconditional reverence for the law. Mowgli breaks "no word of the Law of the jungle" (Ibid.) and is thus uncritically included by Akela among the intimate circle of 'us'. Akela recognises Mowgli as "our brother in all but blood" (Ibid.), thereby foregrounding an ideal of brotherhood that is founded not on origin but on identical manner of habitation under the authoritative governance of law.

This brotherhood that is founded not on the ideal of origin but co-habitation has the axiom ""We be of one blood, ye and I"" (Ibid., 26) as the "Master word" that Mowgli learns with ease from Baloo. The Master word, as Baloo—the learned counsel at law confides to Bagheera—the Panther, is the passcode to safety in the jungle and armed with it, Mowgli "can now claim protection, if he will only remember the words, from all in the jungle." (Ibid., 25) What we thus have is a polity that prioritises a governed model of habitation over origin and determines fraternity in lights of the former. To survive in this polity, it is essential that the singular suspends all considerations of purity and origin-ality and with prompt conviction, submits, and hence accommodates itself within the lineage of the other.

The volatilisation of purity and its consistent turn towards hybridity is fundamental to Kipling's evaluation of the nature of Empire. Unlike the dominant imperialist strains which relied on a clear hierarchical and binarified distinction between the colony and the host, between the racially subaltern native and the superior master, Kipling saw the binaries as blurred and often vanishing in their symbiotic exchange with each other. In a letter to George F. Beans dated 15th August, 1897, Kipling mentions his "dislike" for the word "colonies". He finds the word to be "out of date and misleading, besides being provincial." (Kipling 1990, 309) His celebrated poem "A Song of the English", which ends with a dialogue between the children and the mother (i.e., the various representative cities of the Empire living under the colonial condition and the imperial England) emphasises the inclusive ideal of Empire as Mother England emphatically assures her 'children' colonies (Kipling, of course, does not use the word colonies): "...So long as the blood endures/ I shall know that your good is mine: ye shall feel that my strength is yours:" (Kipling n.d., A Song) Kipling's England adores her colonies as "Sons of The Blood", thus problematising her own claim to hierarchical superiority which has been, historically, a constant accompaniment to English imperialism. The children are bonded to their Mother in a love that is "deeper than speech" and bound by a "tether" that is "stronger than life". In return, the children only have to ensure "That Our House (Empire) stand together and the pillars do not fall". (Ibid.) The pillars of the Empire are hence protected and procured through a compromise of English purity whereby the colony (and thus the colonised) is accredited a status within the lineage of the coloniser and is thereby acknowledged by the imperial Mother as "Sons of The Blood" (Ibid.).

It is interesting to note that Kipling's poem was first published in 1893 and thus in immediate precedence of *The Jungle Books* which in turn, according to most scholars, was published roughly around the period of 1894-95. Hence, the striking resemblance between Mother England's proclamation "Because ye are sons of The Blood" (Ibid.) and the Master word of the jungle "We be of one blood, ye and I" (Kipling 2005, 26) that can unfailingly protect Mowgli from an impending danger is more than coincidental. It is suggestive of Kipling's non-apprehension of hybridity and his non-obsession with purity of origins and lineage, especially when it comes to governing or sustaining within a political community. For Kipling, the equilibrium of governance in a political community is only possible when both the governing and the governed are ready to compromise their obsession with purity that is grounded on the question of origin. The Empire can sustain when Mother England accepts the colonies as "Flesh of the flesh that I bred, bone of the bone that I bare" (Kipling n.d., A Song) and the Jungle can thrive if it accepts the man's cub as its recognised inhabitant turned subject. Reciprocally, the colonies are supposed to "speak to your (their) kinsmen...After the use of the English/ in straight-flung words and few." (Ibid.) and Mowgli is expected to "faithfully" (Kipling 2005, 13) obey the Law of the Jungle. For both the accommodator and the accommodated, the acknowledger and the acknowledged, the contention of origin or purity is a tertiary consideration to be made for the materialisation of a political model of existence. Instead, it is the question of the proper that is more fundamental and primary.

Mowgli is rigorously taught the importance of being proper rather than pure by his tough taskmaster Baloo. He is rebuked by Baloo for his amiable socialisation with the "Bandar-log" i.e., the monkeys. In the story, the monkeys are described as a lawless mass of ungoverned "outcasts" (Ibid., 28) who "...were always just going to have a leader, and laws and customs of their own, but they never did, because their memories would not hold over from day to day..." (Ibid., 29). Both Bagheera and Baloo describe them as "the people without a Law" (Ibid., 27) and even when Mowgli is scientifically right to develop a fondness and fellow-feeling for his origin-al brothers of the primate family and, unacquainted to the

Darwinian thesis, contests his case on the empirical observation that "They stand on their feet as I do", he is immediately warned by Baloo that "Their way is not our way" (Ibid., 28).

This is a significant juncture in the novel for it explores the nuances between the proper and the pure and the politics of governance in the Mowgli stories. Baloo's categorical distinction between "they" and "us" elucidates before Mowgli two contradictory models of inhabitation or existence in the jungle. One is 'our' (emphasis is mine) way of living, in reverence and obedience of an archaic law that is "as old and as true as the sky" (Ibid., 165) The other is 'their' (emphasis is mine) way of existence in a precarious state of lawlessness. Owing to the resemblances in origin, Mowgli is naturally prone to develop a fellow-feeling towards the lawless monkey clan who in turn adore him as "blood-brother" (Ibid., 28) and promise him leadership. However, he must sternly control his instinctive and natural desire for the origin to be accorded subjecthood and thereby recognised as the proper subject of the jungle.

The Bandar-log's self-complacent assertion "What the Bandar-log think now the jungle will think later" seemingly parodies the eminent Indian National Congress Leader Gopal Krishna Gokhale's oft-quoted statement "What Bengal thinks today, India thinks tomorrow". Nina Martyris observes that Kipling was largely dismissive of political bodies like Indian National Congress which were pre-dominated by mimic men who were "…Western-educated, English-speaking Indian intellectuals…who held debates and put forward petitions for increased political representation for Indians." (Martyris 2018) Hence, it is not unreasonable to read the Bandar-log (monkey clan) as an allegorical representation of the native who is critical of the law of the Empire and increasingly resists the imperial mode of governance. Yet, at a more general level, the lawless monkeys are embodiments of the ungoverned which possesses the potential to upset any systemic model of governance and are thus absolutely otherised by and in a governmental and governmentalised regime. They are, to quote Baloo, the outcasts with whom the Jungle "…have no dealings…" (Kipling 2005, 28). The governed 'we' "do not drink where the monkeys drink…do not go where the monkeys go…do not hunt where they hunt…do not die where they die." (Ibid.) In his letter to the French writer Andre Chevrillon, Kipling observes that the Bandar-log were faithful reflections of "my views on the Great God "Democracy"" (Kipling 1999, 576). As a form of governance that was founded on "popular opinion" (Ibid.), democracy, for Kipling, lacked the sanctity of rule and was a political model where the authority of law was essentially compromised. Praising Canada for not having achieved yet the status of an ideal democracy, Kipling opines in *Letters to the Family* that "...the law in Canada exists and is administered, not as a surprise, a joke, a favor, a bribe...but as an integral part of the national character..." (cited in Martyris 2018) The rule by law is Kipling's politico-philosophical/philosophico-political obsession. The intimations of the alien do not intimidate his political understanding; the premonition of lawlessness does. On the contrary, he is repelled at the thought of a political community which is pure in terms of origin but is lawless in nature.

Under the watchful and governing eyes of Baloo and Bagheera, Mowgli evolves as the lawful subject of the jungle. He avoids company of the lawless monkey-clan, he slays Sher Khan, the transgressor of law. His initial return to his origin, i.e., the natives in the village, is marked by his dystopic realisation that the "Men Folk" "...have no manners" (Kipling 2005, 51) and that they resemble with the lawless "gray ape" (Ibid.) in behaviour. Subsequently, he abandons the village and chooses to return to the Jungle to lead the wolves who are now "sick of lawlessness". (Ibid., 66) Complacently, he reveals to Ka, the python, that "It is better in the Jungle" (Ibid., 239). Although he makes occasional visits to the village to meet his biological parents, yet his happy reconciliation with humanity is impossible without the intervention of the Empire. In other words, the Empire serves as the only possible interface between Mowgli and the homo-sapiens. At the initiative of Gisborne and Muller, the white men, Mowgli is absorbed as a forest guard in the service of the Empire. He is now supposed to assist the "Government in the matters of Woods and Forests" (Kipling n.d., In the Rukh). In the Empire, Mowgli finds an accepting human world that is not inhabited/ saturated by narrow minded natives like Abdul Gaffur who are obsessed with purity parameters like origin, race and caste. Instead, it is populated by idealistic white men who do not "trap men" (Ibid.) but enfranchise them, if only they are ready to obey and serve properly.

Notes:

1. See, for instance "Kipling, the Orient, and Orientals: "Orientalism" Reoriented?" by David Scott published in *Journal of World History*, Vol. 22, No. 2
2. The Black Act, passed in 1836, dissolved the Provision of Charter Act of 1813, which allowed a British suitor an appeal to the Supreme Court in suits where Indians generally were entitled to appeal to the Sadar Dewani Adalat. The Second part of the Act did not except any person 'by reason of place of birth or by reason of descent' from the jurisdiction of the civil courts of the Company, barring the munsiff's court.
3. Please see "The Fruits of Macaulay's Poison Tree" in *Empire and Nation: Essential Writings 1985-2005* by Partha Chatterjee. Publication Details are available in Bibliography.

Bibliography:

Agamben, Giorgio. 1998. *Homo Sacer: Sovereign power and Bare Life*. trans. Daniel Heller-Roazen. Stanford: Stanford University Press.

Bhaba, Homi K. 1985. "Sly Civility". *October*, Vol. 34 (Autumn): 71-80. JSTOR. https://www.jstor.org/stable/778489. Accessed on 13th January, 2021.

Chatterjee, Partha. 2012. *The Black Hole of Empire: History of a Global Practice of Power*. Princeton: Princeton University Press.

...2012. *Empire & Nation: Essential Writings 1985-2005*. Ranikhet: Permanent Black. (b)

Dharker, C.D. 1946. "Introduction". In *Lord Macaulay's Legislative Minutes*. London: Oxford University Press.

Foucault, Michel. 1984. "The Right of Death and Power over Life". In *The Foucault Reader*, edited by Paul Rainbow, 258-272. New York: Pantheon Books.

...2008. *The Birth of Biopolitics: Lectures at the College de France, 1978-79*. edited by Michel Senellart and translated by Graham Burchell. New York: Palgrave Macmillan.

Hardt, Michael and Antonio Negri. 2000. *Empire*. Cambridge: Harvard University Press.

Islam, Shamsul. 1975. *Kipling's Law: A Study of his philosophy of life*. London: Macmillan.

Kipling, Rudyard. 1990. *The Letters of Rudyard Kipling: Vol.2 1890-99*. edited by Thomas Pinney. New York: Palgrave Macmillan.

... 1999. *The Letters of Rudyard Kipling: Vol. 4 1911-1919*. edited by Thomas Pinney. Iowa City: University of Iowa Press.

....2005. *The Jungle Books*. New Delhi: Peacock Books.

.... n.d. "A Song of the English". EBook. Retrieved from Project Gutenberg. http://www.gutenberg.org/files/37091/37091-h/37091-h.htm. Accessed on 12th February, 2021.

...n.d. "In the Rukh". Retrieved from kiplingsociety.co.uk. http://www.tel elib.com/authors/K/KiplingRudyard/prose/ManyInventions/ru kh.html. Accessed on 1st March, 2021.

...n.d. "The White Man's Burden". Retrieved from the official website of The Kipling Society. http://www.kiplingsociety.co.uk/poems_burd en.htm. Accessed on 13th February, 2021.

Macaulay, T.B. 1835. "Minutes on Education". Retrieved from http://hom e.iitk.ac.in/~hcverma/Article/Macaulay-Minutes.pdf. Accessed on 16th January, 2021.

...1946. *Lord Macaulay's Legislative Minutes*. London: Oxford University Press.

...1976. *The Letters of Thomas Babington Macaulay: Vol. III, January 1834-August 1841*. edited by Thomas Pinney. Cambridge: Cambridge University Press.

Martyris, Nina. 2018. "The Laws of the Jungle". *Lapham's Quarterly*, May. https://www.laphamsquarterly.org/roundtable/laws-jungle. Accessed on 24th February, 2021.

McBratney, John. 1992. "Imperial Subjects, Imperial Space in Kipling's "Jungle Book"". *Victorian Studies*, Vol. 35, no. 3 (Spring): 277-293. JSTOR. https://www.jstor.org/stable/3828034. Accessed on 19th February, 2021.

Randall, Don. 1998. "Post-Mutiny Allegories of Empire in Rudyard Kipling's The Jungle Books". *Texas Studies in Literature and Language: Local Habitations*, Vol. 40, no. 1 (SPRING): 97-120.

Said, Edward. 1994. *Culture and Imperialism*. New York: Vintage Books.

Scott, David. 2011. "Kipling, the Orient, and Orientals: "Orientalism" Reoriented?". *Journal of World History*, Vol. 22, no. 2: 299-328.

Skinner, Quentin. 1978. *The Foundations of Modern Political Thought Vol. I: The Renaissance*. Cambridge: Cambridge University Press.

Sullivan, Zohren T. 1993. *Narratives of Empire: The fictions of Rudyard Kipling*. Cambridge: Cambridge University Press.

# Making the Chessboard Smooth: Popular as "Nonsense" in *Through the Looking Glass*

Arnab Dasgupta

Alice, the young girl, who is in constant state of engagement with surfaces deep and inverted, occupies a critical space in literary discourses. Lodged in the generic confluence of children's literature, the nonsensical and the popular, she is endowed with multivalency as a literary symbol. Along with literary figures such as Peter Pan, Pinacchio, and Nutcracker she disavows straight jacketing into a specific genre and continuously spills over her textual space of containment. In cultural history Alice is omnipresent, from the writings of Virginia Woolf to cartoon films of Walt Disney, from Grace Slick to the cyber generation, from Tim Burton's adaptations to futuristic e-texts like *Alice for the iPad*, the curious adventures of Alice have woven their way into the intertext of lives and letters of many generations. Alice's adventures, much like Peter Pan's exploits, constantly forfeit closure and consequently her character has become a veritable leitmotif in the contemporary popular psychology.

The issue of being, is central to both the *Alice* novels and particularly so in *Through the Looking-Glass, and What Alice Found There* (1871). The novel with its language games and the simulacra mirror world in(to) which Alice slips/sleeps contrives the motif of the game of chess in which Alice seeks to move to the eighth square, to be crowned the queen thereby, narrates the journey of "becoming woman" for Alice. The journey of Alice through the mirror world has been a regular subject of investigation for the psychoanalysts drawing upon Lacanian understanding of the mirror stage and the objet petit a–the unattainable object of desire which in the novel is symbolised by the world of the looking glass. The reader of the novel is constantly invited, as Helene Cixous puts it, to "take the whole adventure for a figurative representation of the imaginary construction of self, ego, through reflexive identification, the other side of the mirror never being anything else but this side" (Cixous and Maclean 1982, 238). Clearly the narrative centres around issue of subjectivity, its play in the surface and territoriality of simulation, as it explodes between a dream and an improbable game of chess which is played with no intent of "checkmate" and even if the intent is present its utterance is in ellipsis or erasure giving the game a morbius like jiggered continuity. This point of duality and infinite rupture which plays itself out in the surface of the mirror is the point of contest and conflict between the real and symbolic as well as the smooth and the striated. This is the point where "Pure events escape from the state of affairs" (Deleuze 2004, 21). Lewis Carroll's invocation of mirror causes disruption of the continuity and causality in the novel and turns Alice's adventures into a pure event.

Alan Badiou notes regarding Deleuze's concept of event "The event is always that which has just happened and that which is about to happen, but never that which is happening" (Badiou 2007, 38). Badiou elaborates further that "the event" does not take place 'between' a past and a future, between the margins of two worlds rather it is "encroachment and connection: it realizes the indivisible continuity of Virtuality." (Ibid.) This encroachment is exactly what transpires as Alice enters the virtual world of looking glass. For instance, when Alice moves through the looking glass:

> The first thing she did was to look whether there was a fire in the fireplace, and she was quite pleased to find that there was a real one, blazing away as brightly as the one she had left behind.... Then she began looking about, and noticed that what could be seen from the old room was quite common and uninteresting, but that all the rest was as different as possible. For instance, the pictures on the wall next the fire seemed to be all alive, and the very clock on the chimney piece (you know you can only see the back of it in the Looking-glass) had got the face of a little old man and grinned at her. (Carroll 1994, 135-136).

Alice's transference into the simulacra world of the Looking-glass is without any intervallic void between the two spaces- the space of her Victorian room and the mirror and their respective temporalities. The same fire which was burning in her room is present in the same position in the Looking-glass world and the visual motifs which are reflected from the real world too hold their consistency. Yet the two rooms are not identical and it is the mirror world which seems to encroach on the real as it endows a face to the chimney clock and make paintings come real. Event, unlike bodies, lack corporeal depth of present. It subsists in both the past and the future, in becoming. The room into which Alice enters through the Looking-glass folds the pre-given past of Alice's living room with unattainable virtual future which awaits Alice in a homogenous manner. Thus, in *Through the Looking-glass*, in contrast to *Alice in Wonderland*, "Movements of penetration and burying give way to light lateral movements of sliding; the animals of the depths become figures on cards without thickness" (Deleuze 1998, 21).

According to Deleuze, events have the propensity to drift on the surface of bodies and cannot be said to ex-ist. Instead, they subsist or *per-sist* in the inter- relations of the bodies. The game of chess in *Through the Looking-Glass* is an instance of such an event as the game sub-sits through its patterns and series rather than exist through its set pieces. A traditional game of chess is often prearranged and has strict striations of space—both physical and abstract. Displacement through space is greatly controlled and the pieces played with are formalised through consolidation of identities which are hierarchically controlled and they singularly act and move in pre-designated patterns. Deleuze and Guattari write in *Treatise on Nomadology- the war Machine* of *A thousand Plateaus*:

> Chess is a game of State, or of the court: the emperor of China played it. Chess pieces are coded; they have an internal nature and intrinsic properties from which their movements, situations, and confrontations derive. They have qualities; a knight remains a knight, a pawn a pawn, a bishop a bishop. (Deleuze and Guattari 1988, 352)

It is clear that "chess pieces entertain biunivocal relations with one another" (Ibid., 353), and they are limited to function within a limited space. The chess as institutionalised war, unfolds in a closed space where the game dictates occupation of maximum territory through minimum moves and there is possibility of retreat, elimination as well as attack. In chess the pieces are codified, and the board is stratified as chess is an instance of state apparatus. The game of chess as Carroll presents however is a game of 'difference' (emphasis is mine) rather than a game of negation, as in Carroll's chess board there is no stratification or hierarchy, merely 'difference' (emphasis is mine).

Unlike a conventional game of chess, the chess-world of *Through the Looking-Glass* is played with non-stratified non-coded pieces. For instance, the red queen invites Alice to the game with a total disregard for her material reality "You can be the White Queen's pawn, if you like, as Lily's too young to play: and you're in the second square to begin with: when you get to the Eighth Square you'll be a Queen" (Carroll 1994, 150). This non-stratified nature of the game makes it akin to the game of Go where in contrast to the chess pieces the tokens or pieces of the game "are pellets, disks, simple arithmetic units, and have only an anonymous, collective, or third -person function: "It" makes a move. "It" could be a man, a woman, a louse, an elephant. Go pieces are elements of a non-subjectified machine assemblage with no intrinsic properties, only situational ones" (Deleuze and Guattari 1988, 352-353). Indeed, Alice is a woman as she becomes a white pawn in board. There are no rear movements or retreat in the game in which Alice participates, there is only a gradual and steady linear thrust as Red queen predicts the map or design through which Alice will move to the final square to be crowned the Queen:

> A pawn goes two squares in its first move, you know. So you'll go very quickly through the Third Square- by railways, I should think- and you'll find yourself in the Fourth Square in no time. Well, that square belongs to Tweedledum and Tweedledee- the Fifth is mostly water–the Sixth belongs to Humpty Dumpty...the Seventh Square is all forest- however, one of the Knights will show you the way- and in the Eighth Square we all shall be Queens together, and it's all feasting and fun! (Carroll 1994, 153).

This passage makes it difficult to treat the game of chess in the novel in the conventional sense as the occupation of territory is not intrinsic to the discourse of chess but rather capture and movement are the essential play in chess. One finds permanent residents on the board of the chess like Tweedledum, Tweedledee and Humpty Dumpty who are not only immobile piece but are inconsequential as they let the pawn Alice through to the next Square without any resistance. Carroll indeed, through such rupture seems to invite the reader to participate in a nomadic chess, which much like his real life invention of chess-board game "Lanrick", inverts the stratifications of the board. There are various other un-chess like moves in the game played by Alice in the Looking-glass world which Martin Gardner points out in an analysis of Carroll's game in *The Annotated Alice*. For instance, at two points the White Queen gives up a chance to checkmate and on another instance she runs away from the Red Knight when she could have captured him. The mere occupation of territory by pieces, the lack of intentional movement and the sudden lunging forward of the pawn piece make the game of chess more like the game of Go. As Deleuze and Guattari point out "In Go, it is a question of arraying oneself in an open space, of holding space, of maintaining the possibility of springing up at any point: the movement is not from one point to another, but becomes perpetual, without aim or destination, without departure or arrival (Deleuze and Guattari 1988, 353)." Even though the game is played with the pretext of moving Alice to the Eighth Square it is defined by Alice's meandering, wanderings, deviations and even getting lost. This wandering is best typified in the Fifth Square of water- a smooth space. This space produces wandering of a peculiar form as it is defined by continuous reaching out and never arriving at or reaching a destination. As in the Sheep's shop, Alice discovers the complementarity of "the empty shelf" and the "bright thing always in the shelf next above, that is a place without occupant and occupant without a place" (Deleuze 2004, 41).

The fifth chapter titled *Wool and Water*, capsulate the journey of Alice through the Fifth Square and here the reader encounters the alternate sense making through which the white queen continuously becomes. The white queen experiences the time in a backward trajectory and as she points out "there's one great advantage in it, that one's memory works both ways". (Carroll 1994, 181) This means that the white queen's movements through the chess board are non-linear and are continuously in progress through time and are extremely discontinuous and fractured as she passes through regimented striated spaces. This explains to an extent the peculiarity of her movement across the board as her move cannot be plotted on a timeline that goes continuously from past to future, nor located as points in a continuous diagram or map like the one of the chess board Carrol produces at the beginning of the novel. As James William notes in his discussion of Deleuzian event as philosophised in *Logic of Sense* "No event is one-sided and no event is limited since they take place in infinite and multiple series that only exist as continuing mutual variations". (Williams 2008, 2) Deleuze splits time into two different concepts, Aiôn and Chronos, and resist linearity and continuity in time. This peculiar non-linear temporality of the game and the novel in which the game unfolds takes them beyond the realm of what Deleuze terms as good sense for it "affirms that time unfolds in one direction only, from the past to the future, and that logical thought proceeds from the most to the least differentiated, that is, from the particular case to the universal concept" (Stivale 2005, 66). In the domain of the Carrol's chess board, it is not merely the present temporality that takes the accountability of ordering the flow of time; but it is the future which curiously, is also the past that dictates the temporal sense of what is to come. Hence the declaration by the white Queen "The rule is, jam to-morrow and jam yesterday- but never jam *to-day* (Carroll 1994, 181). According to Helen Cixous, this negation of the present is a negation of meaning to the reader as "This stresses allegorically the nongratifying which this book establishes with the reader: no day meaning, but there is meaning on one side and on time of reading, meaning both promised and inaccessible" (Cixous and Maclean 1982, 237). This establishes the text as "extremely mobile empty space" or "an occupant without a place" (Deleuze 2004, 41) as there is an excess of the signifier over the signified in the novel; in the White Queen's worlding as in Carrol's the today is not reducible to other terms of the series "It's jam every *other* day: to-day isn't any other day, you know (Carroll 1994, 181). This incorporeal today is an instance of pure event as it has an essence of "an impossible incorporeal entity"; and it "belongs to no series; or rather, it belongs to both series at once and never ceases to circulate throughout them. It has therefore the property of always being displaced in relation to itself, "of being absent from its own place," its own identity, its own resemblance, and its own equilibrium (Deleuze 2004, 29).

Sense-events according to Deleuze are immanent to structure, yet they make the structure possible. This holds particularly true for the nonsense words which are present in the novel *Through the Looking-Glass*, particularly in the poem "Jabberwocky". Words such as "outgrabe", "rath" and "mome" are completely without signifiers and have no existence apart from language. These words in no way denote real objects, make obvious the beliefs and desires of real persons, or signify meaningful concepts. Yet, these nonsense words convey sense, and therefore avow the immanence of sense to language itself. The esoteric and nonsense words, which include portmanteau words like "slithy", or "frumious", or the self-referring words used by the gnat like "Rocking-horse-fly", or "Snap-dragon-fly" are "not only to connote or to coordinate two heterogeneous series but to introduce disjunctions in the series", a variable movement (depending on the type of esoteric word employed) of "connection", of "conjunction" and of "disjunction" between series (Deleuze 2004, 47).

These displacements, disjunctions or conjunctions are however permitted under certain rules which annul or limit the "play" "on the chessboard, in the cyclical frame of the seasons, and in the limited frame of the totality of the countryside: fences, streams, fences and high points" (Cixous and Maclean 1982, 244). The rules of the board however are abrupt and spontaneous. With each jump, which Alice makes over the six little brooks, she moves into the next square. She enters a completely new set of patterns and these shifts between the squares are marked by abruption, sans beginning or end. When Alice jumps over the first brook abruptly, she finds herself inside a train which she never boarded and immediately "Tickets, please!" said the Guard.... In a moment everybody was holding out a ticket" (Carroll 1994, 155). Similarly, as the train jumps over the brook to move from the third square to the fourth, the goat's beard which Alice was holding on to as the train jumped arbitrarily "seemed to melt away as she touches it, and she found herself sitting quietly under a tree- while the Gnat (for that was the insect she had been talking to) was balancing itself on a twig just over her head, and fanning her with its wings (Ibid., 158). This trend of melting of space and time continuous every time Alice moves a square by jumping a brook and these shifts like events "exposes unity of passage which fuses the one-just-after and the one-just-before" (Badiou 2007, 38).

In the haptic vision of the chess like landscape in which Alice moves constantly, all her actions can be understood as a single event propelling Alice to her eventual state of being and as Badiou points "there is no contradiction between the limitless of becoming and the singularity of the event". (Ibid.) The complete game of chess is then a singular event which unfolds and in turn folds all the concatenations of the game into the being of Alice as pawn- queen. Carroll's chess board as is his writing "is the domain of the action and passion of bodies: things and words are scattered in every direction, or on the contrary are welded together into nondecomposable blocks" (Deleuze 1998, 21). Indeed, the Carrollian text also wields surfaces together- surface of real world and dream world, surface of depth and flatness and the surface of the lateral and that of the real. Martin Gardener writes in his book *The Universe in a Handkerchief*:

> *Through the Looking-Glass* is even richer in mathematical humor than the first Alice book. This is partly due to its pervasive chess themes, but also to the fact that Alice's journey into the reversed world behind the mirror allowed Carroll to indulge in all sorts of bizarre reversals of space and time. Left and right symmetries and asymmetries abound. The Tweedle brothers, for instance, are mirror images of each other. (Gardener 1996, 2-3)

There is continuous subversion of the landscape and constant doubling abounds throughout and particularly through the Tweedle brothers. Tweedledee and Tweedledum not only are doubled and repeated as the product of the prismatic effect of the mirror. This doubling also holds true of the sign posts which point towards their house for as long as Alice went on the road "there were sure to be two finger-posts pointing the same way, one marked "TO TWEEDLEDUM'S HOUSE", and the other "TO THE HOUSE OF TWEEDLEDEE"" (Carroll 1994, 164). There is a sequence of series through which such a prismatic effect unfolds as the gyre like garden/mirror landscape is sensed to be around the house which in turn is around the room which is around the mirror and consequently "the embedding of themes demands a polysemic reading of what appears to be a plaything as well as a game, a piece of machinery" (Cixous and Maclean 1982, 245). This textual machinery causes incessant doubling as it continuously challenges good sense and common sense through repetition. On the other side of the looking glass, as Deleuze observes,

> "the Hare and the Hatter are taken up again in two messengers, one going and the other coming, one searching the other bringing back, on the basis of two simultaneous directions of Aion. Tweedledee and Tweedledum testify to the indiscernibility of the two directions, and to the infinite subdivision of the two sense in each direction, over the bifurcating route plotting to their house" (Deleuze 2004, 79).

Along with these is the figure of the Red king who, as Alice's double, is constantly dreaming Alice as Alice dreams him in the Looking-glass world. The doubles make improbable all limits of becoming, any semblance of fixity and thus nullify causality bound confines of good sense. The doubling works on a meta level also as the text itself contrives to be a mirror and the mirror is itself reflectively constituted by those mirrors of memory which are the spaces of fields, the sea, the streams, and obviously the chess board. Carroll's text then, is a "vision of the world as planisphere, an illusion of different levels which is given the lie by the chess game, flattening of the order of meaning, and dispersals of relationships" (Cixous and Maclean1982, 245).

Deleuze points out emphatically that "In Lewis Carroll, everything begins with a horrible combat, the combat of depths: things explode or make us explode. (Deleuze 1998, 21) This sense of combat and explosion is present in the ending of *Through the Looking Glass* through the effect of flattening- rendering of things smooth and nonsensical. The mirror which contains the text, permits the various character to exist, retains them and continuously plods them into play is flattened by Alice's awakening. Once Alice reaches the Eight Square she is crowned the Queen and she attains a telescopic and haptic vision which makes all the residents of the Looking-glass visible to her simultaneously. Yet precisely this is the point that this world of the chess board/Looking-glass becomes intolerable. In a repetition of her violent rejection of Wonderland and its denizens, in *Alice in Wonderland* where she had declared "You are nothing but a pack of cards!" (Carroll 1994, 117) Alice gets increasingly annoyed at the end of text and cries "I can't stand this any longer!" and she catches hold of the Red Queen and tells her "I'll shake you into a kitten, that I will!" (Ibid.) This flattening or annihilation of the Queen is the effacement of the rights and privileges Alice had just acquired as Queen. Consequently, her waking up and the melting of the dream world Red Queen and the real world kitten flattens and dilutes the surfaces between real and dreamlike/ virtual, the two dimensional chess/mirror world and three dimensional reality and the simulacral and the corporeal. The proliferation of the nonsense in the realms real and virtual dismantle the state apparatus and its hierarchical structure and it flows from the virtual and surface domain of the convoluted looking-glass chess board of Lewis Carroll as event incorporeal- as affects, memories, desires and reflections. Deleuze notes this propensity of the surface (of two dimensionality) to produce nonsense which function like pure event and writes in the conclusion of his essay on Lewis Carroll in *Essays Critical and Clinical* "It is not that surface has less nonsense than does depth. But it is not the same nonsense. Surface nonsense is like the "Radiance" of pure events, entities that never finish either happening or withdrawing" (Deleuze 1998, 22).

Bibliography:

Badiou, Alain. 2007. "The event in Deleuze." *Parrhesia*, Vol. 2: 37-44.

Cixous, Hélène and Marie Maclean. 1982. "Introduction to *Lewis Carroll's through the Looking-Glass* and the *Hunting of the Snark*." *New Literary History*, Vol. 13, no. 2: 231-251.

Carroll, Lewis. 1994. *Alice's Adventures in Wonderland and Other Stories*. New York: Barnes and Noble.

Deleuze, Gilles, and Félix Guattari. 1988. *A Thousand Plateaus: Capitalism and schizophrenia*. London: Bloomsbury Publishing.

Deleuze, Gilles. 1998. *Essays critical and clinical*. London: Verso.

… 2004. *Logic of sense*. London: Bloomsbury Publishing.

Gardner, Martin. 2007. *The Universe in a Handkerchief: Lewis Carroll's mathematical recreations, games, puzzles, and word plays*. New York: Springer.

Stivale, Charles J. 2014. *Gilles Deleuze: Key Concepts*. New York: Routledge.
Williams, James. 2008. *Gilles Deleuze's Logic of Sense: A Critical Introduction and Guide*. Edinburgh: Edinburgh University Press.

Narrative Function and Identity in Paulo Coelho's *The Alchemist*

Mitarik Barma

Paulo Coelho's novel *The Alchemist* (first published in 1988 in Portuguese; the English translation was published in 1993) has been translated into 72 languages and has sold over 65 million copies. The novel remains a bestseller to this date and there are specific reasons behind the continuing popularity of this particular narrative. Coelho in the Preface of his novel admits the fact that he is unaware about the reasons behind the popularity of the narrative, but emphasises on the religious aspect of the narrative. However, the narrative has been accepted by readers belonging to a diverse group of religion quite possibly due to the fact that the Christian religious motifs are not directly enforced and rather have been presented through allegories. There also seems to be little or no religious jargon in place, and the major characters in the narrative take quite a liberal attitude towards non-Christian religions. Moreover, it seems Coelho has borrowed religious motifs common to non-Christian religions as well, which might have resonated with readers more inclined towards other religious beliefs. The allegorical nature of the narrative that talks about overcoming real life obstacles in the path of one's spiritual journey makes it easier to transpose those motifs in non-religious settings as well. Also, Coelho takes up quite an optimistic outlook towards life, interpersonal relationships and the problems of life in the narrative. Perhaps for these reasons, the narrative also works as a self-help text and garners a universal appeal in a society where at the height of individualisation self-help industry sees a surging popularity. Therefore, the narrative serves three distinct categories, the religious, the novel readers and those seeking motivations in self-help narratives. In the following discussion I intend to show through a structural, linear analysis of the narrative how Coelho manages to blend elements of motivational religious themes (both Christian and non-Christian) with existential beliefs to his advantage to create a narrative that remains open to interpretation to readers belonging to a diverse group of religious communities (although it seems the target audience might primarily be the members of Abrahamic religions).

The narrative begins with the description of an abandoned Church where a shepherd boy has taken refuge. The ruined Church with an enormous sycamore tree immediately evokes Christian motifs as Zacchaeus (Hebrew for innocent, or pure) in the Bible climbed a sycamore tree to see Jesus and later gave away half his wealth. In Coelho's narrative the shepherd boy Santiago (whose name refers to Spanish 'santo' for saint and also carries certain other Christian motifs) embarks on a journey which over time transforms into a spiritual one and he has to climb a mountain in the end to be able to converse with God. He also ends up giving part of his wealth away, and has been portrayed as pure hearted in the narrative. If the statement "Blessed are the pure of heart, for they shall see God" from Matthew 5:8 is taken as a reference to Zacchaeus, then that statement would assert the shepherd boy Santiago's spiritual experience near the end of his journey in the narrative. However, these religious references are not always emphasised in the narrative and while they may appeal to the devout Christians, they present no obstacles for comprehension to the casual reader otherwise unaware of these religious motifs. The narrative talks about how the boy Santiago has become accustomed to the routine of his herd and therefore provides an implicit suggestion that in order to bring change in one's life, one needs to break out of their habitual routines. Suggestions like these replete throughout the narrative enforces the self-help elements of the narrative. Similar suggestions appear later in the narrative when the boy starts working with a crystal shop owner.

The fact that the boy is in search of a treasure he sees in a dream adds to the theme of spiritual quest and at the same time brings in an element of detective fiction in the narrative, since the boy has to find out not only the exact location of the treasure but also the alchemist who comes later in the narrative. The element of romance introduced early in the novel with the boy's romantic interest being the girl of a merchant quite possibly attracts attention of readers who would expect emotional, romantic affairs in popular narratives. This also adds to the character of the boy since it establishes the innocence in his character while at the same time throws light upon his interpersonal relationships and suggests that despite his spiritual inclinations the boy is not an ascetic saintly figure. The narrative states here,

> "As the time passed, the boy found himself wishing that the day would never end, that her father would stay busy and keep him waiting for three days. He recognized that he was feeling something he had never experienced before: the desire to live in one place forever. With the girl with the raven hair, his days would never be the same again. But finally the merchant appeared, and asked the boy to shear four sheep. He paid for the wool and asked the shepherd to come back the following year." (Coelho 2019, 5-6)

Coelho emphasises upon the element of change here since later the boy thinks, "We have to be prepared for change," and at the same time by bringing in economic transactions he is normalising the boy. While this particular section of the narrative might intrigue young readers with interest in romance, it also sets up Coelho's theme of changeability in life, since later in the narrative the shepherd boy Santiago would feel greater emotional attachment to another girl named Fatima, who also provides him spiritual guidance by showing him the direction of the alchemist's abode. Needless to say, Fatima (who in the narrative is a subscriber to Islam) not only bears significance in Islam where it is the name of the prophet's daughter, but also is a reference to Portuguese title of Virgin Mary Nossa Senhora de Fátima, formally known as Our Lady of the Holy Rosary of Fátima based on Marian apparitions reported in 1917 by three shepherd children at the Cova da Iria, in Fátima, Portugal.

The narrative at this point emphasises the desire for travel in the shepherd boy Santiago and would later show how spiritual travel corresponds with physical travel. The narrative states,

> "His parents had wanted him to become a priest, and thereby a source of pride for a simple farm family. They worked hard just to have food and water, like the sheep. He had studied Latin, Spanish, and theology. But ever since he had been a child, he had wanted to know the world, and this was much more important to him than knowing God and learning about man's sins. One afternoon, on a visit to his family, he had summoned up the

> courage to tell his father that he didn't want to become a priest. That he wanted to travel." (Ibid., 8)

This description establishes the reasons behind the spiritual beliefs of Santiago and at the same time his father's statements regarding his decision in life points out that change should not only be external but also internal. His father states that travellers across the globe visit their village to observe and enjoy the natural beauty there but despite their search for novel elements in life they remain the same person when they leave that place.

The narrative states,

> "People from all over the world have passed through this village, son," said his father. "They come in search of new things, but when they leave they are basically the same people they were when they arrived. They climb the mountain to see the castle, and they wind up thinking that the past was better than what we have now. They have blond hair, or dark skin, but basically they're the same as the people who live right here." (Ibid.)

Here Coelho is not only stressing upon the need for internal transformation by making the paternal figure state that regardless of the color of the hair or skin all travellers are the same inside when they leave, but also subtly suggesting that religious transformations are not dependent upon race. While the father's insistence on the beauty of the native people makes him more realistic, the multicultural religious suggestiveness inherent in his statement might be one of the reasons behind the cosmopolitan fascination regarding Coelho's narrative.

The shepherd boy Santiago who is intent on following his dream thinks at this point that, "It's the possibility of having a dream come true that makes life interesting." (Ibid., 10) Coelho repeats this motif later in the narrative when the shepherd boy Santiago starts working in a crystal shop and the shop owner states that he prefers to dream rather than trying to realise his dream since the reality might lead to disappointment. It is unclear whether the glass windows installed in that shop following Santiago's request is a reference to stained glass windows, or bears any implicit reference to Job 28:17 or Revelation 4:6, although the falcon as a motif has been used later in the narrative.

Nonetheless, the boy's visit to the oracle and his insistence on the prognosis offered by his dream is in line with Joel 2:28, which states that old men should dream and young men should see visions.

While looking for the psychoanalytic nature in the encounter of the boy with the oracle, an old gypsy woman might not prove fruitful, the scene also underlines the importance of exchange value in life.

> "You came so that you could learn about your dreams," said the old woman. "And dreams are the language of God. When he speaks in our language, I can interpret what he has said. But if he speaks in the language of the soul, it is only you who can understand. But, whichever it is, I'm going to charge you for the consultation."
> "Tell me more about your dream," said the woman. "I have to get back to my cooking, and, since you don't have much money, I can't give you a lot of time." (Ibid., 12)

The oracle would part her wisdom with an interpretation of the dream of Santiago for an economic exchange, an exchange that is placed in future and the boy not only agrees to this set up near the end of the narrative he proves his saintly nature by respecting that agreement. Later in the narrative when Santiago meets the old man (again another Christian figure) who claims to be the King of Salem he also states that in life everything has a price. Coelho keeps stressing upon the importance of exchange value throughout the narrative. These exchanges are not necessarily always spiritual in nature but often involve physical exchange of gold and money to mark the commodification inherent in life itself. On the other hand, the oracle underlines the hermeneutic nature of the symbolic elements in life. There are multiple instances in the narrative where it is stated that the universe provides omens and signs to those who are open to it. It seems that Coelho highlights the positive aspects of these omens in the narrative which support a certain kind of optimism in the readers and at the same time goes in line with the optimistic attitude displayed by Coelho through his narrative. Likewise, when the boy meets the old man, another biblical figure, Melchizedek (whose old Canaanite name means "My King is Righteousness"), he too asserts that people have control over their lives and they believe differently.

The old man, apparently the king of Salem from the Bible, claims that true desire for anything originates from the 'soul of the universe' and implies the destiny of the people who are subject to such desire. Here it seems that Coelho is implying that these kinds of desires are generally positive in nature and are felt by everyone. Otherwise, the religious undertone of Coelho's narrative would falter to say the least.

> "when you really want something, it's because that desire originated in the soul of the universe. It's your mission on earth." (Ibid., 21)

The statement made by Melchizedek, "that people are capable, at any time in their lives, of doing what they dream of" (Ibid.) is reminiscent of French philosopher Jean Paul Sartre's existential philosophy as Sartre stated "you can always make something out of what you've been made into." (Sartre 1977, 101)

However, Coelho is a man of faith and therefore the character of Melchizedek claims that,

> "At other times, at a crucial moment, I make it easier for things to happen. There are other things I do, too, but most of the time people don't realize I've done them." (Coelho 2019, 22)

This statement positions him as a benevolent God-like figure who would help people in different forms. This again is a common trope in most of the major religions, and therefore is in line with Coelho's religious motifs in the narrative. As it has been mentioned before in this article, Coelho brings in the issue of exchange value in life through this character, which seems to be an important lesson for the protagonist Santiago, who would have to exchange money, time and emotions later in the narrative in various situations. By employing instructional discourses and later calling back to them in the narrative therefore Coelho prepares the readers for Eureka effects in sections of the narrative, which enforces the readers' continual interest in the narrative.

When the boy, Santiago, feels 'jealous of the freedom of the wind' (Ibid., 27), Coelho sets up the plot for another Eureka effect as later in the narrative the boy is tasked to turn into the wind.

The statement (which seems to be part of the thought-process of the protagonist) that, "The sheep, the merchant's daughter, and the fields of Andalusia were only steps along the way to his destiny." (Ibid.) is in itself problematic in nature as it implies a certain kind of selfishness on the protagonist's part as it makes that journey towards authentic self-realisation, detached from social responsibilities. Coelho, however, is able to manipulate narrative complications like these since he portrays his characters as innocent and empathetic and yet driven by certain kind of self-interests.

In this part of the narrative again, Coelho asserts the recurring motif of omens and introduces the divinatory stones from the bible, Urim and Thummim, a reference to Exodus 28:30 and Samuel 1. The story regarding the shopkeeper's boy who is told by the wisest of wise man to roam around his palace, observe the marvels and yet keep the drop of oil in the teaspoon held by him might have been borrowed from Hindu scriptures, since there are references to a similar incident featuring the Hindu King Janaka Videha and the Rishi Shuka dev (Vivekananda 2016, 92-94). Coelho's variation of the same narrative however seems to be more focused on the practical aspect of life against the religious goal of self-abnegation set by Hindu scriptures. Whereas in the Hindu narrative Shuka dev remains focused on his goals without any attention to the outside distractions, in Coelho's variation it states,

> "'Well, there is only one piece of advice I can give you,' said the wisest of wise men. 'The secret of happiness is to see all the marvels of the world, and never to forget the drops of oil on the spoon.'" (Coelho 2019, 30-31)

It is quite possible that Coelho's simpler, pragmatic variation of the same narrative might be more suitable for the casual readers whom Coelho might be targeting his text at. The protagonist after losing his money to the trickster thinks,

> "I'm like everyone else—I see the world in terms of what I would like to see happen, not what actually does" (Ibid., 38)

This goes in line with Coelho's primary character's goals in the narrative, who is transformed through his journeys in life, a transformation that Coelho implies is as fantastic as the transformations made by the process of alchemy. His transformation however is brought out through his interactions with others who help him in his spiritual and material quest. This is in line with Coelho's suggestion that the universe or destiny itself is benevolent towards beings who are on this quest of self-discovery. At the same time this underscores the importance of interpersonal relationships. On the other hand, the event of being robbed shows that the protagonist is not completely flawless. Despite the cautionary tale of the drop of oil, his attention flounders when he sees the beautiful sword, which serves no other function in the narrative. The statement made by the protagonist seems to suggest that the world should be seen as it is, and not how one intends to interpret it. However, with his continual use of biblical imageries and suggestions about specific viewpoints, Coelho seems to subtly impose a particular kind of perspective upon the readers instead of encouraging them to take a complete objective assessment of the external world.

Coelho also uses continual reassertions in order to forward his religious motifs to the readers. For example, following the meeting with the Melchizedek when the boy later loses his money to a trickster and thinks of his meeting with Melchizedek he thinks of the following statement again, "When you want something, all the universe conspires in helping you to achieve it." (Ibid.) Likewise, his thoughts regarding the Candy Merchant,

> "This candy merchant isn't making candy so that later he can travel or marry a shopkeeper's daughter. He's doing it because it's what he wants to do," (Ibid., 41)

reasserts the premise that everybody should follow a particular goal in line with their desire. Here, Coelho's statement evokes the concept of authenticity as espoused by existential philosophy of Jean Paul Sartre and Martin Heidegger. (Varga and Guignon 2020, n.p.)

As it has been mentioned in this article before, Coelho sets up his premise to create the Eureka effect in his readers and when the boy meets the crystal merchant near the desert, the attitude of the crystal merchant affirms the statements made before by the character of Melchizedek. The narrative states regarding the crystal merchant,

> "He had lived thirty years of his life buying and selling crystal pieces, and now it was too late to do anything else." (Coelho 2019, 42)

It is the boy whose presence would change both the crystal merchant's economic position and his attitude towards his commercial enterprise. The crystal merchant who remains helpful towards the boy is also portrayed as a devout Muslim and remains in line of Coelho's liberal and positive attitude towards Abrahamic religions. The religious motif of the narrative is emphasised through the conversation of each of the characters with the boy and that remains true here as well. The crystal merchant made the boy clean the crystal,

> "Because the crystal was dirty. And both you and I needed to cleanse our minds of negative thoughts." (Ibid., 44)

Here Coelho's character correlates physical activity with that of the spiritual, physical cleaning with that of spiritual cleansing. It is possible to find similar themes in all major religions, particularly in Japanese Buddhism, where cleanliness remains supremely important. (Matsumoto 2018, n.p.)

On the other hand, Coelho sets up the character of the crystal merchant as dispassionate but somewhat realistic in his attitude towards life. This sets him up as a contrasting character to the shepherd boy Santiago, who would grow only after facing opposing viewpoints from the crystal merchant and thereby would fulfill the narrative expectations of the readers. Conversely, the emotional attachment formed by the protagonist with the crystal merchant and later with his love interest Fatima supports his authentic self-formation, which seems to be his main goal. The characters with whom the protagonist forms emotional attachments seems to form the 'horizons of significance' for the boy. Charles Taylor in his *Ethics of Authenticity* (1991) seems to suggest that authentic self-realisation is presupposed by 'horizons of significance' (Taylor 1991, 52).

While Taylor is critical about the flawed notion of authenticity in the modern times that leads to soft-relativism (Ibid., 15), in Coelho's narrative we find that Coelho is able to avoid the problem of soft-relativism by portraying most of his characters in a positive light who end up being helpful towards the protagonist. When the crystal merchant learns about the dream of the protagonist boy as his reason behind his journey, he scoffs at the boy stating the impossibility of such a dream being fulfilled. However, he provides the boy not only food but a place to work so that he is able to work towards the fulfilment of his dream. We also find that at this point in the narrative, for the first time, the boy is truly disheartened after losing all his money with the fear of crossing the desert. The narrative here states,

> "There was a moment of silence so profound that it seemed the city was asleep. No sound from the bazaars, no arguments among the merchants, no men climbing to the towers to chant. No hope, no adventure, no old kings or destinies, no treasure, and no Pyramids. It was as if the world had fallen silent because the boy's soul had. He sat there, staring blankly through the door of the café, wishing that he had died, and that everything would end forever at that moment." (Coelho 2019, 44-45)

This is quite possibly one of the most important sections in the narrative since this section adds depth to the character of the protagonist and at the same time prepares the readers emotionally for the follow up narrative of success. Readers of motivational self-help narratives as well as the readers who are inclined to religious narratives would expect a positive reversal of faith marked by dedication and hardwork and Coelho provides that in Part II of the narrative. This apparent lack of faith in the boy therefore also marks the beginning of Part II of the narrative where his faith is restored and his beliefs renewed.

Part II of the narrative begins with the crystal merchant's lack of faith in himself and his unpreparedness for reality. For him, the pyramid holds no wonder since he sees them at their most basic element, neither deriving pleasure nor wonder in their structural, historical or cultural value. He states,

"I don't know anyone around here who would want to cross the desert just to see the Pyramids
...
They're just a pile of stones. You could build one in your backyard." (Ibid., 51)

One might notice that Coelho uses the characters of merchants in contrast to his more religious characters. The shepherd boy Santiago's first love interest was a merchant's daughter and his interaction with the merchant is economic. Later the narrative also implies that the merchant's daughter would likewise prefer economic prosperity against a pursuit driven by spiritual dreams. Since Coelho sets up the crystal merchant as a devout Muslim, he is portrayed as more favourable character who would dream but not act on these dreams. These dreams in line with Coelho's motifs are dreams of spiritual journeys. As the crystal merchant states to the boy, "you want to realize your dreams. I just want to dream about Mecca." (Ibid., 52-53)

The crystal merchant who does not know how to deal with change and is happy with his situatedness is therefore representative of an inauthentic being against whom the boy with his constant desire for change is an exact opposite. Therefore, it is against this character that the protagonist is able to continue his identity formation. The protagonist is able to earn enough money from the crystal merchant's prospering business (the reason behind such economic progress being the protagonist's commercial insight's regarding certain marketing changes) and thereafter he embarks on his journey much to the dismay of the crystal merchant, who prefers to live his life without much change.

In order to make the protagonist and the setting seem realistic Coelho makes him doubt about the journey through the desert and the boy thinks,

"On the other hand, I don't know if the desert can be a friend, and it's in the desert that I have to search for my treasure. If I don't find it, I can always go home. I finally have enough money, and all the time I need. Why not?" (Ibid., 62)

However, the narrative later shows that regardless of the apparent dangers throughout his journey the boy is able to fulfill his dream. The optimistic possibility of the realisation of his dream is marked by his thought process in this part of the narrative where the narrative states,

> "But he was able to understand one thing: making a decision was only the beginning of things. When someone makes a decision, he is really diving into a strong current that will carry him to places he had never dreamed of when he first made the decision." (Ibid., 65)

This again is evocative of Sartre's conception of individual's choice and their responsibilities toward such choices. Sartre notes that, "values derive their meaning from an original projection of myself which stands as my choice of myself in the world." (Sartre 1992, 77)

In his pursuit of the treasure in his dream the protagonist meets the Englishman who reasserts the belief held by the protagonist when he states,

> "Everything in life is an omen." (Coelho 2019, 66)

When the protagonist brings out the biblical divinatory stones, Urim and Thummim, the Englishman states,

> "They're only made of rock crystal, and there are millions of rock crystals in the earth. But those who know about such things would know that those are Urim and Thummim. I didn't know that they had them in this part of the world." (Ibid., 65-66)

Coelho here is setting up the importance of these stones as well as reasserting the importance of omens as he makes the Englishman speak. The Englishman's statement here is in contrast to the earlier statement made by the crystal merchant that pyramids are collections of stones and therefore are nothing to wonder about. At the same time, the Englishman's ability to recognise biblical artifacts and his acknowledgement of Jesus Christ as a spiritual king ("It was shepherds who were the first to recognize a king that the rest of the world refused to acknowledge.") is reflective of his religious devotion. The Englishman who is lured by the ability to turn lead into gold by alchemy is, therefore, set as not an atheist but a devout

Christian. Observant readers might find this interesting that through his pursuit of the dream, the closer the protagonist comes to his aim, the surer he is of his destiny and his beliefs. The narrative states,

> "The closer one gets to realizing his destiny, the more that destiny becomes his true reason for being, thought the boy." (Ibid., 69)

It seems that there is a certain kind of confirmation bias in his attitude towards omens and destinies. Later the narrative states,

> "The boy was beginning to understand that intuition is really a sudden immersion of the soul into the universal current of life, where the histories of all people are connected, and we are able to know everything, because it's all written there.
> ...
> "We make a lot of detours, but we're always heading for the same destination." (Ibid., 71-74)

The section above is reminiscent of Jung's concept of the collective unconscious in the "The Significance of Constitution and Heredity in Psychology" published in November, 1929 (Jung 1991, 111-112). However, Coelho uses that to reassert his belief in faith and destiny.

These reassertions become prominent once the protagonist boy reaches the oasis where he meets his second love interest, Fatima. When he arrives at the oasis the narrative states,

> "He was at home with the silence of the desert, and he was content just to look at the trees. He still had a long way to go to reach the pyramids, and someday this morning would just be a memory. But this was the present moment — the party the camel driver had mentioned — and he wanted to live it as he did the lessons of his past and his dreams of the future." (Coelho 2019, 82)

This scene evokes a kind of Buddhist presentism as espoused by Buddha in Bhaddekaratta Sutta (Nanamoli and Bodhi 2015, 1039), but it remains important for the fact that the oasis in the middle of the desert as a form of miracle also marks the fast onset of spiritual transformations in the protagonist. Coelho places greater emphasis on the spiritual motifs throughout the rest of the narrative. The verbal interactions between the protagonist shepherd boy and his love interest seems to be much more removed from everyday interactions compared to the earlier interaction of the protagonist with the wool merchant's daughter. For example, at one part the narrative states,

> "The day after we met," Fatima said, "you told me that you loved me. Then, you taught me something of the universal language and the Soul of the World. Because of that, I have become a part of you."
> ...
> "Maktub," she said. "If I am really a part of your dream, you'll come back one day." (Ibid., 93)

These interactions in highly metaphoric language laden with spiritual motifs are in stark contrast to the relatively more realistic conversations held by the boy near the beginning of the narrative. His interactions with the wool merchant's daughter seemed to be much more sensible and age appropriate. There might also be a slight orientalist attitude apparent here as Andalusian women are shown to be more pragmatic compared to the women in the desert who are shown to be more spiritually inclined with greater faith in destiny.

At the same time the importance of destiny is reasserted through the realisation of the fear of failure by the Englishman, who states,

> "It was my fear of failure that first kept me from attempting the Master Work. Now, I'm beginning what I could have started ten years ago. But I'm happy at least that I didn't wait twenty years." (Ibid., 94)

The camel driver's thoughts regarding the protagonist boy Santiago's vision also assert Coelho's hermeneutic emphasis on life being full of omens and signs projected by a benevolent being. This is visible through the following statements in the narrative,

> "One could open a book to any page, or look at a person's hand; one could turn a card, or watch the flight of the birds... whatever the thing observed, one could find a connection with his experience of the moment. Actually, it wasn't that those things, in themselves, revealed anything at all; it was just that people, looking at what was occurring around them, could find a means of penetration to the Soul of the World." (Ibid., 96-97)
> ...
> "God had shown the boy a part of the future, the camel driver thought. Why was it that he wanted the boy to serve as his instrument?" (Ibid., 99)
> ...

"And, as the camel driver had said, to die tomorrow was no worse than dying on any other day. Every day was there to be lived or to mark one's departure from this world." (Ibid., 103)

One may notice that here also the camel driver's thought is reflective of the existential philosophy of Sartre as demonstrated in Act 10, sc. 2 of his play *The Devil and the Good Lord* (1951).

It seems plausible that Coelho's narrative is able to hold the readers' attention due to the fact that the protagonist is portrayed as a character with doubts, rather than a character who would stay on the course of his faith against all adversity. When Santiago meets Fatima, he wonders whether he should abandon his quest for treasure in the land of pyramids. When he asks the alchemist what would happen if he decides to say, the alchemist who is also good at prophecies, prophesises a future where the boy is able to live a happy life but lives with a sense of unfulfillment. He tells the boy that by the end of his fourth year in the desert,

"you'll be a rich merchant, with many camels and a great deal of merchandise. You'll spend the rest of your days knowing that you didn't pursue your destiny, and that now it's too late." (Ibid., 115)

The alchemist states that love is the language of the world and therefore Fatima would be able to understand Santiago's quest and his reasons behind it seems like a necessity for the plot. Fatima not only asserts her love for the boy, Santiago, by agreeing to let him go but also declares the symbolic importance of his presence in her life. The narrative goes as following,

"" I'm going away," he said. "And I want you to know that I'm coming back. I love you because..."
"Don't say anything," Fatima interrupted. "One is loved because one is loved. No reason is needed for loving."
...
Fatima went back to her tent, and, when daylight came, she went out to do the chores she had done for years. But everything had changed. The boy was no longer at the oasis, and the oasis would never again have the same meaning it had had only yesterday. It would no longer be a place with fifty thousand palm trees and three hundred wells, where the pilgrims arrived, relieved at the end of their long journeys. From that day on, the oasis would be an empty place for her." (Ibid., 116-117)

Coelho at this point is able to garner the readers' sympathy for the characters of Fatima and Santiago. Both of them have to accept certain personal sacrifices for the sake of Santiago's spiritual quest. The protagonist Santiago even wonders whether the alchemist has any experience with romantic love,

> "It was difficult not to think about what he had left behind. The desert, with its endless monotony, put him to dreaming. The boy could still see the palm trees, the wells, and the face of the woman he loved. He could see the Englishman at his experiments, and the camel driver who was a teacher without realizing it. Maybe the alchemist has never been in love, the boy thought." (Ibid., 118-119)

Here, like the final section of part one of the narrative, nostalgic recollection along with self-doubt is used to add emotional depth to the character of the protagonist. And in line with Coelho's hermeneutic aims, the boy is unable to decipher the emerald tablet with the secret of making alchemic gold even after the alchemist shows him the tablet. The narrative states,

> "It's a code," said the boy, a bit disappointed. "It looks like what I saw in the Englishman's books." "No," the alchemist answered. "It's like the flight of those two hawks; it can't be understood by reason alone. The Emerald Tablet is a direct passage to the Soul of the World."
> "The wise men understood that this natural world is only an image and a copy of paradise. The existence of this world is simply a guarantee that there exists a world that is perfect. God created the world so that, through its visible objects, men could understand his spiritual teachings and the marvels of his wisdom. That's what I mean by action." (Ibid., 121)

The alchemist tells the protagonist that he is unable to understand the tablet because it is not his destiny. His spiritual objectives are different and the material world only aids in one's spiritual quest. Coelho therefore offers asseveration of the religious aspect of the material word and the omens to be observed there. The alchemist states,

> "The desert will give you an understanding of the world; in fact, anything on the face of the earth will do that. You don't even have to understand the desert: all you have to do is contemplate a simple grain of sand, and you will see in it all the marvels of creation." (Ibid., 122)

As it has been noted in this article before, Coelho's mysticism is much more pronounced in the second part of the book. Here the emphasis on the importance of omens and the all-pervasive nature of those spiritual omens is accentuated in the alchemist's statement who is portrayed like a messenger of God. Earlier in the narrative, the alchemist tells the protagonist that if he were to stay in the desert without fulfilling his destiny, he would remain unsatisfied. During his journey when Santiago asks why he should keep listening to his heart the alchemist replies,

> "Because you will never again be able to keep it quiet. Even if you pretend not to have heard what it tells you, it will always be there inside you, repeating to you what you're thinking about life and about the world." (Ibid., 123)

The alchemist tells the protagonist,

> "Every search begins with beginner's luck. And every search ends with the victor's being severely tested." (Ibid., 127)

This statement is an indirect avouchment of the earlier statement in the narrative that the universe conspires to help everyone in the realisation of their goals in par with their destiny. The character of Melchizedek is shown to be quite similar to that of the alchemist. Akin to Melchizedek, the alchemist too reminds Santiago regarding the nature of exchange and transaction in life and implies that life is more important than money since, "It's not often that money saves a person's life." (Ibid., 135)

When Santiago is caught by the Arabs, the alchemist tells the chief that Santiago is able to turn himself into the wind and buys time before their prospective execution. When Santiago states that he does not know how to turn himself into wind the alchemist tells Santiago that, "There is only one thing that makes a dream impossible to achieve: the fear of failure." (Ibid.)

This again is an avowal of the earlier proclamation made by the Englishman, who said that it is his fear of failure that prevented him from attempting to complete his masterwork of alchemy. On the other hand, the remark made by the alchemist that, "Usually the threat of death makes people a lot more aware of their lives," is reminiscent of Heideggerian conception of authentic self-realisation in the face of death. Heidegger noted that, "with death Da-sein stands before itself in its ownmost potentiality-of being." (Heidegger 1996, 232) It is only at the face of its possibility of death that '*da-sein*' is able to achieve authenticity. Coelho seems to suggest a somewhat less nuanced version of variation of that philosophical concept at this portion of the narrative

It is not clear whether it was intentional on Coelho's part to use conceptions common to existential philosophy but it is possible to find similar parallels in the narrative. Later when Santiago is at the top of the mountain the narrative states his interaction with nature and elements in nature. He looks at the desert and the desert speaks to him,

> "What do you want here today?" the desert asked him. "Didn't you spend enough time looking at me yesterday?" (Coelho 2019, 137)

When Santiago asks the desert to turn him into the wind, the desert tells him, "I don't understand what you're talking about."

To this Santiago replies,

> "But you can at least understand that somewhere in your sands there is a woman waiting for me. And that's why I have to turn myself into the wind." (Ibid., 138)

Coelho is making use of the emotional aspect of his character in order to garner the readers' sympathy for the protagonist who is doomed to die unless he can turn himself into the wind. Following a brief pause the desert replies, "I'll give you my sands to help the wind to blow, but, alone, I can't do anything. You have to ask for help from the wind."

And therefore, the boy asks the wind for the same favour. The wind as a personified force of nature too is shown to have its limits who is unable to fulfil the protagonist's request, and asks him to request the same to the sun. The conversations between Santiago and the different elements of nature are laden with the same spiritual motifs spread across the entire narrative. For example, the narrative reports the following interaction of the boy Santiago with that of the sun,

> "This is why alchemy exists," the boy said. "So that everyone will search for his treasure, find it, and then want to be better than he was in his former life. Lead will play its role until the world has no further need for lead; and then lead will have to turn itself into gold."
> "That's what alchemists do. They show that, when we strive to become better than we are, everything around us becomes better, too." (Ibid., 143)

Here alchemy as a mode of metamorphosis has been applied both in the spiritual sense and in the material sense and confirms an earlier statement made by the alchemist who proclaimed that true alchemists of the past were not only trying to evolve gold but also trying to evolve themselves as persons. (Ibid., 131) When the sun is unable to fulfill the request of Santiago,

> "The boy turned to the hand that wrote all. As he did so, he sensed that the universe had fallen silent, and he decided not to speak. A current of love rushed from his heart, and the boy began to pray. It was a prayer that he had never said before, because it was a prayer without words or pleas.
> ...
> The boy reached through to the Soul of the World, and saw that it was a part of the Soul of God. And he saw that the Soul of God was his own soul. And that he, a boy, could perform miracles." (Ibid., 144-145)

This particular section in the narrative when the protagonist at the face of death is able to communicate with the Soul of God and arrives at the realisation that the soul of the God is his own is quite possibly the utmost spiritual section in the entire narrative. Here too, one might notice that the Soul of the God being one with the Soul of the World with that of the Soul of one's own self is a concept that has been borrowed from the concept of Advaita-vada in Hinduism. The self-realisation of the protagonist of Coelho's narrative is strikingly similar to that of Adi Shankara in Upadesasahasri 11.7, where he states,

> "I am other than name, form and action.
> My nature is ever free!
> I am Self, the supreme unconditioned Brahman.
> I am pure Awareness, always non-dual." (Comans 2000, 183)

Additionally, the protagonist's ability to speak with the forces of nature and his subsequent self-realisation with the help of these natural forces is similar to Sathyakāmā Jabali's narrative in the fourth part of Chandogya Upanishad. (Muller 1879, 60-64)

The fact that the protagonist continues his journey for a material treasure even after the pinnacle of his spiritual experience at this point in the narrative does not add up the gravity of those experiences. Quite possibly Coelho continues the narrative in order to make the text appear less religious in nature than it would have had had the protagonist become a purely religious figure following his communion with the Soul of the God at the height of the mountain and his self-realisation. Christian themes are invoked again when the alchemist before parting with the boy at a monastery tells him a version of the story of the centurion from Matthew 8.8. Despite his ability to perform miracles and to talk with natural elements, the boy is beaten by refugees from the tribal wars who robs him of his gold (created from lead by the alchemist who wanted to demonstrate that he truly was one) and thereafter the leader of that gang tells him,

> "In my dream, there was a sycamore growing out of the ruins of the sacristy, and I was told that, if I dug at the roots of the sycamore, I would find a hidden treasure. But I'm not so stupid as to cross an entire desert just because of a recurrent dream." (Coelho 2019, 155)

Typical to Coelho's narrative style, the statement made by the leader of the rogue Arabs repeats the motif of following one's personal calling. Since, earlier the protagonist is seen to be able to communicate with the Soul of the God with the understanding that it is the same as his own soul, here the enforced realisation of the protagonist that even the material treasure is situated in at his own homeland seems to be a superfluous reiteration on Coelho's part. The protagonist returns to the ruined church and finds the treasure buried there and thinks, "It's true; life really is generous to those who pursue their destiny," (Ibid., 160) which is an avouchment of Coelho's belief regarding destiny. Santiago decides to go back to the gypsy oracle to fulfill his promise (which also proves his righteous nature) and the narrative ends with an optimistic note as he states that he would embark on a journey to reunite with his love interest Fatima.

Coelho's narrative therefore is laden with spiritual motifs belonging to the Abrahamic religions with the primary source being the Christian sect. However, he makes use of concepts which are common to existential theories of Sartre and Heidegger and individuation theory of Jung. He also makes use of concepts and narratives from Hindu theology although he never clearly refers to other religions beyond the Abrahamic ones. While he seems to have certain theological beliefs in place as expressed in his Preface to the narrative and as it becomes evident through a careful analysis of the narrative, his narrative nonetheless appears to be much less dogmatic compared to any religious manifesto, due to its allegorical nature. Coelho does not name most of the characters in the narrative and provides scarce description of the physical appearances of the people and the places in the narrative, which enforces its allegorical nature.

Alternatively, the simple language of the allegorical narrative keeps it open to interpretation and garners widespread public appeal. It is not completely clear as to why he gives the narrative its two-part structure except for the fact that the second part of the narrative sees a more profuse use of the spiritual motifs. Apart from the Prologue where the alchemist reads Coelho's variation of the legend of Narcissus, the primary narrative is tripartite, part one which lacks a headline, part two, where the protagonist slightly falters in his belief and starts working at the crystal merchant's shop, and the epilogue which recounts the protagonist's return to the ruined church with the sycamore tree to find his material treasure. It is not clear whether these partitions were necessary from strictly narrative point of view since Coelho throughout his narrative employs paragraph breaks to mark breaks in the narrative. The spiritual climax of the protagonist in the second part of the narrative, where he is able to commune with God, makes the remaining portion of the narrative logically flawed and paler in their spiritual motifs compared to the earlier section. However, for casual readers who might have been Coelho's target audience, the final section of the narrative might seem a narrative necessity and it is quite possible that people do not observe the narrative ambiguity inherent in those. Not only does Coelho use an allegorical narrative which garners optimism and is in simple language, he also seems to emphasise upon social responsibilities (through the righteous nature of the boy, or the charities of the crystal merchant), element of friendship (between the protagonist and his advisers) and romance (between the protagonist and his love interest), the importance of interpersonal relationships (the protagonist arrives at self-realisation only through his interaction with other people) as well as non-dogmatic theological beliefs which are universally applicable and therefore serves people with a wide range of religious beliefs. By underscoring the importance of social responsibilities, Coelho is able to avoid the soft-relativistic approach towards authentic self-formation of his character. Not only does his text conform to many concepts from existential philosophy, but also by employing the moral elements mixed with social responsibilities in his narrative he is able to avert the problems (related to self-centeredness of his protagonist) involved in the self-formation of his character. One may also note that it is possible to compare the striving for the fulfillment of destiny by Santiago, to the concept of fictional finalism in the work of psychoanalyst Alfred Adler, who noted that,

> "The science of Individual Psychology developed out of the effort to understand that mysterious creative power of life which expresses itself in the desire to develop, to strive, to achieve, and even to compensate for defeats in one direction by striving for success in another.
> ...
> The final goal emerges for everyone, consciously or unconsciously, but its significance is never understood [by the individual himself]. From individual evaluation, which usually causes a permanent mood of inferiority feeling, there develops a fictional goal." (Adler 1956, 92-93)

Adler however believed that it is not possible for the individual to completely comprehend the fictional goal of one's life since this fiction is 'blurred and pliable' (Ibid., 93). He is also of the opinion that this fictional goal is teleological in nature and it is self-imposed and it carries the same function as that of fate as long as the individual remains unconscious regarding the goal. He further notes that,

> "we find concrete single purposes, such as the purpose to operate as a member of the community or to dominate it, to attain security and triumph in one's chosen career, to approach the other sex or to avoid it. We may always

NARRATIVE FUNCTION AND IDENTITY   95

> trace in these special purposes what sort of meaning the individual has found in his existence and how he proposes to realize that meaning.
> ...
> It is the fiction which teaches us to differentiate, which gives us support and security, which shapes and guides our doings and actions, and which forces our mind to foresee and to perfect itself." (Ibid., 96-97)

One may observe the parallels between Adler's concept of self-ideal and Coelho's claims regarding the realisation of one's destiny. In a way, Coelho is not only setting up this form of fictional finalism in case of his protagonist but also inspiring similar kind of self-fashioning in his readers (although Adler's concept is far from conscious self-fashioning, and rather refers to unconscious self-formation). Coelho does so through his repetitive use of theological motifs, many of which are common in popular culture. This might be the reason for which critic S.M. Hart noted in his article on the magic realist elements in Coelho's *The Alchemist*, that,

> "One possible explanation for Coelho's popularity is that he uses the shorthand of literary cliché expertly" (Hart 2004, 304) and that the "play with stereotypes, indeed, is one of the reasons Coelho's work has not always endeared itself to academic audiences, who often see it as pandering to popular taste." (Hart 2004, 305)

He also notes that,

> "Coelho has a column in the online version of the Brazilian newspaper O Globo, and he regularly includes a horoscope column (see http://oglobo.globo.com). In some ways his fiction expresses the rather simplistic ideology of the horoscope writ large; his novels are animated horoscopes. It is also true that Coelho's work is often full of grammatical errors when submitted to his Brazilian publishers. Coelho resists having his "errors" corrected, because it changes the "numerology" of the text." (Ibid.)

As one may note that these spiritual beliefs are also apparent in *The Alchemist*. Nonetheless, having these flaws do not change the fact that Coelho is able to make expert use of popular tropes and literary devices which makes his text appealing to the general populace. Hart notes that,

> "First, it is important to note that Santiago's name is chosen deliberately — alluding to the patron saint of Spain — and yet his journey will take him to the heart of Arabian culture, understood in a generic sense, through

Morocco and on toward the Pyramids of Egypt, such that his journey reenacts some of the topoi of *The Arabian Night.*" (Ibid., 311)

This element of cultural hybridity might also be one of the reasons behind the general appeal of the text. Hart also notes that Santiago resembles the biblical character of Jospeh, as he is a stranger in a strange land like the character of Joseph. (Ibid., 310) However, he is different due to his ability to make divinatory observations through objective phenomena in everyday life. Coelho's narrative therefore carries the implicit suggestion that spiritual truth can be found in everyday life if one knows how to look at it. For this reason, the Englishman is unable to find the truth of alchemy, as he is not able to look at the simple truth. Similarly, it takes the protagonist a series of complicated journeys in order to find the material treasure which was present in the ruined Church where he lived. His journey in the physical as well as in the spiritual plane seems to emphasise the importance of self-discovery or knowing oneself. In that sense, it is a narrative that showcases the journey for Santiago's identity formation. But such identity formation is marked by his simple insight into everyday life. Santiago as a character is presented as a simple being who looks at the world with a certain kind of innocence. He is unable to comprehend complex narratives in books, which becomes evident when the Englishman is unhappy with his simple interpretations of complex books on alchemy. Despite his child-like approach towards life, he is able to find his way to self-realisation through his everyday observations and his interactions with nature. Coelho's expert use of popular literary tropes and his use of the commonplace, the everydayness of spiritual revelations further upholds his universal acceptance.

Bibliography:

Adler, Alfred. 1956. *The Individual Psychology of Alfred Adler.* USA: Basic Books.

Coelho, Paulo. 2019. *The Alchemist.* Translated by Alan R. Clarke. India: Harper Collins Publishers.

Comans, Michael. 2000. *The Method of Early Advaita Vedānta: A Study of Gauḍapāda, Śaṅkara, Sureśvara, and Padmapāda.* Delhi: Motilal Banarsidass.

Hart, Stephen M. 2004. "Cultural Hybridity, Magical Realism, and the Language of Magic in Paulo Coelho's The Alchemist." *Romance Quarterly* 51, no. 4: 304–12. https://doi.org/10.3200/rqtr.51.4.304-312. Accessed on 23rd August, 2020.

Heidegger, Martin. 1996. *Being and Time*. Translated by John Stambaugh. Albany: SUNY

Jung, Carl Gustav. 1991. "The Significance of Constitution and Heredity in Psychology". In Vol. 8, *Collected Works*. London: Routledge.

Matsumoto, Shoukei. "Take It from Me, a Buddhist Monk: Cleaning Is Good for You." *The Guardian*. Guardian News and Media, January 5, 2018. https://www.theguardian.com/commentisfree/2018/jan/05/buddhist-monk-cleaning-good-for-you. Accessed on 10th August, 2020.

Muller, F. Max. 1879. "Chandogya Upanishad". In Part I, *The Upanishads*. Oxford: The Clarendon Press.

Nanamoli, Bhikkhu and Bhikkhu Bodhi. 2015. *The Middle length Discourses of the Buddha*. USA: Wisdom Publications.

Sartre, Jean Paul. 1977. *Life/Situations: Essays Written and Spoken*. Translated by P. Auster and L. Davis. New York: Pantheon.

Sartre, Jean Paul. 1992. *Being and Nothingness*. Translated by Hazel E Barnes. USA: Washington Square Press

Taylor, Charles. 1991. *The Ethics of Authenticity*. USA: Harvard University Press.

Varga, Somogy, and Charles Guignon. "Authenticity." *Stanford Encyclopedia of Philosophy*. Stanford University, February 20, 2020. https://plato.stanford.edu/entries/authenticity/. Accessed on 13th August, 2020

Vivekananda, Swami. 2016. *Karma–Yoga: The Yoga of Action*. Kolkata: Advaita Ashrama.

Section II
Science Fiction

Hail the Monster and Fie the Man: The Construction of Monstrosity in *Frankenstein*

Shirsendu Mondal

Characters of fictions or imaginative writings often find their entry into general culture in a seamless process of reciprocity. They even become icons. Aaladin, Hamlet, Faust or Crusoe have become integral part of popular culture in endless analogues or juxtapositions through allegories, parallelisms, metaphors and emblematic icons. The anecdotal presence of these fictional figures interprets reality and produce meanings in a curious meaning-making process. Perhaps the most powerful of such widely circulated myths in modern literature is offered by Mary Shelley's *Frankenstein*. But in no other case as in *Frankenstein*, general culture castigates one figure by naming another. In a complex process of cultural reception and appropriation, the novel becomes a metaphor for the rise of diabolical evil in the form of a monster erroneously called by the name of its creator, Frankenstein. The actual Frankenstein, whose dangerous science brought man to the brink of disaster, mostly comes out unscathed. Most of us, I presume, have grown up hearing about the novel as the apocalyptic tale of a primitive dark force. The deprecatory impatience of branding the monster as evil incarnate hardly notices that the monster is made unique by the combination of brute strength and intellect (Zuk 2013, 141). Unfortunately, the novel becomes synonymous and gets fixated with the horror of a gigantic scale identified in the monster metonymically named Frankenstein. The shadow of the monster hides the monster in Victor Frankenstein.

Producing a Villain

Replacing the central character from the focus, the novel undergoes a change in orientation. It is no more a story of the angst of a man who should be standing perplexed between dispassionate science and ethical responsibility of its outcome, usurping godly creativity and pathetic human limitation and between defying nature and nature's revenge. *Frankenstein* definitely showed the promise of engaging with the dialectic that concerns the fundamental dilemma of a scientist-creator and his soul-searching. But instead of recognising and endorsing the nuanced encounter of humanity and monstrosity, the narrative became busy painting in large, lurid letters the villainy of the monster. This shift of focus screens off Victor and the turbulence of complex forces he is composed of. The text is made more amenable to the culturalist project of identifying an 'other' and justifying the populist allegorical understanding based on the dichotomy between the benevolent creator and ungrateful creation.

With the substantial corpus of Frankenstein criticism in the background, it is both a cliché and an uncontested observation that the creature is a victim of blind social hatred and persecution. His desire for revenge is directly and absolutely traced to the gross injustice and abandonment hurled at him both by his creator and the society at large. And since revenge, by intimidation, ensures survival against withdrawal of all life-support, the actions of the monster turn out to be just and necessary. But the concept of justness, propriety, and normative behavior are the exclusive reserves of civilised humans. The creature, although more closely resembling humans than any other kindred beings, is read a 'monster' of diabolical intent. He cannot be brought in the fold of human community; therefore, the rules of human world do not apply to him although he must be governed by the same set of rules. The creature could be abandoned, hounded and pelted with stones but he could never pick up the stones and hurl them back at the perpetrators. I wonder how a 'proper' human being with similar physical and mental status would react under similar circumcision. The creature is made a monster at will by the arbitrary logic of opportunistic human calculation. Friedman and Kavey cogently ask the parameters which can define monstrosity and frame monstrous behavior. To put it simply, anything that violates the conventional ideas of the natural and contradicts the understandings of natural law and progression can be monstrous. Yet Frankenstein's creature, like many other literary monsters, is made a monster because of the "twisted acts" committed in response to their "hysterical often violent receptions of the human beings" (Friedman & Kavey 2016, 3).

Crossing the Alps, Victor catches a fleeting, almost spectral glance of the creature. Without pausing to verify, he concludes the creature to be the murderer of William. Luckily, it turns out to be true. It is understandable that the death of William and the presence of the creature in the scene, under the backdrop of Victor's reckless abandonment of his creation can make the creature a prime suspect. But notice the language of assertion and conviction in the words of Victor. Even before the actual crime was committed, the criminality was believed to have been predetermined, preordained in the creature. All of it just because he looked different:

> Could he be (I shuddered at the conception) the murderer of my brother? No sooner did the idea cross my imagination, than I became convinced of the truth; my teeth chattered, and I was forced to lean against a tree for support... ... Nothing in the human shape could have destroyed that fair child. He was the murderer! I could not doubt it. The mere presence of the idea was an irresistible proof of the fact. (Shelley 2015, 55)

I contend that as the creature is more akin to a human being in every sense, yet looking weird as it were; there is a greater desperation to brand him a monster. In all his activities, the creature, truly speaking, is following a human logic of understanding (Sim 2008, 156). A monster would not have wasted time to look for connections between Victor and William and seek out the child for wreaking vengeance on his elder brother. He would come down heavily on the creator and would be consumed in the retributive fury. The paraphernalia of indirect revenge and the logic of seeking justice by avenging the villain's associates are complexly human. No monster or forces of the irrational would follow the extensive and circuitous route of revenge for derivative justice. The monster, in killing Victor's wife, also doles out an 'equitable' (emphasis is mine) punishment as the one suffered by him. Both the 'father' and 'son' (emphasis is mine) are cut loose without the prospect of a wife and progeny. While God gratifies Adam's desire for Eve, the human over-reacher, assuming Godly creativity and defying mortality, shudders at the possibility of 'conceiving' a race of monsters through the creation of a female. As Victor scuttles to demolish the half-finished rag-tag (mis)creation of a female species, the monster launches into a systematic annihilation of Victor's family.

Surprisingly, the text is blandly devoid of a single human figure who counters the monster-making discourse through a self-criticism of the crimes committed by man. It appears that Mary Shelley herself is only pushing forth the cause of the creature for a sympathetic audience. And here we encounter the central problematic of the text because the loathsome creature, abhorred and vilified by the superior man, is given a highly refined sensibility of a rational, compassionate being. In a lengthy exchange between the Creator and the Creation, the latter clearly stands out and far surpasses the former in his logical thinking, clarity of understanding, reasoned judgment and humanitarian outlook. It seems that the author took particular care to shape the mind of the monster with the pure essence of Enlightenment principle. This is completely against how Mary Shelley evolved to become a distinct personality as she moved away from the shadow of Godwinian reformist ideology. For a variety of reasons, "she rejected her utopian and radical heritage and opted for a more conservative and pessimistic view of the world" (Sterrenburg 2015, 243). Yet in building the monster, Mary Shelley unmistakably manifests the Enlightenment concerns that her celebrity parents so assiduously propagated against the pervasive orthodoxy of the day.

Mary Wollstonecraft's intellectual effort had been a constant striving towards a just and equitable society and an assertion that the individual is both endowed with and entitled to self-improvement. Dedication to the cause of women's development and progress of man in general, was enjoined with Godwin's vehement rejection of all oppressive, restrictive institutions preventing individuals to grow. If Wollstonecraft's *A Vindication of the Rights of Women* is a powerful rebuttal of the conservative opinion of women, the immensely influential *Enquiry Concerning Political Justice (1793) by William Godwin* ushers in a radical new age of man's emancipation. Certainly, Godwin's impassioned espousal of the cause of human liberation translated the spirit of radicalism in Utopian terms. But the essence of Godwinism lies not in the literalness of the exalted ideas, the excess of utopia or the exaggeration of the emotional revolt but in the belief in the emergence of ordinary man against tyranny and oppression. In the context of Enlightenment, when conservatism was contested by liberalism; the new 'man' (emphasis is mine), inevitably, had to have an articulation of its own.

The self-educated, persevering, soft-hearted, benevolent, monster develops a strong veneration for the culture of man. In his attempt to emulate the best in man and in order to salvage himself from the dungeon of wretchedness owing to his blighted birth, the monster ironically reaches the extremity of goodness. He not only makes himself a man but represents all the best that man should embody. Against the elevation and moral superiority of the monster, Frankenstein is a pathetic disgrace who is both incapable to justifying his cruel rejection of the creature and is a prisoner to his own incomprehensible hatred.

For the monster, the feeling of bliss and gratitude at having been born in the middle of such wonderful earth soon evaporates as his deformity makes him the obnoxious and evil 'other'. The depth of human revulsion is suggested by the indiscriminate use of hate-words against him. And hatred is immediately translated into actions of potential persecution suggestive of killing the 'other' before it wreaks havoc. On two occasions the monster is brutally assaulted, once beaten with a cudgel and next injured severely by a gun-shot. The incident of being fired at is a culminating point in his gradual disillusionment with the goodness of man, for immediately before that, he saves a young lady from being washed away by gushing water of a rapid stream. As he frantically tries to revive the girl, her companion, a young boy tears her away from the caring hands of the monster. Aghast and curious, the monster follows them and instantly receives the bullet that crushed his bones. From this point on, the monster is irrevocably launched into a permanent antagonism against man and seeks to vent his anger through avenging the wrongs done to him. The Lockean mind of the monster, the *tabula rasa*, receiving knowledge through the imprints of acculturation, turns malign in response to the evil observed in man.

The bottom-line of the monster's charges against his master would simply boil down to the fact that willful desertion and wanton rejection caused him endless misery which in turn made him sinister. He also questions the human construct of the notion of justice, for Frankenstein's conduct is tantamount to a travesty of the principles of equitability, clemency and compassion. The false God, ironically named Victor, creates a 'fallen angel' (emphasis is mine) as it were, instead of an Adam. This however, is spoken not with the menacing defiance of an adversary looking to supplant his master but with the submission of a loyal beneficiary. The supreme ability of composure in the face of dire crisis confers upon him a rare unimpeachable personality. Admittedly, for a being of such refined sensibility, a sudden transformation into a child murderer out of vengeance against his father is hardly justifiable. The process of cultural improvement out of base nature is rather too soon disbanded. But if we suspend our judgments on the Monster's choice of victims and consider his late moral 'decline' consequential, he certainly raises questions that have wide ranging ramification:

> Cursed creator! Why did you form a monster so hideous that even you turned from me in disgust? God in pity made man beautiful and alluring, after his own image; but my form is a filthy type of your's, more horrid from its very resemblance. Satan had his companions, fellow devils, to admire and encourage him; but I m solitary and detested. (Shelley 2015, 101)

What arrests my attention is the observation that while Adam takes after God who has the power to reproduce his own image, the creature looks like the filthy type that Frankenstein is capable of making. But if it means that the creature shares the same filthy form with Frankenstein and the resemblance is horrifying, then it is simply an inheritance of the creator's monstrosity. His identification with Satan is both a critique of how God produced a devil and a legitimisation of his war against his own god. But as a human agent, Frankenstein has a lot more to answer:

> I am malicious because I am miserable; am I not shunned and hated by all mankind? You, my creator would tear me to pieces, and triumph; remember that, and tell me why I should pity man more than he pities me? You would not call it a murder, if you could precipitate me into one of those ice-rifts, and destroy my frame, the work of your own hands. (Ibid., 113)

For the noble human, intention to kill its procreation and extinguishing the half-formed life never appears as murder. The scientist, on the contrary, would be hailed victorious if he rids the earth from the 'monstrous' (emphasis is mine) creation. The monster, in choosing not to be unilaterally good, has found out the disturbing anomalies of what humans profess as principle or virtue. The irreverent being shall now be unstinted in returning kindness and infinitely vengeful if confronted with cruelty. Frankenstein is clearly defeated and shamed by the 'justice of his agreements' (emphasis is mine) and is forced to acknowledge to himself that he has neglected the responsibilities of the creator for making provisions for the happiness of his creation. The momentary realisation, however, soon gives way to the sight of "filthy mass that moved and talked" and his "feelings were altered to those of horror and hatred." (Ibid. 116) The possibility of considering the creature as a subjective entity endowed with rationality and judgements, is lost with objectifying him as a lump of uncouth flesh. Like the self-defined human propriety of nurturing and murdering, the notion of aesthetic is made to stand on the shallow foundation of external appearance.

Mary Shelley's depiction of Dr. Frankenstein as a disinterested, socially alienated, self-absorbed scientist who aspires for the secret of human immortality can be a metaphor of how the conservatives viewed a Godwinian reformer. The presumptuous Victor who is incapacitated to render a perfect form and who fails miserably to own up his own creation appears to be the subject of authorial censure. The progenitor is haunted and hunted down by the humiliation hurled against him. It does appear that the text celebrates the inception of the natural man, the proletarian victim as it were, against the gross injustice and persecution of the superior social and economic class. This is borne out by the apparent critique of Frankenstein's efforts and endorsement of the monster as an essentially neutral being, capable of turning good or evil under the impact of social forces. Mary Shelley repeatedly emphasises the inherent goodness of the creature and makes Frankenstein admit that the monster is deprived of care and nurture. The trajectory of the text should be defined at this point, that Frankenstein should go down in disgrace paving the way for the emergence of the new man.

Yet, the project of sympathising with the wronged creation and condemning the 'unnatural' (emphasis is mine) scientist is cancelled out in favour of the scientist. Mary Shelley still has loads of sympathy for the scientist who faces an apocalyptic threat in the course of his millennial scientific achievement. For that matter, she has never been critical about the disinterested, a-social and self-centric objective of Frankenstein's discovery. Except the satisfaction of his monstrous ego, Frankenstein never proclaims to cater to any grand social-humanitarian cause. His obsessive isolation and dislike of human company coupled with his near-hysteric preoccupation with stealing the ultimate secret of life makes him a spectral presence within human community. The author shuts her eyes on the disguised violence and magnifies the violent actions of the creature with a predetermined mind of locating evil in him. David Punter captures this ambivalence:

> She wants, on the one hand, not to blame the monster for being as he is, while on the other not blaming Frankenstein for hating him with a furious, bitter, and almost incoherent hatred, ... Constantly in the book Mary Shelley tries to produce in the reader an alienation from the monster, which misfires because it really seems that the original reason for Frankenstein's rejection of him was mere aesthetic disappointment. (Punter 2015, 279)

The Authorial Dilemma

Why does Mary Shelley suddenly abandon the creature whom she nurtured with so much care and had him articulated? Why does she finally take sides with the egotist scientist who aimed at a-sexual reproduction and produced an 'unnatural' superhuman? The authorial motivation or obligation for asserting the demonic in the monster and sympathising with an anguished scientist, however, does not preclude the critique of bad science and neglected parenting. There may not be any straight unproblematic answer to the question of why the author promoted a fixed perspective to the monster.

Frankenstein is a text of subversive ideology and many contesting worldviews flow into it making it amenable to a multiplicity of mythos. In June, 1816, when the story germinated in a waking dream, the eighteen-year-old Mary had already left her father after her elopement with Percy Shelley. Eighteen months back, she had seen her first child die and had given birth to her second child in January 1816. The death of her first child had produced a recurrent traumatic dream in which she had visions of her baby coming back to life and warmth (Mellor 2003, 10). The genesis of the novel also coincided with two suicides-that of Fanny, Mary's half-sister and Percy Shelley's wife Harriet Shelley. At home, the lofty, disinterested idealism of Percy Shelley and his predilection for adulating women was at odds with the bold, imperious personality of Mary. Anne Mellore points out that the haunting dreams about the dead child may have reflected on the deep-seated anxiety of new mothers who often fear giving birth to deformed children (Ibid). But more importantly, the anxiety of procreation was metaphorically expressed in her frantic efforts to produce a ghost story that her husband, Byron and others mutually agreed to write as a friendly contest. Both Godwin and Percy Shelley wanted to see her as writer of repute as her mother was. And facing "that blank incapability of invention which is the greatest misery of authorship, when dull nothing replies to our anxious invocations" (Ibid.), Mary was definitely under tremendous pressure of performance. Describing the text as "hideous progeny" in the Introduction to the 1831 edition, Mary translated the hideously painful process of composing and producing the story. The monster as evil became the embodiment of her nightmare. It was terrible to produce the terrible.

Under such tumultuous emotional crosscurrents, a horror story involving a laboratory-engineered creature, must have assumed an apocalyptic dimension. The monster got animated with superhuman power and mythical capacity for destruction, none of which was consciously programmed and controlled by the scientist. Recalling the process of executing the principles of life, Victor finds himself bestowing animation on the body from the outside. The ultimate knowledge of providing the spark of life is described in terms of a sudden light breaking upon him. Alongside, in contradiction to the above, Victor observes with wonder the inscrutable laws of correlation of constituent parts, collected from the cemetery and charnel houses and the 'minutiae of causation' (emphasis is mine) that animate them. Frankenstein's method envisages the uncertain union of the opposing perspectives of John Abernethy and William Lawrence; his creation shares the indeterminacy arising out of the unknown ways of origin.

Contemporary experiments with electricity and excitement surrounding its phenomenal power had naturally made its entry as the defining element of the vital principle of animation. But the colossal power of electricity was as much feared for its uncontrollable capability as it was hailed as an agent of revolutionary change. If Frankenstein's monster is taken to be animated by the strange force of vital currents, then it serves to represent the pervasive threat that the creature might go out of bounds. Mary consciously models the monster on this horrifying uncertainty as it "can result in such an uncontrollable recombination of organic particles that the use of life science to bring about a better state of humanity, Victor Frankenstein's initial aim (Shelley 2012: 33), can ultimately produce monstrosities because of the largely unknown nature of vitality itself" (Hogle 2018, 28).

A monster suffused with human kindness and devoid of wild terror was the last thing that Mary Shelley would like her monster to appear in public. Rendering the monster thoroughly comprehensible within the linguistic capacity of humans and fix the meaning of this strange 'aberration' (emphasis is mine), would deprive the text of its sublime appeal. It is suggested that by withholding to name the monster, the author consolidates the monster's identification with the dark unknown.

Making something known by a specific name is seen as an instrument of control and disciplining (Tropp 2007, 14). The monster is consistently associated with the wild desolation and overwhelming expanse of Romantic nature. As a necessary objective correlative, the mystery of nature-a-moral, inexorable, unlegislated and preternatural, flows into the formative elements of the monster, making him a part of the sublime. For Shelley's creature is definitely located with the abstruse in sublimity, "a word used to describe the human mind's confrontation with the unknowable, the overwhelming, the infinite". (Mellor 2003, 22) But the sublimity in the monster cannot be accommodated within the familiar philosophical discourses of the time. The human understanding and judgment of evil is either an invention or a linguistic construction, imposed on the unknowable (Ibid., 23) in order to contain or eliminate threat to evolving order of things. The monster is let loose in the vast icy deserts of the Alps, in the bleak frozen nothingness of the North Pole or in the insurmountable mountain cliffs so that it grows and gains in the meaning of limitless ferocity.

Keeping in view the factors that evoked Mary Shelley's visualisation of the monster she was conceiving, the representation of Gothic fear embodied in the giant proportion of monstrosity is undeniably evident as authorial agenda. We learn that the vision of the monster was induced in Shelley's vision when she, Percy Shelley, Byron and Polidori read together from *Fantasmagoriana*- a collection of French Gothic fictions at villa Diodati on a rainy night in 1816. In the 1831 edition, Mary Shelley recalls how her reading evoked one of the images-'a gigantic, shadowy form, clothed like the ghost in *Hamlet*, in complete armour', whose kisses withered children. This image, having close resemblance to one of the two principal spectral presences in Walpole's *The Castle of Otranto*, anticipates Frankenstein's monster in a big way. J. E. Hogle finds that Shelley's monster has its foundation in Horace Walpole' Gothic image which itself is inspired by Shakespeare's specters. He observes that the Gothic in the monster has to be found,

> ...in his Alfonso-esque enormity, his composition out of divisible pieces like those of Alfonso's ghost, his haunting of Victor Frankenstein with both the latter's and his culture's sins (such as grave robbing), his being the revenant both of the dead bodies that compose him and of an entirely artificial being (like Walpole's ancestral portrait or statue), and his abrupt and unsettling animation out of inanimation as he suddenly 'breathed hard', like Ricardo in *Otranto*, while 'a convulsive motion agitated his limbs'(Hogle 2018, 22)

At the ground level, the nameless, indefinable creature of superhuman stature is more horrible than the classic monsters of legend. Standing midway between man and machine, life and death, the creature exhibits an assemblage of features that humans necessarily construe as repulsive. The reception of the creature in the human community is testimony to the circulation of the semiotic meanings of ugliness and beauty. The monster's appearance pushes human minds to the limits of tolerance, so much so that the probability of his emergence as a kind and compassionate being is cancelled out by the perversity of ugliness in the socially conditioned psyche. Walton, at the end of the story, confronted the monster in the full knowledge of what he was going to see. Yet he exclaimed "I dared not again raise my eyes to his face, there was something so scaring and unearthly in his ugliness". (Shelley 2015, 176) The notion of the uncanny and bizarre, harbouring intentions contrary to human interests, is based on this sense of unearthliness.

Focusing on the yellow skin, black lips and the contorted muscles barely covered by the flesh; the monster has been viewed as a victim of racial otherness. There is no denying that Frankenstein's monster does function as a potential metaphor for the entire range of proletarian, dispossessed, culturally marginalised representatives in their relationship with the superior European. But in this case, the agent in question is not a human agent and the author, in spite of her best intentions, is rendered powerless to convince her fellow men about the 'humanity' (emphasis is mine) of the non-human. Like the dual nature of her monster, Mary Shelley is also perennially divided between her allegiance to the humanity and the enlightenment of the monster and to the cultural demand that the monster be branded as evil. But what is more disquieting is the doubt that independently, without having to act in support of the supremacy of man, Mary Shelley might have been inevitably prejudiced against the monster. At the end of the day, sympathising with the monster must part ways with fighting for the cause of the victim against man. This would mean leaving the scepter to the force of the unknown and its unpredictable ways of motivation and action. Realistically speaking, Frankenstein's abrupt change of decision to abort the project of creating a female for the monster saved man from the haunting paranoia of having a crowd of monstrous progeny. And this fear was not the least shared by the author. Frankenstein's monster could be a good monster but a monster nonetheless.

Frankenstein brings forth a profound sense of unease about the fear of the ugly, the unknown and the disruptive. Human civilisation throughout history has suspended judgement in the face of the alien. The fear may have been an invention of the troubled mind, yet it is alive and universal as the vigilant mind keeps watch over the unpredictability of the unknown. "Frankenstein may have committed a heinous sin, or a social crime, but in the end he is 'one of us': the monster may not be wholly blameworthy, even for his later acts of violence, but nonetheless he is different, and must be chastised as such". (Punter 2015, 280)

The Monster in Man

If the monstrosity of the monster is the causation and consequence of our belief and action, then can we hold Frankenstein responsible for making the evil manifest? Precisely, as the creature traces its origin to the dangerous science of Frankenstein, is he expressing the evil that has always been lurking in the dark secrets of the self-absorbed maker? The novel has variously been seen as an exposition of the forced erasure of women from the role of procreation. The unhallowed arts of Victor's godlike science replace the organised human creation with a hasty patch up of disparate materials. Critics have noted in the text the centrality of "charged homoerotic" relations displacing the role of female sexuality altogether. This in itself would not have been harmful had there not been an inevitable backlash in the concomitant withdrawal of motherly nurturing from the maker's heart. In the absence of a procreating female and object of heterosexual desire, the monster becomes both the coveted child and expression of his physical union. Peter Brooks goes as far as to suggest that the creature is the demonic projection of Frankenstein's own self which, bereft of social ties and absorbed in self-serving pursuits, hopes to be signified in the monster's form. Frankenstein and his monster are inextricably tied together in a pathetic battle of hunting each other down and the creator is aware "that the monster's death will be his own death-that in destroying the daemonic side of himself, he will also destroy the whole of self" (Brooks 2015, 335).

Victor had no emotional urge for creating the being; the creature was the produce of his audacious hubris in usurping or replicating the process of nature. Male motherhood is monstrous as it ensues from the mind or the will rather than the heart of the creator. Like the mythical omnipotent creators, the birth of the being was supposed to have been a satisfaction of the master's megalomania related to the exercise of power and control over a powerless subject. Mary Shelley wants us recognise that the male-births, in so far as they issue from motives other than love, are in varying degrees unnatural—that the true monster here is not the creature but the creator (Hatlen 2015, 292).

Denied of the glory of heavenly creation, the monster finds the rejection and fierce vengefulness of Satan his own. As the Epigraph from Milton's *Paradise Lost* shows Adam confronting God with his legitimate demand, so the monster challenges Frankenstein's authority with the eloquence of a rhetorician. Frankenstein on the other hand, potentially defies God's authority by a scientific imitation of cosmic thunderbolt and redefining the laws of reproduction. In the excitement of transgression, he identifies himself with the arrogant defiance of Lucifer, "I trod heaven in my thoughts, now exulting in my powers, now burning with the idea of their effects." The interplay of Frankenstein/Monster and Lucifer/Satan relations ultimately conflate the two avatars with the dreaded suggestion that the monster's villainy expresses the evil of its maker-Frankenstein (Tropp 2007, 6).

By the way of a postscript, the benign monster, turned violent by circumstances, however, is not to be absolved in academics and popular culture. He is still called by Frankenstein and is forced to share the darkness of his creator. He is also indiscriminately associated with a host of inherently diabolical characters who far surpass in cruelty and violence. Elizabeth Young cites filmmaker Michael Moore critiquing US foreign policy in the post 9/11 global scenario. He is quoted as saying, '"We liked playing Dr. Frankenstein. We created a lot of monsters—the Shah of Iran, Somoza of Nicaragua, Pinochet of Chile..."' In the same breath Moore, talking about Saddam Hussain, conflates the two figures when he says, '"We had a virtual love fest with this Frankenstein whom we (in part) created. And, just like the mythical Frankenstein, Saddam eventually spun out of control"' (Young 2011, 369)

Who then is the Frankenstein, the US or Saddam Hussain? Even though we know who the real Frankenstein is, the creations always appear to share a good portion of the maker's infamy. In the same way, the destiny of our good old monster is shaped by the burden of our schizophrenia about evil in things not looking like us.

Bibliography:

Brooks, Peter. 2015. '"Godlike Science/Unhallowed Arts": Language, Nature, and Monstrosity'. In *Mary Shelley, Frankenstein*, edited by Maya Joshi, New Delhi: Worldview Publications. (reprinted by permission from *The Endurance of Frankenstein*. Ed. Levine, George & Knoepflmacher, U.C. Berkley: University of California Press, 1979, pp. 205-220).

Friedman, Lester D. and Allison B. Kavey. 2016. *Monstrous Progeny*. New Jersey: Rutgers University Press.

Hatlen, Burton. 2015. "Milton, Mary Shelley and Patriarchy". In *Mary Shelley, Frankenstein*, edited by Maya Joshi, New Delhi: Worldview Publications. (From Burton Hatlen. 'Milton, Mary Shelley and Patriarchy'. Bucknell Review 28, 1983, pp.19-47).

Hogle, H. Jerrold. 2018. "The Gothic Image and the Quandaries of Science in Mary Shelley's *Frankenstein*." In *Global Frankenstein*, edited by Carol Margaret Davison and Marie Mulvey-Roberts, 21-35. Switzerland: Palgrave Macmillan. E-book.

Mellor, K Anne. 2003. "Making a "monster": an introduction to Frankenstein". In *The Cambridge Companion to Mary Shelley*, edited by Esther Schor, 9-25. Cambridge: Cambridge University Press.

Punter, David. 2015. "Gothic and Romanticism". In *Mary Shelley, Frankenstein*, edited by Maya Joshi, New Delhi: Worldview Publications. (Extracted from Punter, David. *The Literature of Terror*. London: Longman, 1980).

Sim, Stuart. 2008. *The Eighteenth Century Novel and Contemporary Social Issues: An Introduction*. Edinburg: Edinburg University Press.

Sterrenburg, Lee. 2015. "Mary Shelley's Monster: Politics and Psyche in *Frankenstein*". In *Mary Shelley, Frankenstein*, edited by Maya Joshi, New Delhi: Worldview Publications. (reprinted by permission from *The Endurance of Frankenstein*. Ed. Levine, George & Knoepflmacher, U.C. Berkley: University of California Press, 1979, pp.143-171).

Shelley, Mary. 2015. *Frankenstein*, edited by Maya Joshi. New Delhi: Worldview Publications.

Tropp, Martin. 2007. "The Monster". In *Mary Shelley's Frankenstein*, edited by Harold Bloom, 13-28. New York: Chelsea House Publishers.

Young, Elizabeth. 2011. "Frankenstein as Metaphor". In *Frankenstein* (Norton Critical Edition), edited by J. Paul Hunter, 330-337. New York: W. W. Norton & Company.

Zuk, D, Peter. 2013. "Is the Monster Free". In *Frankenstein and Philosophy: The Shocking Truth*, edited by Nicolas Michaud, 98-108. Chicago: Open Court Publishing. 2013, E-book.

All textual quotes are taken from *Mary Shelley*.

Rethinking Sciences, Situations and Bamboo-groves in Ray's Science Fictions: *Guessing Who Speaks What*

Rajadipta Roy

> "Arise. Heed the prophecy... Learn all the wisdom and all the secrets of the white man. But do not follow his vices. Be true to your people and the ancient rites."
> Ngugi wa Thiong'o.

The premise of Bengali Science Fictions (henceforth abbreviated as SF), and more specifically that of Satyajit Ray's science fantasies, has long been a fiddly ground of political negotiations between the colonially surcharged discourse of western science and the subversive counter logic produced immediately against such colonial manoeuvres to let out the steam of its cultural hegemony. With such an awareness of ambivalence underpinning one's knowledgebase, it is frequently observed in the process that SF of the western canon may easily be looked at as an expression of the politico-cultural transformation that originated in European imperialism and was inspired by the ideal of a single global technological regime. Well documented for years in the contributions of such writers like Jagadish Chandra Basu (1858–1937), Hemlal Dutta (?), Jagadananda Ray (1869–1933), Rajshekhar Basu (1880–1960), Sukumar Ray (1887–1923), Hemendrakumar Roy (1888–1963), Premendra Mitra (1904–1988), Khitindra Narayan Bhattacharya (1909–1990) etc., the slow yet decisive reallocations in the specific genre of SF in Bengali literature, which was albeit a creature of imperialism and inspired by a world-view of techno-scientific empire, have gradually lead towards a paradigmatic shift in the culture of writing SF's in the hands of Satyajit Ray in the context of post-Independence nation-building of the Indian postcolony by the second half of the last century.

Any perfunctory study of the positivist philosophy of science reveals that an intricate colonial schema of normative power relation ordinarily prefigures in the binary identification of the idea of science as qualitatively demarcated from the area of history in the western epistemology as such. This proposition also stimulates the generic membrane of SF's futuristic agenda in the western literary world. The stereotype of an a-historical value-neutrality has therefore remained central to this literary product of western scientism for long. Logically then, the cult of this popular genre in the context of the Indian postcolony invites a huge discursive inspection as the crucial historicity of the Indian society immediately calls for adaptive re-configurations of the literary form's generic scope along the ethical lineage of Indian scientism.

Deeply trained in his family lineage formed by such doyens like Upendrakishore and Sukumar, Satyajit Ray has always exhibited a culturally synthesised sensibility in his idea of science which is predominantly honed by the thoughts of the much talked of Bengal renaissance of the late nineteenth century. It is not hard to detect a relentless authorial effort to entwine the cultural values of our society into the larger ethical perspective of his story's elemental scientism which is concomitant to the collective psyche of the indigenous populace, and hence, assures a paradigmatic shift in the field in the Indian context. While speaking on Ray's cinema, Suranjan Ganguly sheds light on the ambivalent authorial position of Ray and subtly investigates the vector of the postcolonial cultural synthesis operating behind such paradoxes in the maestro's mind. He writes:

> "Such paradoxes are common in a cinema generated within a postcolonial society, especially one that is characterized by bewildering diversity. Ray's upbringing and cultural inheritance make the situation all the more complex since he is the product of a unique East-West fusion. As the sociologist Ashis Nandy has remarked, 'Ray ... lived with a plurality of selves, and a part of him was as deeply Indian as a part of him was Western.' Thus, his struggle to define himself within the framework of his legacy involves a larger struggle to define the India within which he functions as an artist." (Ganguly 2000, 1-2)

This claim of exhibiting a "plurality of selves", which is applicable to his cinematic authorship, is also equally tenable for his literary authorship of SFs and other stories. From several other anecdotes and sources, it is evident that Ray himself was aware of this cultural plurality operating heavily not only behind his mind but also in the creative milieu of India in general by the middle of the twentieth century. While talking to the legendary artist Binode Behari Mukherjee (1904–1980), who was Ray's professor of art during his brief but culturally decisive period of stay in Santiniketan, Ray harps on the idea of "absorption of foreign influence" in the artist and himself coins the term "synthesis" to appreciate Mukherjee's brilliant fusion of western "composition" and Indian "climate" in his works (Ray 2020, 24–25). Ray's SFs invite a lot of debate in including and synthesising non-normative incidents such as that of parapsychology, the occult and clairvoyance etc. into its folds so far so that these are often popularly identified more as speculative fictions than pure Science Fictions in line with its western counterpart. This attempt in addressing the cultural "climate" of his tales in general often makes not only the character of the scientist but the very idea of science itself pretty adventurous in his SFs and cut an altogether different curvature in the generic route map of Bengali SFs. Suranjan Ganguly examines a persistent effort functioning behind the political intent of Ray the film maker in describing "the making of a nation as it emerges from its feudal past and its experience with colonialism to become a new hybrid, postcolonial entity", which is uniformly pertinent to Ray as the writer of SFs (Ganguly 2000, 4). As a result, a cultural synthesis of western form and composition with Indian tone and climate becomes historically central to the postcolonially plural texts of Ray in all their aspects from the cinematic to the literary, as Ganguly further comments:

> "For Ray, the modern is inseparable from this sense of the plural that incorporates within itself its history of multiple dislocations." (Ibid.)

The nineteenth century colonial interface facilitated epistemic inputs of Western science into the social fabric of Bengal and witnessed the upsurge of an inevitably ethos-neutral scientism in the so-called Bengal Renaissance of the period. Consequent to the ubiquitous colonial system of knowledge, the rubric of Bengali SF initially was habituated to weigh this hegemony primarily into the newly introduced generic space. The power of the West in the idea of science during the era was sacrosanct in itself until it was reclaimed and relocated historically in the early part of the twentieth century by such thinkers like Acharya Prafulla Chandra Ray (1861–1944) or Acharya Brajendra Nath Seal (1864–1938). Acharya Ray's *A History of Hindu Chemistry from the Earliest Times to the Middle of Sixteenth Century* (first volume published in 1902; second volume published in 1909) helped immensely to make inroads into an antiquarian Indian lineage of scientific thoughts parallel to that of the prevalent Western hegemony.

Dhruv Raina offers a significant proposition on the ethico-moral gravitas of scientific thought in India down the ages and refers to the post-positivist repositioning of the archive of ancient body of knowledge in his article "Scientism and Romanticism" to facilitate a historical understanding of the idea elaborately enough (Raina 2011, 19–48). "In studies on the history of science and technology in India", writes Raina, "the historiographic frames are structured by a multitude of factors, such as the nature of the interaction between traditional forms of knowledge and new knowledge" (Ibid., 19). The historiographic urgency and the cultural impetus behind such relocation of the philosophy of science in the essentially localised context of the Indian society is further clarified by Raina in more economic terms in the following statement:

> "Further, epistemological approaches to the study of the sciences in the developing countries have had to break with the standard or Big Picture of the history of science and technology ... An epistemological view of the sciences in the developing countries may be grounded in a socio-economic theory of marginalization. An investigation of science, technology, and development in India has frequently been undertaken within the frames of the politics of knowledge, centre and periphery, and metropolis and province. The necessity for such a theory resides in both global and local contexts of science and politics." (Ibid., 20)

Once resolved that in India the "seeds of a modern indigenous scientific tradition were first sown in Bengal" (Ibid., 24) during the late nineteenth century, the Bengali psyche witnessed the dovetailing of both the Eurocentric and the revitalist projects of scientific thoughts in shaping the nation's consciousness in the following decades of its self-expression, finally maturing into the hugely complex idea of Indian modernity. Such a historically important revitalist tract of cultural scientism traces back its origin more in the writings of the philosopher—Acharya B. N. Seal—who relentlessly and impeccably posited a logical communication between the Indian philosophical tradition and the positivist philosophy of science in praxis in his astounding book *The Positive Sciences of the Ancient Hindus*, first published from London in 1915. Seal embarks upon the understanding of the Nyaya logic and "represented it in the idiom of inductivist philosophy of science" (Ibid., 27). V. Shekhawat in his article "Emergence of a New Paradigm and the Onset of Sastra Phase" approaches this issue of locating the idea of science in the Indian philosophical tradition and offers an interesting discursive opportunity in placing the idea of indigenous 'sastra' as a signifier of the 'science', saving the latter's incumbent political connotation of being loaded with hegemonic hangover of the western epistemology (Shekhawat 2007, 49). Shekhawat insists on the recognition of the "heterogeneity of cognitive pursuit" (Ibid.,106) elsewhere in the book and insists on the philosophical cognition of the idea of science in the cited article beyond the paradigm of the western epistemology:

> "Indeed, if sastra represents the acme of Indian cognitive systemization, then what is of greatest historical significance is the study of the conditions under which this concept originated and was fashioned more and more thoroughly. Sastra represents the Indian conception of science, and it is during the study, pursuit and growth of sastras that knowledge was reclassified and re-systematized." (Ibid., 49)

Satyajit Ray, coming to write SF in 1961 and writing exclusively for the Bengali children of the post-independence era, primarily writes within the cultural matrix of this inevitable postcolonial interface where "heterogeneity of cognitive pursuit" is translated in terms of ideational plurality. But to suit his purpose of resisting the Western practice of stereotyping the trope, Ray has considerably reinvented that plurality. He had largely adapted the genre of SF into a form of science fantasy that constantly offers a strong ethical base to his idea of science(s) and the scientist(s). Ray's long honed awareness of the legacy and richness of Indian culture also extends itself to shape his open-ended attitude to the ethical scientism working in the collective imagination of a Bengali child. He attempts to narrate culturally rooted science fantasies for his young readers who are located on the postcolonial crossroads and are inescapably in the habit of negotiating their reading experiences between cultures.

The pluralistic interpolations of the ideas of science(s) and scientist(s) in the speculative imagination of Ray, where the mysterious cohabits the empirical, fact cohabits fiction and the causal cohabits the arbitrary leading to a more infusive and cultural scientism, are well dispersed over the generic oeuvre of SFs produced by him over a period of three decades from the year 1961 up to the last draft titled *The Incident of the Drexel Island* in 1991 built on the adventures of his much popular protagonist, Prof. Shonku, who turns 75 on October 16 in the unfinished tale. Ray's whole bulk of SFs can broadly be divided into two categories: namely, the 'Shonku' tales and the 'non-Shonku' tales. Ray burst into the field of Bengali SFs with two tales serialised in the difference of merely some months in the renowned children's magazine **Sandesh** back in the years 1961 and 1962. *The Diary of a Space Traveller*, the first ever published tale featuring Ray's amusing and extraordinary inventor cum scientist Prof. Shonku, was serialised in the September, October and November issues of *Sandesh* in 1961, while his first and probably one of the best ever non-Shonku SF, *Bonku Babu's Friend*, was published in the February issue of the same magazine in 1962. Ray's culturally sentient idea of science and his postcolonial plurality hold the mainstay of all the forty tales of Prof. Shonku, both finished and unfinished, and his other non-Shonku SFs in general, the grain of which might easily be perceived in the very inception of such a unique scientist in his imagination who is an apotheosis of an ethical Indian identity.

In several interviews and talks, found all over the web platforms, Ray has repeatedly made it clear that he modelled his inimitable character of the scientist cum inventor, Professor Trilokeshwar Shonku, on the literary image of Professor Heshoram Hushiyar, made immortal in *Heshoram Hushiyarer Diary* by his father and his literary predecessor in the line of SFs—Sukumar Ray.

Ray exploits this intertextual scope of building up Shonku's adventures around the extensive encounters with different peoples, animals and cultures of the world to figure out a completely new, original and effective genre of science-fantasies conducive to the taste and environ of a reader rooted in a postcolonial cultural climate. Ray is unavoidably aware of the cultural limitations of a writer writing in a vernacular language but transcends the same by making his tales live heavily within the culture that he is writing of. An observant eye like that of the famous writer Chitra Banerjee Divakaruni does not miss this point as she examines that,

> "Professor Shonku is not merely a scientist fashioned after the heroes of Jules Verne or H. G. Wells and plunked down in Calcutta. Ray has given his adventures a definite Indian dimension that is at once appealing and unique. The professor (whose curiosity and stubbornness are constantly landing him in trouble) moves with ease from the world of futuristic invention to one of timeless magic; to encounter a dead ancestor who looks just like him, or a vengeful sadhu who knows a spell to bring dead animals back to life, or a magician who can turn a lizard into a Chinese dragon, or an Egyptian mummy and its modern day descendant whose lives are somehow linked." (Ray 2008, viii)

Ray's deliberate subversion of the colonially tempered tradition of SF writings as such locates a difference voicing out resistance between the lines of his popular texts which are deeply steeped in the Indian climate. Way back in the years around the sixth decade of the last century, when the colonial hangover in the social structure of India was still quite thick and the blazing consumerism of the global market did not quite bedazzle our imagination to a callously cloned mimic mediocrity of extremely oblivious cultural awareness, Ray narrated the experience of an alien encounter amidst a dark bamboo grove somewhere in the provincial localities of suburban Bengal in *Bonku Babu's Friend*. With such acclimatisation of a trope endlessly produced and reproduced in the western genre of SFs, Ray thus immediately initiates a crucial but much awaited cultural adjustment in the collective psyche of a quintessentially Bengali adolescent reader with respect to his or her aesthetic reception of a science-fantasy in terms which are at once historically nuanced and politically alert. As a result, it does indeed amount to a departure in the field of SFs in the Bengali literary canon as the genre, as a typical outgrowth of intense colonial enterprise in the field of knowledge as such, stands adequately redefined by Ray in the context of the changing socio-cultural atmosphere of Indian scientism. Ray's canon denies to appropriate science and technology solely as colonising tools which always attempted otherwise to politically calibrate our idea of the same in the sole light of the positivist philosophy of the western world.

The literary alacrity with which Ray makes his somewhat singular idea of science coil into the cosy corner of his reader's mind while adequately bending the genre of SF to fit his postcolonial pluralistic purpose is something brilliant in itself. The charm of this extraordinary literary acumen often mesmerises the average reader to remain impervious to the significance of Ray's vital idea of science that has stimulated a much-animated debate of late among the critics usually camped on opposite poles. Ray's rubrical praxis in discourse, however, encloses within its folds almost all events labelled as magical with events labelled as futuristic, hence scientific, and resists the normative rehearsals of western epistemology traded to us by our heavy colonial legacy. Such ideational culturalism results in a confluence of perceptive binaries, as those of science and history, which are externally suspect of an alarming imaginative anomaly alien to the construction of any systematically developed scientific imagination. Biswajit Ray addresses the trouble of this unique ideological configuration of science in the fundamental imagination of Ray in his book *Professor Shankur Sesh Diary* (The Last Diary of Prof. Sanku) and successfully brings into focus that Ray's scientism "does not always approve of the state regulated idea of science" (Ray 2013, 68) where the 'state' should be taken as a veritable colonial construct. Ashis Nandy criticises the insistent claim of the role of culture in Ray's formulation of a somewhat 'meta-scientific outlook' operating within the creative framework of his SFs and ponders on the phenomenon rather cynically as he tends to diagnose an element of crass populism in Ray's essential aesthetics (Nandi 2011, 257). Reckless violation of the fundamental codes applicable to the specific form of art and the commercial prescription of gross sentimentality, the two most conspicuous negative regularities which characterise the so-called faulty aesthetics of popular Hindi movies in India are, according to Nandy, alleged to be ironically ingrained within the textual world of Ray's popular fictions. In his remarkable article "Satyajit Ray's Secret Guide to Exquisite Murders", Nandy observes that, "[not] only do magical elements return in the guise of superscience to play an important part in his science fiction, so does the element of predictability in his crime stories" (Ibid.).

Nandy's censure continues to draw a drastic parallel between the commercial populism of the average movie market and the working aesthetic venture of Ray's SFs that makes the former comment that "Ray's identification with his scientist-hero... is at least partly powered by his self-image as a Renaissance man, straddling the disjunctive cultures of the humanities and science" (Ibid., 258). Once treated in doubt, the cultural scientism of Ray is immediately pointed out by Nandy as Ray's emblematic effort of self-fashioning induced by the three generation Renaissance fetish of his illustrious forefathers. He embarks upon a plausible pathology of Ray's scientism replete in the creative imagination of the latter's SFs and blurts out at length in the following vein:

> In popular fiction, however, his commitment to the worldview of science is romanticized. Specially in his science fiction, the events on which he builds his stories often reveal an openness to experiences (such as paranormality and extra-sensory perceptions of various kinds) that might be taboo to the [film maker] Ray. Ideologically, he may be more closed in his popular works, methodologically he is much less encumbered. Even a casual reader quickly finds out that Ray is not a perfectionist in his popular writings: he is less careful about his workmanship and his imagination is less controlled. (Ibid.)

However inadvertent that critical laceration might be on Nandy's part, any watchful reading of his critique and consequent disapproval of Ray's scientism unearths perhaps the most crucial cue to the culturally insightful author's outstanding treatment of the idea of science in his literary productions. Nandy emphasises an attitudinal 'openness' to experiences traceable in Ray's idea of science and that openness owes a lot more than what usually meets the eye to the developing idea of science in Indian history in and around the time when Ray was fashioning out his science fictions for the young generation of Bengali readers living with the social awareness of their unique spatio-temporal reality. Ray's culturally tempered presentation of science in his science fantasies, or more appropriately in his speculative fictions, are often put into comparison to the same literary praxis of his father Sukumar Ray or that of his grandfather Upendrakishore Ray Chowdhury. Nandy relates the heavy Renaissance fervour of the latter two to the psychological grooming of Ray as even a child in somewhat a caustically blasé manner (Ibid.) and Biswajit Ray attempts to locate the immediate legacy of Satyajit Ray as a writer of SFs in the perspective of his father and grandfather respectively being the eminent literary men in the genre of popular science in the very early part of the twentieth century (Ray 2013, 59).

It is wise to assume that the immediate fallout of a genealogical attempt in studying the scientism of Ray with an eye to determine it instantaneously and on a much larger scale as an offshoot of a Renaissance mindset like that of Sukumar or Upendrakishore does not go scot-free of the charge of overt and blatant generalisation. Sukumar was an academically trained student in the schools of western science, procured his degree from the British colleges and wrote with a frank and free preference of interest to the archive of western scientism though he had no less concern for the nationalist sentiment of his contemporary Bengali society of the pre-independence days. Sukumar's preferential fulcrum generally inclined heavily to the Eurocentric ideas of anything scientific as such and the issues of culture were neatly differentiated from his discussion of that 'scientific', be that in the form of a fictional account of a scientific invention or that of a scientist's (European indeed) biography. But the table turns almost a full circle, and perhaps a little oddly enough, if we try to read the essentially cultural primer of Satyajit's scientism jumping a generation back in linkage to the historically nuanced scientism of his grandfather Mr. Upendrakishore Ray Chowdhury. Upendrakishore was a fine product of the so called nineteenth century Bengali Renaissance that resulted from the complete colonisation of Bengal and yet a strong awareness and obligation to his historical locale in fashioning his exquisite tales of popular science is unmistakably mapped out in him. In the enlightening write-up on the paleontological creatures of extreme antiquity titled *Sekaler Katha* (Tales of the Days Gone By), published in the form of a monograph in the year 1903, he offers a splendid literary excursion to the Jurassic and the Triassic worlds and finishes the fascinating tale with a subtle but sure clue to the geographical situatedness of some of these creatures and events in the very localised pre-historical past of India. The ploy at once attracts the attention of an Indian, in this case Bengali, reader and serves to qualify the claim of literary verisimilitude to an authentic degree of scientific imagination and cultural intimacy. Upendrakishore procures, if we are allowed to quote Coleridge verbatim in this instance, for these creatures of scientific imagination their needed "semblance of truth" (Jackson 1985, 314) in absolute cultural terms by locating their existence on the very soil of Indian pre-history when he mentions the presence of paleontological species like the Tigodons and Shivatheriums in the Sivalik ranges near Dehradun in India (Chowdhury 2013, 189).

The interlacing of culture with science, be that for the sake of guaranteeing a justifiable historical locale to his literary fictions of popular science or else to understand and represent the very idea of science in unsmudged ethico-moral terms, is certainly an awareness that Satyajit incurs from his family line especially more from the psycho-cultural adjustments of Upendrakishore than from the Eurocentric appropriations of his father Sukumar. Nandy is ruthless in locating the presence of this ethical element in the scientism of Ray and ascribes the origin of the same in the long-standing tradition of British, therefore colonial, culture of novel writing. For Nandy, the effort is nothing but appropriation of the western tradition and he reads Ray, the writer of popular SFs, more as a replicator of the colonial monolith of Baconian "inductionism and empiricism" (Nandy 2011, 256). Despite, however, the disapproval of Nandy, the ontology of this entwined awareness remains singularly crucial in understanding Ray's science fictions if we read into that awareness in relation to the history of science in India.

The unavoidable logical outcome of such a contested legacy of discursive practice in theorising a culturally conducive idea of science entwines the spatio-temporal configuration adapted to the required ethical standardisation of the much-professed value-neutrality of science in the local context. Nandy does exactly detect the urgency of such a historical necessity in his article "Defiance and Conformity in Science: The World of Jagadis Chandra Bose" and observes that in the individual psyche of the great Indian scientist, on whom the article is essayed, the "cultural psychology of scientific creativity also allows one to probe the creativity of individual scientists as link between cultural and individual needs" (Nandy 2004, 18).

The reconciliation of the theoretical components of positivist thought and the elements of Indian historicity are central in the literary approaches to explore the full scopes of popular science writings in India as one has to take into account the anxieties and confusions of such a project at large which an Indian writer trying hands in the genre of SFs is inevitably fated with. Nandy further explores the historical limitation of the value-neutral scientific thoughts in the same article when he warns his readers that,

> "Scientific creativity, like any other form of human creativity, assumes the ability to use one's less accessible self in such a way that the primordial becomes meaningful to the community and the individual scientist. Out of this ability comes not only the creative scientist's sense of being driven, but also his distinctive approach to concepts, relationships, and operations, the order that he imposes on his data, and the limits he sets on his insights. The scientific community prescribes where and when professional assessments begin, but it can never fully control what at any point of time is accepted as objective, impersonal, and formal scientific knowledge." (Ibid., 86-87)

The measure to "control" the unbridled implementation of scientific exegesis in the form of hyper-technologically materialistic enterprises of western futurism in an imperially consumerist manner does call for an ethical re-standardisation of the ideas that eventually give birth to the socially sanctioned initiative of cultural scientism duly put in vogue by the "Needham project" (Habib and Raina 2001, 281). The ethical message on which almost the whole oeuvre of Ray's SFs conclude are briskly put to criticism by Nandy, and he labels Ray's psychic bent as a prototypical derivative of the Eurocentric scientism when he derides the author as a tame and "uncritical believer in the emancipator and educative role of Enlightenment values" (Nandy 2011, 260). The placement of the hegemonic a-historicity of western science against the ethical historicity of cultural values, as that is put into praxis in the SFs of Ray much to the critical discomfort of Nandy, may be shielded by Habib and Raina's focus on the changing scenario of scientism in the whole world since the middle of the last century as they weigh the situation elaborately enough in their article "The Missing Picture: The Non- emergence of a Needhamian History of Sciences in India":

> "By the end of, what Hobsbawm [...] calls, 'the Age of Catastrophe', a number of scientists and scientists-turned-historians of science attempted to project science as a cultural activity that enjoined humanity — this moral vision was to fill the vacuum left by the two wars. From Sarton [...] to Bernal and Needham an attempt was underway to redefine humanism, wherein science would provide a cultural affirmative for the West ruined by two world wars. This 'moral' vision of science was to strike a sympathetic chord within the nebulous scientific communities of newly independent nations like India where the bonds between state and science were mutually reinforcing...." (Habib and Raina 2001, 283)

Many of the pieces of the puzzle of Ray's cultural scientism that immediately calls into action a thoroughbred historico-philosophical reading fall into places if Ray's treatment of science is stripped of the usual 'overdeterministic' metaphors of the western epistemology which finds a politically insinuated binary proposition in the 'underdeterministic' ideation of history and culture and ethics thereof (Fuller 2001, 121). Consequently, when Ray comes to write his SFs by the sixth decade of the last century exclusively for the children of Bengal the general vision of science with both its utopian and dystopian possibilities must have been very open to him as it might logically be inferred from his well-trained exposure to the cultural on-goings and shifts in the western societies. His assured awareness of the historical evolution of the idea of science was not perhaps absolutely novel and unique for his generation, but his cultural adjustment of the 'scientific' put into the praxis of his SFs is certainly sentient with that deep knowledge of the historical contextuality.

Consequent to this historical contextuality, the speculative products of high western scientism like the UFOs, aliens, the humanoids or androids meet the average Bengali people like Bonku Babu in the most ordinary situations of mundane life amidst such indigenous locales like a bamboo grove in the SFs of Ray as uneventfully as possible. The cultural construct that he foregrounds in the narratives have an inexorable historical authenticity to make them appear as less falsifiable and more and more plausible in nature, context and ethical reach. The localisation of the ideas contributes to the adaptive authenticity of these tales of Ray, the onus of which unavoidably falls not on the western specificity of the genre but on the assimilative re-positioning of the 'glocal' (global + local) open-endedness of the same that might be traced in the long track of evolution of scientific thoughts in India as well as in the relatively young generic history of the Indian science fictions.

In Ray's early SFs on alien encounters, *Bonku Babu's Friend* and the other culturally loaded alien-story of *The Maths Teacher, Mr. Pink and Tipu* (1982), the author reveals his proposition of cultural scientism in the most effortless literary style, which is non-metaphorical and therefore direct and quintessentially authentic to the experiences of inhabitants of the Indian provincial towns known as Mofussils. His reading of the power politics embedded within the textual frameworks of western SFs is impeccable when he mocks the mimic attitude of a 'cultural amphibian's' (Said, as quoted in Raina 2011, 25) perceptions over the possibility of encountering a UFO in the rural setting of Bengal in *Bonku Babu's Friend* with a certain tinge of satire:

> Bonku Babu repeated his words, his tone still gentle: 'Suppose someone from a different planet came here?'
> As was his wont, Bhairav Chakravarty slapped Bonku Babu's back loudly and rudely, grinned and said, 'Bravo! What a thing to say! Where is a creature from another planet going to land? Not Moscow, not London, not New York, not even Calcutta, but here? In Kankurgachhi? You do think Big, don't you?' (Majumdar 2012, 3)

The fictional identity of an alien, a Martian or a UFO is typified by the futuristic colonial version of western science and therefore the possibility of such an encounter on the human part must be a privilege for the western people only. This restrictive attitude is a cultural fetish with far reaching implications to construct distorted notions of anything non-western as stereotyped by the sheer absence of science. The hegemonic fetish of this complementary interdependence of colonialism and science is subtly indicated by Ray in a short fiction apparently not dealing with science and yet which puts out a dialogic discourse on the configuration of the set of binaries like the logic/mystery, west/non-west or the British/Indian etc. all of which are finally contributing to the unconditional acceptance of the binary set of science/culture in the common psyche. In the story *The Hunting Lodge of Dhumalgarh* (1984), one of the characters pass a seemingly naive comment which in due course breaks the fifth wall to the critics of culture with a considerable effectiveness. Although the story is modelled on one of Ray's favourite topics, the supernatural air affected by ghosts and wraiths, it betrays a delicate mindset in Ray all alert to the colonial gaze in which India is often represented to the western readership. Pratapnarayan, the power-hungry prince faulty of the surreptitious murder of his own elder brother in the story offers a caustic comment on this colonial gaze and blurts out in contempt,

> 'Macardy thinks that India is a store house of ghosts and spirits. I could not convince him otherwise. The Sahib used to assume every abandoned house as a haunted one. It was set deep in his imagination.' (Ray 2009, 417)

This colonial gaze is inextricably intertwined with the generic limitations of SFs whose origin is concomitant with and complicit to the fundamental project of the west-oriented colonial hegemony. John Reider scrutinises this complicity of the genre richly in his fascinating book *Colonialism and the Emergence of Science Fiction* and lights up the issue with the following logic:

> Emergent English language science fiction articulates the distribution of knowledge and power at a certain moment of colonialism's history. If the Victorian vogue for adventure fiction in general seems to ride the rising tide of imperial expansion, particularly into Africa and the Pacific, the increasing popularity of journeys into outer space or under the ground in the late nineteenth and the early twentieth centuries probably reflects the near exhaustion of the actual unexplored areas of the globe – the disappearance of the

white spaces on the map, to invoke a famous anecdote of Conrad's." (Reider 2008, 4)

The most critical twist in Ray's *Bonku Babu's Friend*, is perhaps stored in the dual employment of the cultural signification of this last cited phrase—"unexplored areas of the globe" — as the representative mimic-mediocrity of the common Indian mindset, glossed with colonial knowledge, does not find any logic even in the utter theoretical probability of an alien landing in a waste and retrograde land as that of India. The Bengali phrase "pora desh", translated as "God-forsaken place" by Gopa Majumdar (Majumdar 2012, 3), is a qualifier to describe the inferior status of India in the hierarchy of power offered and attested by the western epistemology that successfully replicates the colonial binary of the civilised / savage construct in the story. All the characters present in the story are unaware of this inherent politics ingrained in their collective psyche, save that of the protagonist. Therefore, the rich host of the weekly hangout, lawyer Sripati Majumdar, whose profession is a deliberate indication of his Eurocentric outlook and has a touch of colonial superiority, might easily conclude with authority and consensus in the story that the aliens must not be fools to come to any insignificant rural part of Bengal and they must be "sahibs, and they will land in some western country, where all the sahibs live" (Ibid.). The helplessly meek (tame to an extent) and patient Bonku Babu, the village school-teacher of Kankurgachhi, never found words to reason with the dominant Sripati Babu or his cronies who were the regular leg pullers of the former in these weekly meetings. It was almost a custom with Bonku Babu to leave these meetings dumbfounded following many sarcastic gibes and humiliating jeers. The day on which the events of the story were shaping up was also no exception to this routine. But Bonku Babu did not support the opinion of the meeting regarding the sole possibility of an alien encounter only in some foreign and remote metropolitan city of his imagination and kept thinking of the phenomenon of the moving point of light of the very evening in the northern sky on his way back to home. The phenomenon of the mysterious light triggered off the whole discussion on the UFOs and the aliens. En route to a short cut through the bamboo grove of Poncha Ghosh in the pitch-black darkness of the night, goose bumps break out on Bonku babu's body as he involuntarily bumps into a UFO and an alien amidst the small pond at the centre of the grove. What follows next is narrated with Ray's usual literary acumen. Once over with the initial awe and aura the earthling and the alien break into a communication which is of the most crucial import for our discussion of Ray and his cultural scientism in context. The alien is, marking a departure in the dystopian treatment of such fictional bodies in the colonial projects of western SFs, not inimical to Bonku babu and hits up a working mentor-pupil relationship with the latter almost in no time. After a short while, he leaves with an ethical advice to Bonku Babu leaving him both mesmerised and elated at once. Ang, the alien that represents a version of not only technologically but also ethically superior civilisation in the story, echoes the immaculate humanism of Tagore that is philosophically value loaded, and not value-neutral, and culturally oriented around the age-old wisdom of the Indian Vedantas. Ethical insinuation prefigures in Tagore's poem "Nyay Danda" that reads "Anyay je kore ar anyay je sohe/ Taba ghrina jeno tare trinasama dohe" [He who does ill and he who tolerates ill/ Let them both burn like weeds in your wrath] (Tagore 2000, 442). The same insinuating note erupts out of the prophetic suggestion made by the alien to Bonku Babu:

> Look, I have been watching you. And I have examined your arms and legs. You belong to a much inferior species. There is no doubt about that. However, as human beings go, you are not too bad. I mean, you are a good man. But you have a major fault. You are much too meek and mild. That is why you have made so little progress in life. You must always speak up against injustice, and protest if anyone hurts and insults you without provocation. To take it quietly is wrong, not just for man, but for any creature anywhere. (Majumdar 2012, 7)

The rest is a logical outcome of the literary design as Bonku Babu is transformed into a spirited man with his wits and stands against all the cronies of Sripati Babu with a harmless but hilarious retaliation. The alchemisation of the image of a common man in Bonku babu is definitely a cue to Ray's secret criticism of the members of the Bengali community who are often charged with the symptoms of mental sloth and moral laxity. A clandestine intimation to take over a revolutionary stand against all situational odds underpins the affable and comic hit-back of Bonku Babu. But what is more noteworthy is the alien's attempted pathology of not only the spatio-temporally bound social situation of a timid Bengali man like Bonku Babu, but his more universal observation of the existential ethical crisis and its salvage on the cultural level of both the personal and the collective psyche of any race of beings whatsoever. The ethical condition pressed hard in the utterance of the scientifically superior alien is less Darwinian but more philosophical in essence when he blurts out unequivocally that to take any injustice quietly "is wrong, not just for man, but for any creature anywhere."

This is exactly where Satyajit Ray finds his cautious self-fashioning tales of science-fantasies for his young readers, fastened to their unique cultural location and climate of a postcolonial social space by the 60's of the twentieth century, in the juvenile republic of India only a few years after its hard-earned freedom from British rule back in 1947. Ray, in fact, took to the writing of SFs keeping an alert eye upon his readership sated in this complex urban and semi-urban social dynamics of a historically suffering Bengal, desperately struggling to cope with the toddling economy of a nation that has just won its freedom from a long-drawn colonial rule at the cost of riots, refugees and reckless political instabilities. As it falls out, the socio-historical situatedness of his characters and events narrated in the SFs are conceived to work up the ambience of a veritable social narrative for the text that candidly makes room for may be the rudimentary but definitely fundamental scientism of the mundane and yet traditional Bengali life with ease. Thus, the textual experiences of the characters in the fictive spheres are happily shared by the real-life experiences of the children for whom these are narrated which, in turn, contribute to the historical credibility of the characters in the texts.

Textual credibility of Ray's scientists, androids, robots and UFOs relies on the historicity of his scientism, which might be at times reaching out to limits to raise questions against the very epistemology of science taught to us by the western system of knowledge. Ray finds the ontological foundation of his ideas in the pre-colonial Indian texts and myths in a manner that has much to do with the resistance put to the west's appropriative re-examinations of its so-called scientific superiority even in the dystopian years following the great wars of the last century. Therefore, Ray's science fantasies do not anymore remain complicit to the epistemic pre-eminence of the western scientific thoughts at the expense of the gross stereotyping of non-western ideas of science, but engages with debates of real merit on the cultural cognition of the idea of science more significantly on the onto-cultural level. Ray does not tend to limit the idea of science to the mere application of certain law- governed methodologies imbibed and sanctioned by the western epistemology so far, but goads us to traverse newer paths, breaks the barriers of over-deterministic dogmas and tends to implant the spirit of enquiry into such realms and phenomena which are usually identified as areas of study pigeonholed by the sheer absence of science. The recognition of a value-oriented discursive space for science is the driving force of Ray's science fictions and his cultural scientism might well be read as an attempt to ascribe to science "the quality of a cultural universal" (Cunningham and Williams, 1993, 411).

The ethical input preached at the end of *Bonku Babu's Friend* indeed have a Renaissance smack of humanism in it as it is rightly assumed by Nandy's suspicion of "the integrative capacities at the disposal of his self" (Nandy 2011, 260) in Ray. But that fervour of Renaissance humanism does not necessarily reduce the scope of the author's cultural reading of Indian scientism to a single monolithic structure. Renaissance was not a homogenous idea even to Ray's grandfather Upendrakishore in whom we have already traced a certain culture consciousness contributing to the formation of the Indian psyche. Upendrakishore, despite being enlightened in the colonial legacy of Renaissance thought in the second half of the nineteenth century, was openly critical of the anthropocentric project of humanism that formulated its bedrock of being. He concludes the monograph *Sekaler Katha* with the following words that critiques the sacrosanct hegemony of western anthropocentric ideology passed in the name of science and leaves the text open ended with possibilities favourable to the culturally tolerant imaginative mind of an Indian reader:

> A lot remains untold of the animals of the days gone by. You will grow up and will read of them. We sometimes think that the world was perhaps created only for us. I hope that this misunderstanding is now going to be resolved. Bubbles brew up and then disappear in the same water. Since its creation until now, all life forms are coming to being and are ceasing to be some day in this pattern. All relishes it for a day and then disappear in days. Now, what right do we the human beings have to claim that we have come to stay for some more days? (Chowdhury 2013, 191)

For Ray, as it might be worked out of his exquisite SFs with little efforts, the conjunction of the 'scientific' with the 'cultural' within the historical dynamics of the Indian society definitely has an anxiety embedded in its substratum of self-fashioning motive. The event of Renaissance is often criticised for professing a straight jacketing syncretic view of human endeavours to the extent of appropriating the given power structure of the imperial order and for establishing a hegemonic position to the European scientism as sacrosanct and value-neutral that finds in the non-European nations its stereotype of the 'other' characterised with the absence of science. Science and culture, more importantly its ethical values, are well demarcated in the western positivist thought process which is induced with the political ideology of Renaissance teachings. But this indictment of binary standards is not prevalent in the social fabric of the Indian knowledge system where knowledge, be it scientific or cultural, always is perceived not necessarily as power but as a mode of achieving emancipation which is rich with the ethical credence of the philosophical sublime. In his fascinating study on Bankimchandra Chattiopadyay's philosophical orientation in "The Moment of Departure: Culture and Power in the Thought of Bankimchandra" Partha Chatterjee discusses the fundamental premise of the Sankhya system of knowledge in the Indian tradition and opines that the Sankhya philosophers did "recognize the need for gaining a knowledge of the world", but "the goal of knowledge was salvation", and not power, for them (Chatterjee 2012, 57). It is in his inclusive attempt to explore and foreground the greater position of the "knowledge of the world", of which scientific knowledge is merely a part, that Ray in his SFs for the Bengali children could never take his eyes off the immediate ethical adjustments required for his readership. An amount of ethical and generic adjustment and adaptation is indispensable on their part for a proper appreciation of this vigorously colonial genre relocated adequately to fit into their strictly localised conditions. Ray's narratives deny to appropriate the praxis of western SF and are indeed less technographic but more ethnographic to adapt to the very fabric of culture that he writes within and writes for.

Notes:

- All textual citations of the works of Satyajit Ray and Upendrakishore Ray Chowdhury are copyrighted to *The Estate of Satyajit Ray*. The writer of the present article owes indebtedness to the 'Estate' and all due authorities thereof for using excerpts strictly in academic interest from the works of Ray and Chowdhury.
- The quote at the beginning of the article is taken from p. 20 of Ngugi wa Thiong'o's celebrated novel *The River Between*. The source is cited below.

Bibliography:

Chatterjee, Partha. 2012. *The Partha Chatterjee Omnibus*. New Delhi: Oxford University Press.

Chowdhury, Upendrakishore Ray. 2013. *Upendrakishore Rachanasamagra*. Vol. 1. Ed. Anathnath Das and Amal Paul. Kolkata: Ananda Publishers Pvt. Ltd.

Cunnigham, Andrew and Perry Williams. 1993. "De-centring the 'Big Picture': The Origin of Modern Science and the Modern Origins of Science". *British Journal of History of Science*, 26: 407-32.

Fuller, Steve. 2001. "Prolegomena to a World History of Science: Recovering a Sense of Historicity in the History of Science". In *Situating the History of Science: Dialogues with Joseph Needham*, edited by S. Irfan Habib and Dhruv Raina, 114-151. New Delhi: Oxford University Press.

Ganguly, Suranjan. 2000. *Satyajit Ray: In Search of the Modern*. New Delhi: Penguin Books.

Habib, S. Irfan and Dhruv Raina. 2001. ed. *Situating the History of Science: Dialogues with Joseph Needham*. New Delhi: Oxford University Press.

Jackson, H. J. 1985. "Introduction" in *Samuel Taylor Coleridge: The Major Works*, edited by H.J. Jackson. Oxford: Oxford University Press.

Majumdar, Gopa. 2012. tr. *Classic Satyajit Ray*. New Delhi: Penguin Books.

Nandy, Ashis. 2004. *Return from Exile*. New Delhi: Oxford University Press.

... 2011. *The Savage Freud and Other Essays on Possible and Retrievable Selves*. New Delhi: Oxford University Press.

Raina, Dhruv. 2011. *Images and Contexts: The Historiography of Science and Modernity in India*. New Delhi: Oxford University Press.

Ray, Biswajit. 2013. *Professor Shankur Sesh Diary* (The Last Diary of Professor Shonku). Kolkata: Lalmati.

Ray, Sandip. 2020. ed. *Satyajit Ray: Sakshatkar Samagra* (Compilation of all Interviews of Satyajit Ray). Kolkata: Patra Bharati.

Ray, Satyajit. 2009. *Golpo 101*. Kolkata: Ananda Publishers Pvt. Ltd.

Ray, Sukumar. 2010. *Sukumar Sahitya Samagra*. Vol. II. Ed. Satyajit Ray and Partha Basu. Kolkata: Anada Publishers Pvt. Ltd

... 2011. *Sukumar Sahitya Samagra*. Vol. III. Ed. Satyajit Ray. Kolkata: Anada Publishers Pvt. Ltd.

... 2012. *Sukumar Sahitya Samagra*. Vol. I. Ed. Satyajit Ray and Partha Basu. Kolkata: Anada Publishers Pvt. Ltd.

Reider, John. 2008. *Colonialism and the Emergence of Science Fiction*. Middletown, Connecticut: Wesleyan University Press.

Seal, B. N. 2001. *The Positive Sciences of the Ancient Hindus*. Ed. Jyotirmoy Gupta. Kolkata: Sahitya Samsad.

Shekhawat, V. 2007. *On Rational Historiography: An Attempt at Logical Construction of a Historiography of Sciences in India*. New Delhi: Project of History of Indian Science, Philosophy and Culture (PHISPC).

Tagore, Rabindranath. 2000. *Sanchayita*. Kolkata: Viswabharati Gronthonbibhag.

Thiong'o, Ngugi wa. 2015. *The River Between*. New York: Penguin Books.

Utopia as Dystopia: Subjectivity at the Limits of Subjection in Ray Bradbury's *Fahrenheit 451*

Jaydip Sarkar

"What is it to govern? To govern according to the
principle of raison d'État is to arrange things
so that the State becomes sturdy and permanent,
so that it becomes wealthy, and so that it becomes
strong in the face of everything that may destroy it."
The Birth of Biopolitics
Michel Foucault

"I doubt if anyone has ever been warmed to desire himself a citizen in the Republic
of Plato; I doubt if anyone could stand a month of the relentless publicity of virtue
planned by More…"
The Modern Utopia
H.G. Wells

Freedom consists in knowing that freedom is in peril.
Totality and Infinity
Emmanuel Levinas

The Subject, a contested category, has often (almost helplessly) returned like the repressed within the aesthetic imaginary and the porous limits of Western epistemology. While the birth of modernism is identified with the sacrilegious Death of God and the fragmentation/disintegration of the subject of transcendental significance into multifarious conditions of subjectivity, the subsequent aesthetic-philosophical commitments have increasingly questioned the very status and stature of subjectivity itself. The limited aim and scope of the present chapter does not allow such conceptual interrogations into the nuance, paradox and ambiguities pertaining to the notions of subject and subjectivity within the loosely categorised epistemic-cultural field of Continental Philosophy. However, for the strategic purpose of reading the notion of subjectivity and its profoundly intimate correlation with the trope of dystopia and Utopia in Ray Bradbury's novel *Fahrenheit 451*, the chapter chooses to begin with a synoptic consideration of the idea of the subject. The chapter will interrogate into the status of the subject within the political condition and pre-consideration of the biopolitical State. Through exhaustive references to (arguably) poststructuralist thinkers and philosophers like Michel Foucault, Jean Luc Nancy, Emmanuel Levinas among others, the chapter explores the condition of subjection as the only sanctioned notion of subjectivity within the naturalised political limits of existence of the bio-political State. The chapter subsequently engages in a conceptual reading of Ray Bradbury's novel to exhibit how the transgression of subjection and the possibility of an uncompromised subjectivity renders the otherwise naturalised notion of the bios-politicos as a dystopia. The chapter proposes to locate the dystopic not within the imperatives of the unnatural or abnormal but in the perilous moment of transgressing the naturalised for an admiration of the excess that is a possible other of the natural.

Freedom, an otherwise unproblematic idea in Political theory when conceptualised in context of sovereignty, has been thoroughly problematised by Michel Foucault in his epistemic oeuvre. Foucault elucidates the changing notion of freedom in a liberal State as "completely different" (Foucault 2008, 66) from the notion of freedom organised around the question of sovereignty (the question of liberty). For Foucault, the consideration of freedom in a Liberal State does not necessarily refer to the "external protection of the individual". (Ibid.) Instead, it is associated with "interests" (Ibid.) and the "...liberal art of government, is forced to determine the precise extent to which and up to what point individual interest, that is to say, individual interests insofar as they are different and possibly opposed to each other, constitute a danger for all." (Ibid. 65) Foucault identifies the notion of 'interest' as the determinant drive of political machination and it is on this principle of interest that the rationale of governmentality is reorganised and to an extent, reconceptualised. As such, Foucault interrogates the notion of freedom within the axiomatic principles of governmentality of the liberal State and concludes

> "...liberalism is not so much the imperative of freedom as the management and organization of the conditions in which one can be free, it is clear that at the heart of this liberal practice is an always different and mobile problematic relationship between the production of freedom and that which in the production of freedom risks limiting and destroying it....Liberalism must produce freedom, but this very act entails the establishment of limitations, controls, forms of coercion, and obligations relying on threats, etcetera."
> (Ibid. 63-64)

This notion of production of freedom within limits and the subsequent perpetration of it is inseparable from the idea of regulative subjectivity, which elsewhere Foucault defines as the docile body. For Foucault, the docile body is a "subjected and practised body" (Foucault 1995, 138) which may be "subjected, used, transformed and improved." (Ibid. 136) Foucault's notion of the body does not necessarily remain pre-fixed within an anatomical referential paradigm. It is also a profound consideration of the behavioural and the performance of the individual; that which Foucault, in passing, refers to as 'conduct'. (Ibid.143) The individual, under Foucaultian considerations, is a regulated individual determined, moulded, ritualised and constructed upon the premises of 'tactics' and 'practice' (emphases are mine).

Foucault's 'hermeneutics of the subject' (reference to his title, a detailed discussion of which is however beyond the scope of the present chapter) problematises the consideration of sovereign subjectivity and his disorientation of the notion of 'proper subject' has often been identified as the motive turned motif of his historic-philosophical meditations. In an interview anthologised in *Politics, Philosophy and Culture* Foucault observes that he has been lifelong apprehensive of the notion of a sovereign subject, i.e., "a universal form of subject to be found everywhere." (Foucault 1990, 50) On the contrary, he has believed that the "subject is constituted through practices of subjection, or, in a more autonomous way, through practices of liberation, as in Antiquity, on the basis, of course, of a number of rules, styles, inventions to be found in the cultural environment." (Ibid.) The subject, particularly of modernity, is constituted and formulated. It is a being in becoming.

Jean Luc Nancy's epistemic question "Who comes after the subject?" has been fundamental in exhibiting the nuances and ambiguities pertaining to the notion of subject and subjectivity within the varied and heterogeneous purview of Western epistemology. Nancy elucidates his rhetorico-philosophical question thus

> "The question...bears upon the critique or deconstruction of interiority, of self presence, of consciousness, of mastery, of the individual or collective property of an essence." (Nancy 1991, 4)

Nancy's subsequent problematisation of the notion of the subject opens up considerations pertaining to essence, existence, identity and presence--all of which are located within the prevalent questions of Being and Becoming. The subject for Nancy is a deferral, valid within the perpetual state of 'arriving' and this subject is "never the subject of itself." (Ibid.7)

Harping upon this perpetual removal between the being and becoming of the subject, the French philosopher Balibar affirms "after the Subject comes the citizen". (Balibar 1991, 38) For Balibar, the status of the citizen is that of 'subjectus', one who is born in subjection, a (Foucaultian) discursively constituted subject "whose constitution and recognition put an end (in principle) to the subjection of the subject." (Ibid., 39) Within the engulfing condition of the biopolitical, it is only within a performative of citizenship that recognition is restored to the subject. The question of freedom accorded to the Subject, to go by Balibar (as also with Foucault), is formulated, processed and sanctioned in subjection. Balibar, in his politico-allegorical reading of the Descartian notion of freedom in subjection observes that "...freedom can in fact only be thought as the freedom of the subject, of the subjected being, that is, as a contradiction in terms." (Ibid., 36) Political validation of identity is proposedly performed in subjection and it is thus that subjection attains its correspondence/ correlation with citizenship. For Balibar, the status of the Subject and its freedom is founded on an ethics of 'obedience'. (Ibid., 42)

The foundation of the biopolitical State, which Foucault genealogically locates in the Liberal State, is located in this principle of obedient freedom or freedom in/through obedience. As such "control, constraint and coercion" (Foucault 2008: 67) is fundamental to the Foucaultian notion of freedom, leading to the evolution of the

'Panopticon' structure of the State. Control, surveillance, regimentation and the likes are not necessarily "counterweight to freedom". (Ibid.) On the contrary, Foucault observes that "it (Control) becomes its (freedom) mainspring" (Ibid.) subjecting the subject to a design of homogeneity which perpetuates a condition of becoming and not being. The subject, to attain his/ her subjectivity, must ascribe to the conditions upheld by the dictums of the libertarian paradox where the natural is indistinguishable from the political. Or rather, the natural is a formulated category that is a necessary aftertruth to the political. This ambiguity pertaining to the intricate interdependence of the natural and the political is the kernel which formulates the possibilities of Utopia-Dystopia.

The hyphenation that conjoins the apparently contradictory categories of the good and thus nowhere (Greek prefix 'eu' later compressed into 'u') and the ill (Greek prefix 'dys') contains the premonition of a paradox. Yet, this paradox is not novel and devoid of an intellectual tradition of its own. The inter-related status of Utopia and Dystopia is longstanding and they are not essentially mutually contradictory categories. Michael D. Gordin, Helen Tilley and Gyan Prakash observes "Every utopia comes with an implied dystopia- whether the dystopia of the status quo, which the utopia is engineered to address, or a dystopia found in the way specific utopias corrupts itself in practice...the dialectic between the two imaginaries, the dream and the nightmare,...beg for inclusion together..." (Gordin et al. 2010, 2) The two separate categories are presumably not distinct; they are suggestive of an interdependence that is contingent upon the "conditions of possibility, conditions of imaginability." (Ibid.) As such, like other categories which are discursive subjects of an epistemic, cultural and political rationale, the essence, notion and implication of dystopia and utopia are not in liberation from the possibility of ideological intervention. They are situational and are profoundly associated with a politics of perspective.

Ray Bradbury's novel *Fahrenheit 451* foregrounds this politics of perspective and nuances the notion of Utopia-Dystopia in correspondence with the status quo of subject and the event of subjectivity. The novel has been thoroughly read as a text that is critical of a totalitarian State order that materialises and sustains itself within a regime of technocracy. With its intimidating world of surveillance and repression, the worldview in the nameless city in Bradbury's novel is unquestionably dystopic. The machinations of the State and its mechanised measures of regimentation and regulation overrule the possibilities of evolution of a bare agency. The enfranchisement of the self is formed in subjection and it is through an immaculate performance of citizenship, which is unquestionably in resonance with the principles of governmentality, that the subject is sanctioned recognition. Departures from this unitary model of governmentality and governance are scathingly repressed and annihilated by the various modalities of State apparatus and the State emerges as an enclosed epistemic territory of controlled knowledge regime, inhabited by docile bodies, whose subjectivities are formulated in subjection.

Guy Montag, the protagonist in the novel, is initially one of those docile bodies that "hoard and sleep and feed" (Tennyson 2014, 265) in ways prescribed by the State. He is employed as a fireman — an "amazing conductor playing all the symphonies of blazing and burning to bring down the tatters and charcoal ruins of history." (Bradbury 2008, 9) His ingenious and "fierce" smile, provoked at the sight of burning books and the plight of crumbling columns of deviant wisdom, stays with him — a smile of satiation that is suggestive of an absolutely complacent agency that is uncritical of its formulation and propagation. Montag's state of being is in perfect coherence with the juridico-legal prerogatives of a totalitarian State, it is the seminal condition of a pre-consumption of the ethical by the ideologues of the political. Judith Butler observes that "the state is supposed to service the matrix for the obligations and prerogatives of citizenship…" (Butler and Spivak 2007, 3) which makes it a binding force that hyphenates the state of being of the citizen and the principles of the Nation State. Montag's smile is the material manifestation of a happy hyphen — one that has conjoined rather than dissociated.

While the protagonist smiles in complacence at his precision in preserving the authoritarian regime of the Nation State by actively participating in the ravage of repression, the ideological is propagated in form of a culture that is synthetic and simulacral. In the worldview that Bradbury constructs and Montag inhabits, entertainment is provided by tapioca-bland television that broadcasts sentimental mush throughout the day. Montag's living room has become a 3-D televisual environment for his wife Mildred or Millie, who dreams of adding a fourth wall-screen so that the room will seem no longer theirs but of "exotic people's" (Bradbury 2008, 31). The dispossession of room is significant; it is suggestive of a profoundly interpellated consciousness that willingly surrenders the material questions of existence for a fetish of the distant and the non-real. Simultaneously, it is also suggestive of a dissolution of the authentic real and its unequal substitution by an alternative (mis)conception of reality. The questions pertaining to priority, truth and reality are increasingly problematised as readers encounter the following conversation between Montag and Mildred, a husband and wife:

> """...How long you figure before we save up and get the fourth wall torn out and a fourth wall-TV put in? It's only two-thousand dollars."
> "That's one-third of my yearly pay."
> "It's only two thousand dollars," she replied. "And I should think you'd *consider me* (emphasis mine) sometimes. If we had a fourth wall, why it'd be just like the room wasn't ours at all, but all kind of exotic people's rooms. We could do without a few things."
> "We're already doing without a few things to pay for the third wall. It was put in only two months ago, remember?"" (Bradbury 2008, 30-31)

The material considerations of being are increasingly substituted and superseded by a falsified prioritisation of the non-real, that which is disseminated by the machinations of a culture that is obsessed with simulacra. What is further problematic is the 'consideration' that Mildred seeks. Consideration is essentially an act of recognition of desire and Mildred's urge that Montag *'considers'* (emphasis is mine) her implicitly involves a desire quotient. Her urge to be recognised makes her desire functional, not within a psycho-sexual economy of libidinal desire though. It is instead aroused within a fantasy of the non-real. Hence, Montag's performance of the 'considerate' (emphasis is mine) husband does not happen within the normative schema of phallic and philic performance. It is evaluated on his potency to sustain as relevant within the modes of production, commodified yet productive within the greater structure of technocratic capitalism. For the fourth wall to arrive in the room, it is essential that Montag unconditionally renders himself effective within the predominant mode of a technocratic capitalist economy and correspondent modes of production.

If one overlooks the predominant climate of technocracy that overpowers the novel, Montag's state of being is curiously identifiable with the central protagonist in a Victorian novel modeled on a Protestant work-ethic and bourgeois sensibility of work and prosperity. Toil and try and the kingdom of heaven shall arrive on Earth—arrive with all its glory, growth and happiness. Work with vigor, work with reason, work within the hermeneutics of logic and production. For a happy family life, Montag must work, work uncritically and without questioning. The classic case of utilitarian capitalism, the State prospers with the prosperity of self-subject. "…no one is idle, but that each applies himself industriously to his carft…" (More 2020, 54) is the gospel on which Amaurot, Thomas More's archaic Utopia runs. To follow his trade with diligence, Montag must burn more books. The more loads of wisdom he burns, the closer is he towards redemption—a redemption of his impotency to quench his wife's desire that is founded in the lack. Not the lack of phallus but the lack of a fourth wall. The perfect means to a perfect end. A Utopia in place.

H.G. Wells's revision of Utopia begins with a consideration of the Classical notion of Utopia. Among other identifiable features, Wells notes that Older (Classical) Utopias are "perfect and static States" (Wells 2009, 13) where the law of uniformity overrules the possibility of heterogeneity. (One can refer to More's preoccupation with 'regulated', 'regulation', 'regulatory' and 'regular' in his description of the perfect Utopia) This essential presupposition of the uniform celebrates the notion of a conformed subjectivity and Wells is quick to point out that the myth of Utopia is marked by an absence of subjectivity, that "there are no individualities." (Ibid., 17) For Wells, such a condition is "comprehensively jejune". (Ibid.) Wells describes the classical/ stalk notion of Utopia thus

> ...one sees handsome but characterless buildings, symmetrical and perfect cultivations, and a multitude of people, healthy, happy, beautifully dressed, but without any personal distinction whatsoever." (Ibid., 17-18)

It is worthwhile, although a little rampant and non-schematic, to quote a passage from the novel where Beatty, the in charge of firemen explains to Montag, who is now exhibiting a reluctance at his task, the sense and sensibility of the age and its underlying essence:

> We must all be alike. Not everyone born free and equal, as the Constitution says, but everyone made equal. Each man the image of every other; then all are happy..." (Bradbury 2008, 77)

One cannot miss the unfailing resonance between Wells's "a multitude of people...but without any personal distinction" and Beatty's "everyone made equal. Each man the image of every other." Happiness is the homogeneous, to be happy is to be governed within a rationalised eudaemonia that is lived and inhabited not by the subject as self but subject in subjection and following Balabar, as citizen. Do we read Bradbury's nameless city and the ethics of inhabitation that it hosts as suggestions of a characteristic Utopia? The interrogation demands that we introspect further into the notion of Utopia.

In stark contrast to this classical notion of the Utopia of regulated subjectivity, Wells locates the essence of Modern Utopia in "the fertilising conflict of individualities" and Utopias to him are "no more than schemes for bettering that interplay." (Wells 2009, 19) Hence, Well's idea of modern Utopia is formulated in dialogue that, in its conflict, is suggestive of transgression. To conceptualise this modern Utopia is to transgress, to conform is suggestive of a profound dystopia. Frederick Jameson, in his insightful essay "Utopia as Method, or the Uses of the Future", locates the essence of Utopia in "form" rather than "content" and defines it as "not what can be positively defined and proposed, but rather what is not imaginable and not conceivable." (Jameson 2010, 23) Jameson proposes

> "The utopia, I argue, is not a representation but an operation calculated to disclose the limits of our own imagination of the future, the lines beyond

which we do not seem able to go in imagining changes in our own society and world..." (Ibid)

The ethics of Utopia in context of modern-postmodern(ity) is thus suggestive of a transgression from the systemic.

In his "Preface to Transgression", Michel Foucault problematises the relationship between limit and transgression. Foucault argues that limit ceases to exist without the act of transgression and poses an epistemic question of intrigue "...can the limit have a life of its own outside of the act that gloriously passes through it and negates it?" (Foucault 1977, 34) Resonating the Husserlian notion of phenomenological, hence/ thus inter-subjective, Other, Foucault infers

> "Perhaps it is like a flash of lightning in the night which, from the beginning of time, gives a dense and black intensity to the night it denies, which lights up the night from the inside, from top to bottom, and yet owes to the dark the stark clarity of manifestation, its harrowing and poised singularity; the flash loses itself in this space it marks with its sovereignty and becomes silent now that it has given a name to obscurity." (Ibid., 35)

In other words, the condition of limit remains unexposed and possibly unborn, without the act of transgression. It is in transgression that limit is validated and Foucault remarks "The limit and transgression depend on each other for whatever density of being they possess..." (Ibid., 34)

This originary interdependency of transgression and limit is explicated at the very preliminaries of the novel where the regimented and the regulated encounters and subsequently interacts with the excess. In an atmosphere of premonition that exceeds the aural, olfactory and tactile habitations, Montag's path crosses with Clarisse McClellan. Clarisse is "seventeen and crazy" (Bradbury 2008, 14) and "thinks too many things" (Ibid., 16), which suggest in their own way a deviant consciousness that evades the hermeneutic and unilateral logic of a regimented sense. Trivial ficto-factualities about the "dew on the grass in the morning" (Ibid.) or "the man in the moon" (Ibid., 17) are disparate from Montag's lawful revelations about the significance of "numerals 451". (Ibid., 16) The regimentations of repression and the precarious excess counter-pose and very soon it is the latter that starts overpowering the discursive agency of the former in form of a seduction of ecstasy. Montag, in the aftermath of his wife's drug overdose and subsequent technocratic therapy, is enchanted by that excess. As he is drawn by the enchanting laughter flourishing "across the moon-coloured lawn"to Clarisse's house, Montag feels an irresistible urge to "tap on their door and whisper, "Let me come in."" (Ibid., 26)

This urge to 'come in' is suggestive of a transition (a Foucaultian "leap", refer to Foucault 1977, 35) into the praxis of transgression. The transgressive in the novel is Foucaultian in essence, i.e., "it is an affirmation of a division...retaining that in which it may designate the existence of difference." (Ibid., 36) As such it is a dissection, evaluation and critical consideration of the homogeneous and the normative which tends to appropriate and assimilate discontinuities, differences and the plural within a totalitarian economy of the standard. Montag's urge to 'come into' (leap into) the transgressive is suggestive of the originations of a subjectivity in departure.

In his insightful explorations of the intimacy that the Foucaultian notion of transgression shares with resistance, Brent L. Pickett observes that the very intimation of transgression involves "an implicit affirmation of difference." (Pickett 1996, 450) The transgressive, within the erudition of Foucaultian epistemic practices, does not necessarily produce, propagate and disseminate an alternative mode of being. The praxis of transgression does not necessarily foresee a materialised subject-agency as its end point. Instead, the validation of the agency is contingent with transgression; it is in the very act of transgression that the deviant subject is identified. It is in its positional status of being the other of that which it transgresses that the agency of transgression is accorded its own validation. This validation of the subject, without the evolution or even without an anticipation of evolution of a hermeneutic hierarchical organisation propagating the ethicalities of subjectivity, is what characterises Foucaultian Utopia of resistance. What is more, it is in this assertion of transgression as resistance that proposes a concomitance between resistance and the process of subjectification.

It is in transgression that subject formation begins and Montag's gradual motility towards departure identifies him as a transgressive subject. Within the totalitarian atmosphere that Bradbury portrays, this transgression involves a possible reclamation of singular subjectivity, if any. While the singular is the exclusive and the distinct, it is however not removed from the possibility of an ethical consideration of the other. This consideration of the other is significantly different from the consideration that Mildred demands from Montag. It is not overruled on a principle of demand and supply, desire and satiation. Instead, the other arrives as an excess, an enticing beyond that can locate the self outside the regimentations and complacence of a regulated subjectivity. As Montag remonstrates Clarisse and her singularity that, for him, has been in stark departure from the homogeneous ethics of being he realises:

> "But Clarisse's favourite subject wasn't herself. It was everyone else, it was me." (Bradbury 2008, 94)

The singular subject and the intimations of a sovereign consciousness in the novel is not directed inwards. Instead, it is suggestive of a Levinasian ethics of the other — an openness and a genuine interest turned consideration of the other promising a being in alterity (that which Emmanuel Levinas romanticises as infinity). In contrast to the notional stature of a subject vitalised in subjection stands the irreducible subject of precarity, open and unapprehended, ever enticed by the other and its inheritance of excess. The possibility of the irreducible subject that transgresses the regimentations of regulated subjectivity is the precarious subject.

Emmanuel Levinas and his philosophical interventions, that replace the Sartrean phenomenology of the self for a phenomenology of the other, problematises the consideration of the subject as pre-discursive and precedent to the world — impersonated in the stature of the Other. Instead, subjectivity for Levinas, "is a relationship with a surplus always exterior to the totality" (Levinas 1979, 22), where totality is the circumscribed condition of regimentation and the surplus unfurls as the other. Levinas proposes subjectivity "as welcoming the other, as hospitality;" and the Other for him is the presence in which the "idea of infinity is consummated." (Ibid.

1979, 27) Hence, the irreducibilities pertaining to the notional conceptions of self/subject within the Levinasian epistemology, inescapably concerns the other. This "other-regarding way of thought", as John Wild notes in his introduction to Levinas's magnum opus *Totality and Infinity*, "rejects the traditional assumption that reason has no plural, and asks why we should not recognize what our lived experience shows us, that reason has many centers, and approaches the truth in many different ways." (Wild 1979, 16) The acknowledgment of the other is suggestive of a hospitality towards the plural and a subsequent admiration of the heterogeneous. Levinas emphasises this correlative equitability where the Other is synonymous with plurality as he asserts that the Other is in possession of a "radical alterity" (Levinas 1979, 35-36) which is also substitutable as a kind of "radical heterogeneity". (Ibid., 36) The Levinasian Other is "other with an alterity constitutive of the very content of the other" (Ibid., 39) and in the words of Jacques Derrida it is suggestive of a "heteronymous curvature". (Derrida 1999, 10) To formulate selfhood and subjectivity with this "heteronymous curvature" is to indulge a precarity that celebrates subjectivity as openness, whose irreducible essence is influenced by the enticement of the surplus, the Other and consequently the Infinite.

This promise of a precarious subjectivity is foregrounded in the novel in form of books which are materialised tokens of heterogeneous epistemic wisdom and prudence. The totalitarian State, with its conceptualised notion of a regulated subjectivity, identify in books "figments of imagination" (Bradbury 2008, 49) and non-telocentric relativism (and thus a fertile and febrile world of possibilities without finality) which jeopardise the desired materialisation of the homogeneous and the formation turned vitalisation of the docile subject. They are intimations of an exterior that can facilitate an ideal of subjectivity which is consumed by the ecstasy of the plural-exterior and subverts the narrowed and constricted situatedness of the complacent subject. As Derby, the one-time English Professor who has succumbed to the forces of technocracy and now lives a vegetal life, observes

> "The magic is only in what books say, how they stitched the patches of the universe together into one garment for us." (Ibid., 63)

Book, in the novel, becomes a materialisation of the excess and contains the intimation of infinity, which is co-terminus and indissociable from subject formation. One is tempted to refer to the famous tract "Areopagitica" that John Milton wrote in response to the Order passed by the English Commonwealth that *"no book, pamphlet, or paper shall be henceforth printed, unless the same be first approv'd and licenc't by such,* or at least one of such, as shall be thereto appointed." (Milton 1894, 4-5). As Milton defends the Freedom of Press and literature (a legible tract i.e.) against the watchdog gaze of censorship, he puts forward the celebrated proposition

> "...but a good book is the precious-life blood of a master-spirit, embalmed and treasured up on a life beyond life." (Ibid., 6)

"Life beyond life" is the Levinasian infinite that which projects before the subject a possibility of transcendence and which can subsequently prompt the foundation of an authentic ideal of subjectivity. However, Milton's proposed allegation against censorship also involves an accusation of "homicide...whereof the execution ends not in the slaying of an elemental life, but strikes at that ethereal and fifth essence, the breath of reason itself, slays an immortality rather than a life." (Ibid.) Milton identifies the book as a living vitality that hosts "a potency of life in them to be as active as that soul was whose progeny they are" and argues that "they (books) preserve as in a violl the purest efficacie and extraction of that living intellect that bred them." (Ibid., 5) The Levinasian other lives in the book and an indulgence of the beings in print is to indulge an irreducible ethics of the other. Here is a perplexed Montag, self-critical and reflective, profoundly engaged in a consideration of the other, and thus paradoxically, engaged in a transgression into subjectivity beyond subjection.

> "Last night I thought about all the kerosene I've used in the past ten years. And I thought about books. And for the first time I realized that a man was behind each one of the books. A man had to think them up. A man had to take a long time to put them down on paper." (Bradbury 2008, 68)

Book burning, an otherwise prevalent practice in authoritarian regimes, is one of the most vehement spectacles of ideological repression. Such instances of systemic violence are chronic recurrences in States ailing from the pestilence of totalitarianism and there are prevalent instances of such incidents throughout the stretch of global political history. For example, on the night of 10 May, 1933, Nazi followers destroyed piles of books in German university towns. As the flames rose in the square opposite the University of Berlin the Propaganda Minister Dr. Goebbels praised the gathered throng for ending the "age of extreme Jewish intellectualism" and ushering in the new German era: "From these ashes there will rise the phoenix of a new spirit... The past is lying in flames. The future will rise from the flames within our own hearts." (Noakes and Pridham 1974, 345)

However, the act of book burning in the novel, as Faber notes, is not the solitary crisis or agony of the age. Instead, what is a matter of greater concern to him is that "The whole culture's shot through" (Bradbury 2008, 113) reducing agency and subjectivity to surface level existence. For Faber, "books were (are) only a type of receptacle where we stored a lot of things we were afraid we might forget." (Ibid. 107) What is a matter of greater pertinence is the annihilation of a distinct agency that is suggested in the amnesia and rootlessness. Memory and remembrance are suggestive of a validation that authenticates the subject as distinct and exclusive, in resistance of the essentialist politics of identity accreditation and reduction. The very absence of memory and history in the novel and Montag's subsequent urge to restitute the same in form of a resurrection and reclamation of books highlight the question of subject and subjectivity as one of the fundamental considerations that the novel indulges in. One cannot necessarily overlook the estrangement of memory that constitutes the intimacies of everyday existence in the novel. Here is a glimpse of the conversation that Montag has with his wife in the early episodes of the novel:

> "When did we meet. And where?"
> "When did we meet for what?" she asked.
> "I mean-originally."
> He knew she must be frowning in the dark.

> He clarified it. "The first time we ever met, where was it, and when?"
> "Why, it was at—"
> She stopped.
> "I don't know," she said
> He was cold. "Can't you remember?"
> "It's been so long."
> "Only ten years, that's all, only ten!"
> "Don't get excited, I'm trying to think." She laughed an odd little laugh that went up and up. "Funny, how funny, not to remember where or when you met your husband or wife.""
> (Ibid., 57-58)

One cannot definitely overlook the hyperbolisation employed by the author that borders on the level of absurdity and irrealism. Yet, Bradbury's purpose in the novel is to emphasise the irrealism of the technocratic age where facts are indissociable from fiction and identities are empty performances adhering to the principles of an institutionalised homo-normativity, lacking a distinct residual essence that can claim the validation of a heterogeneous agency. In the irrealis of simulacra, the intimations of the lived are bartered for a make belief 'happy' (emphasis is mine) life of existence. It is a world where sterile wives are not anxious of their husbands gone to war (no young girls plucking flowers for their lovers' grave) and prefer to bask in the exotica of parlor rooms.

Harold Bloom observes that the novel indulges a "prophetic hope that memory (and memorization) is the answer" to the age of simulacra which he epitomises as "the age of screen". (Bloom 2008, 1-2) Bloom's syllogistic assertion "If you cannot read Shakespeare and his peers, then you will forfeit memory, and if you cannot remember, then you will not be able to think" (Ibid., 2) proposes books as the *elan vital* of thought. One can take a step further and propose "if you cannot read...you will forfeit memory, and if you cannot remember, then you will not be able to think. If you fail to think, how do you claim the validity of cogito...without a cogito, where is your agency...without an agency are you not a subject in subjection and never a subject endowed with subjectivity?" (emphasis is mine)

An essentialist proposition perhaps, taking into consideration the nuances of Continental philosophy that has long back problematised the cogito and its undisputed claim to sovereign agency. Nuanced, but perhaps not unproblematically empty! The spectral subject survives in narratives of resistance, in the undisputed desire to topple the structures and limits of logic-reason, power and truth. In the questions posed at the institutionalised rationale of power, the transgressive subject is able to validate a Utopia that is beyond the design of *flattened society* that is characteristic of the Classical Utopia. Discussing the transformation of Montag in the novel Jack Zipes observes that "…Fahrenheit 451 is a novel of development in that Montag undergoes a learning experience which lends the book its Utopian impetus." (Zipes 2008, 5) This "learning experience" of Montag, as Zipes highlights, involves a critique of the "consciousness industry of America". (Ibid., 6) Consciousness — the accomplice of subjectivity, that which ordains the subject its status quo. While the totalitarian regime (the present chapter has refrained from a historicist reading of the novel and does not necessarily determine the geo-politicos in the novel as America) produces consciousness and the cult of the subject, Montag must learn to reject the same for a more sovereign state of subjectivity. It is in question of subjectivity that the Utopia/ dystopia in the novel rests. It is only when Montag realises and transgresses into that other design of subjectivity, where the self is conceptualised in a promiscuous proximity of the excess other, that the dystopia of the sustaining regimentation of essentialised and appropriated subjectivity is exposed. The novel can thus be read in departure from the traditional readings of technocracy as dystopia. The dystopia is the unproblematic acceptance and complacence of the subject with a governed notion of subjectivity, which has otherwise been a fundamental essence of the Classical Utopia. The Utopia in the novel is a Deleuzian Utopia of immanence which involves an *opening to the unknown* that is metaphorically ascribed in the novel with Montag's irreducible urge to preserve the last traces of binded wisdom. It is born in the dystopia of transgression, that which questions the otherwise apparently stable Utopia of wholesome existence and conformed subjectivity. The Utopia survives in the question; it is the question that turns Utopia into dystopia and vice-versa.

An After Thought

In Satyajit Ray's acclaimed movie *Hirak Rajar Deshey* (*In the Country of Hirak*) the despotic King of Hirak commands his Minister of Education to burn the stacks of fables and morals, epics and histories that the local school master Udayan possesses and shut down the *paathshala* (village school for elementary education). The king's orders are observed immaculately and as Udayan tries to resist the book burning rituals by exclaiming "Are you insane?" the Minister retorts

> "Beware! Do not interrupt proceedings of State
> Or else, brainwash is your hapless Fate." (Ray 2003, translation is mine)

In Ray's masterpiece, brainwash is simulated in the chambers of *jantar-mantar*, a technocratic invention by the eccentric scientist Gabochandra who lives under the patronage of King. The brainwashed subjects, eroded of reason and rationale, unconditionally hail praises of the sovereign. What is significant is the echo of a Foucaultian great confinement in the disciplining mechanism. There is no category or possibility of transgression. Either you perform your fidelity to the King or else you are 'cured' (thus confined) by the State to become the perfect subject who has no consciousness outside the ideologically imposed. In other words, state of subjection is not a choice, it is an inevitability—an inevitability that is so undisputed and free from any other considerations that it acquires the status of an uncontested self-referential truth. There is no either/or. One is always the subject in subjection. To be the subject is to uncritically accept/perform acceptance of the authority of the sovereign and proclaim/perform proclamation of its benevolence. There is no state of exception to the rule and hence no possibility of the aporia called question.

There are countries and cultures governed by democracies and elected authorities who do not burn books or engage technocratic assets and intelligentsia to devise labyrinths of *jantar-mantar*. They are, however, apprehensive of questions.

Questions, on the contrary, are indispensable to Politico-Social Utopia. A question is the vent through which glares the figment of possibility. The narrow domestic walls of faith and dead habit are broken down, opened up, to herald the consideration of an-other, an excess, a plural.

A Politico-social Utopia is born in the enticement of doubt rather than the enclosures of faith.

Bibliography:

Balibar, Etienne. 1991. "Citizen Subject". In *Who comes after the Subject?*, edited by Eduardo Cadava et al., 33-57. New York: Routledge.

Bloom, Harold. "Introduction". In *Ray Bradbury's Fahrenheit 451 (New Edition): Bloom's Modern Critical Interpretations*, edited by Harold Bloom, 1-2. New York: Bloom's Literary Criticism, 2008.

Bradbury, Ray. 2008. *Fahrenheit 451*. London: Harper Voyager.

Butler, Judith and Gayatri Chakravorty Spivak. 2007. *Who Sings the Nation State: language, politics, belonging*. Calcutta: Seagull Books.

Derrida, Jacques. 1999. *Adieu to Emmanuel Levinas*, trans. Pascale-Anne Brault and Michael Naas. Stanford: Stanford University Press.

Foucault, Michel. 1977. "A Preface to Transgression". In *Language, Counter-Memory, Practice: Selected Essays and Interviews*, edited by Donald F. Bouchard, 29-52. Ithaca: Cornell University Press.

...1990. *Politics, Philosophy, Culture: Interviews and Writings 1977-84*, trans. Alan Sheridan and others. London: Routledge.

...1995. *Discipline and Punish: The Birth of the Prison*, trans. Alan Sheridan. New York: Vintage Books.

...2008. *The Birth of Biopolitics: Lectures at the College de France 1978-79*. Edited by Michel Senellart, trans. Graham Burchell. New York: Macmillan.

Gordin, Michael D., Hellen Tilley and Gyan Prakash. 2010. "Introduction: Utopia and Dystopia Beyond Space and Time", in *Utopia/ Dystopia: Conditions of Historical Possibility*, edited by Michael D. Gordin et al, 1-17. Princeton: Princeton University Press.

Jameson, Fredric. 2010. "Utopia as Method, or the Uses of the Future", in *Utopia/ Dystopia: Conditions of Historical Possibility*, edited by Michael D. Gordin et al, 21-44. Princeton: Princeton University Press.

Levinas, Emmanuel. 1979. *Totality and Infinity: An Essay on Exteriority*, trans. Alphonso Lingis. Boston: Martinus Nijhoff Publishers.

Milton, John. 1894. *Areopagitica*, edited by John W. Hales. Oxford: Clarendron Press. Retrieved from Google Books. Stable URL Link: https://books.googleusercontent.com/books/content?req=AKW5 QafWQIdsFrMzDbQS_8IM2RocM4p-Fa6lQyYHroFso5dZL6lfToXO cCavANP-Ppla5SwLIchDVeLRHQe42fgIF4WmZs5tShyXl7RZ9icXV eCPMB-7gro6ZPHj-taPkdnc2MuEB5y-9279RbMMmCiqYpJ1IwkWn UTACJQUEOPux_Q4YA1AZTw4tCWJXdw3QD_UDWl8rgQVjsws eQZ9dOwP2PITX37QXsUV6NYZqHfM6rjPoZJY6MQ https://www.google.co.in/books/edition/Areopagitica/G3FOa2R XC-cC?hl=en&gbpv=1.

More, Thomas. 2020. *Utopia and Selected Epigrams*, edited by Gerard B. Wegemer and Stephen W. Smith. Texas: CTMS Publishers at the University of Dallas.

Nancy, Jean Luc. 1991. "Introduction". In *Who comes after the Subject?*, edited by Eduardo Cadava et al., 1-8. New York: Routledge.

Noakes, Jeremy and Geoffrey Pridham (ed.). 1974. *Documents on Nazism: 1919-1945*. London: Jonathon Cape.

Pickett, Brent L. 1996. "Foucault and the Politics of Resistance". *Polity*, Vol. 28, no. 4 (Summer): 445-466.

Ray, Satyajit. 2003. *Hirak Rajar Deshey*. Angel Digital Premium.

Tennyson, Lord Alfred. 2014. "Ulysses". In *Tennyson: A Selected Edition*, edited by Christopher Ricks, 264-267. London: Routledge

Wells, H.G. 2009. *A Modern Utopia*. The Floating Press, 2009. e-book. Purchased from www.thefloatingpress.com.

Wild, John. 1979. "Introduction". In *Totality and Infinity: An Essay on Exteriority* by Emmanuel Levinas, 11-20. Boston: Martinus Nijhoff Publishers

Zipes, Jack. 2008. "Mass Degradation of Humanity and Massive Contradictions in Bradbury's Vision of America in Fahrenheit 451". In *Ray Bradbury's Fahrenheit 451 (New Edition): Bloom's Modern Critical Interpretations*, edited by Harold Bloom, 3-18. New York: Bloom's Literary Criticism.

Section III
Crime and Detective Fiction

Reclaiming the Elementaries of Context: Ponderings on Doyle's *The Hound of the Baskervilles*

Pinaki Roy

> It is not Sherlock Holmes who sits in Baker street, comfortable, competent and self-assured; it is we ourselves who are there, full of a tremendous capacity for wisdom, complacent in the presence of our humble Watson, conscious of a warm well-being and a timeless, imperishable content. The easy chair in the room is drawn up to the hearthstone of our very hearts—it is our tobacco in the Persian slipper, and our violin lying so carelessly across the knee—it is we who hear the pounding on the stairs and the knock upon the door...And the time and place and all the great events are near and dear to us not because our memories call them forth in pure nostalgia, but because they are a part of us today.
> Edgar W. Smith, "The Implicit Holmes"

The late nineteenth century European aesthetic imaginary was haunted by crime, with the macrocosmic moral and pathocentric design of punishment and retribution giving way to a more subtle and intricate rational microcosm of detection. Detective fiction, a genre that gained popularity in the nineteenth century, is marked by its greater impetus on deduction than crime, on the resolution of the mystery rather than its intimation. What is more, the intensity of the mystery is significantly dependent on the progress of detection as the mysterious air intensifies with the initiation of the process of detection. It is in the detective's endeavours to unveil the secret that the face of the secret's veil is exposed in its absolute intensity and detail. The mysterious outgrows itself in detection, in detection lies the ripeness of mystery.

This essential devotion towards detection renders the generic traits of detective fiction replicable and the detective novel is often reduced to a literary form that is significantly influenced and reproducible by the formulaic. John T. Irwin observes that "Precisely because it is a genre that grows out of an interest in deductions and solutions rather than in love and drama, the analytic detective story shows little interest in character, managing at best to produce caricatures—those monsters of idiosyncracy from Holmes to Poirot." (Irwin 1986, 1169) The detective is fundamental to the genre of detective fiction; it is never incorrect to tautologically define detective fiction as a genre which figures the detective. This correlative correspondence between the genre and the character is hinted by Heather Worthington as he observes "Central to the accepted developmental narrative of crime fiction is the figure of the detective, and almost equally important is the case structure that is familiar to readers of crime fiction from Sherlock Holmes to the present day." (Worthington 2005, 3) Although Worthington's evaluation of the 'rise' of the sleuth-investigator focuses more on the climate that enhanced the rise and not on the salient traits of the character, it also refers in passing to the recurrent and often repetitive tropes that constitute the greater canon of detective fiction. These tropes (i.e. the case structures) are not novel and cannot claim a historical indeterminacy. Instead, as Worthington's research reveals, they are very much in lineage of a vigorously dominant cultural atmosphere that was preoccupied with crime and criminology. Stephen Knight, very much in resonance with Worthington, observes

> "The vast majority of detective, and indeed crime, stories written in the nineteenth century did not appear in the book form, but in the pages of the elusive magazines and regularly appearing newspapers. This is the sea in which detectives are born and first swim." (Knight 1998, 11)

In this shoal of detectives, Sherlock Holmes is the archaic Ichthys, the mythological *Matsya*, or the Melvillean Moby Dick. Holmes owes his identity as the 'detective primaria' not as much to chronology as to his immense popularity across cultures and continents, age and the anachronistic. For the reading imaginary, which is otherwise, like all other imaginaries, characteristically heterogeneous, Holmes is never out of fashion. As the thought of Africa invites the image of the jungle and animals (pardon the 'orientalistic' overdose and for further references consult Satyajit Ray's screen adaptation of *Joy Baba Felunath* that is also about a popular private detective Feluda), the thought of the detective helplessly invites the image of the pipe-smoking Holmes and the magnifying glass. In the words of Mark Gatiss, the co-creator of a popular web series titled *Sherlock*,

Holmes and his assistant Dr. Watson "is the model". (Armstrong 2016) He is, for due reasons, the 'lion of the jungle' (emphasis is mine).

An immaculate interrogation of all those 'due reasons' (emphasis is mine) is beyond the scope of the present chapter. The reasons are, rather predictably, too diverse and heterogeneous to interrogate within the limits of a chapter. One can only refer in passing to Lawrence Frank who argues that the popularity of Holmes, especially in the Edwardian age, rested considerably on those stories that "...touched on the themes of empire, urbanisation, and work that so preoccupied late-Victorian men and women" (Lawrence 1996, 53) or to Edgar W. Smith who identifies Holmes's stature as a "symbol...of all that we are not, but ever would be" (Smith 1989, 15) as the latent cause of his trans-cultural and timeless reputation. Poula Anderson, in her own distinction, locates Holmes as "the archetype" (Anderson 1989, 135) and stands in between Frank's materialism and Smith's obsession with fantasy. Such distinct yet equally valid explanations and speculations only highlight the impossibility of arriving at a determinable inference that can explain the reasons behind the avid popularity of the Baker-Street detective. What can only be deduced satisfactorily is that Holmes presents before the literary critic a classic case of a 'wilful suspension of disbelief' (emphasis is mine) which a perfect literary work renders possible.

The literary has a typically precarious trans-cultural essence. In its inherent appeal to the imaginative, the literary holds its relevance among the readership. To be more precise, one can claim, that among other features, the imaginative is perhaps the most fundamental to a literary work. In its ability to render the imaginary as relevant, even authentic, the literary is accorded its self-referential status. Following Hillis Miller's assertion that the imaginative "is a basic feature of any literary work" (Miller 2016, 17) one can argue that the imaginative, which suspends, subverts, transgresses and transcends reality, is the fundamental attribute of the literary that enthralls readership. What is more, the imaginative and its aura curtails other ethical readings of the literary that is possible beyond the spectrum of universal/ trans-cultural and seemingly hinders (or transcends?) the possibilities of localising the text within a context. The elementary is eclipsed by a celebration of the timeless that the trans-cultural literary tempts.

The present chapter attempts to restore the elementary to the timeless Sherlock Holmes through an exhaustive historicist reading of *The Hound of the Baskervilles*, the novel that was published in the intensifying ambience of discontent among the readers on Holmes's death in the preceding short story "The Adventure of the Final Problem". The chapter intends to exhibit before the readers the contextual interjections which have now been rendered redundant and anachronistic owing to the outrageous popularity of the detective and his adventure. The chapter does not necessarily presume a critical eye which identifies the popular as an impediment to the literary or aesthetic essence and does in no way regard the reigning popularity of the novel as a malcontent which compromises the literary quality of the novel. On the contrary, the chapter engages in a material-historicist reading of the novel only to unearth the possible literary, aesthetic and stylistic traits and tropes which have significantly contributed to the persistent popularity of the novel.

The Hound of the Baskervilles, serialised in *The Strand Magazine* from August 1901 to April 1902, was the third of the four detective-novels on the exploits of the Scottish investigator Sherlock Holmes and his English associate and superannuated-army-physician John Watson. Although Doyle was 'distracted enough' from his other, 'serious' literary writings to 'kill' Sherlock Holmes 'off' in *The Adventure of the Final Problem* (fighting 'Professor James Moriarty' near the *Reichenbach Falls* in the Bernese Oberland region of Switzerland) which was published in *The Strand Magazine* in December 1893; Holmes's suggested death caused so much of public outcry in England and *The Strand Magazine* suffered so much of financial damages due to constant cancellation of subscriptions that Doyle was forced to 'revive' Holmes—although in a 'pre-Reichenbach-episode-narrative'—in *The Hound of the Baskervilles* just eight years later. Allen Eyles identifies *The Hound of the Baskervilles* as the 'best known of all the Sherlock Holmes stories' (Eyles 1986, 40). Kuiper *et al.* are also of the same opinion (Kuiper 1995, 560). *The Hound of the Baskervilles* is not only a detective novel; it is also a near-gothic narrative and a quasi-historical fiction.

The Hound of the Baskervilles is a gothic narrative—as far as Ousby *et al.*'s definition of the characteristics of the writings of the sub-genre is concerned. Ousby *et al.* note, 'gothic fiction' is usually set in "mountainous landscapes"—among others—and the plot "hinges on suspense and mystery, involving the fantastic and the supernatural" (Ousby 1992, 179). Kuiper *et al.* add characteristic features like 'horror', 'gloom', 'desolation', 'decay' 'superstition', and 'revenge' to the body of gothic writings (Kuiper 1995, 480). Interestingly, almost all these 'features' could be straight-forwardly identified in Doyle's *The Hound of the Baskervilles*. Janice M. Allan notes that the "The Hound of the Baskervilles is saturated with the familiar tropes of the Gothic. Amongst such features are a fragmented narrative (consisting of an ancient manuscript, letters, telegraphs and journal entries), a family curse, questions relating to lineage and inheritance, entrapment (physical and metaphorical), a persecuted woman and 'domestic tyrant' (715), doubles, a tell-tale portrait, aberrant and heightened states of mind and an ancient manor, Baskerville hall, 'a place of shadow and gloom'...". (Allan 2019, 221-222). Yet, for Allan, the element of the Gothic in the novel is not a typical re-presentation of what constitutes the familiar elementaries of the Gothic. Instead, the Gothic is also expounded in a curious juxtaposition of the "desolate landscape of Dartmoor" and "the familiar topography of London". (Ibid., 217) Referring to Nicholas Royle's notion of the "uncanny" as "a peculiar *commingling* of the familiar and the unfamiliar" (Royle cited in Ibid.) Allan argues, in resonance with Freud, that the uncanny "retains its character only 'so long as the setting is one of material reality; [and] where it is given an arbitrary and artificial setting in fiction, it is apt to lose that character." (Ibid.) This realm of natural reality that complements and intensifies the supernatural ir-real is suggestive of a curious poetics of trans-infusion that subverts the nominal law of the genre. The generic traits of detective fiction, which indulges a preoccupation of scientific rationalism, is drawn to an aporia by the infusion of the gothic in the narrative. This contamination of genre promotes a febrility in the novel which appeals to the mass without being neither overtly sensational nor elitist. Allan observes that "In bringing together the scientific detective and the supernatural beast of the ancient legend, *The Hound* occupies a...liminal position, poised between the rational positivism of detective fiction and the uncanny ambiguity of the Gothic." (Ibid., 216) He further notes that this poise between apparently opposing genres, "antithetical in method and intent", highlight their "common ancestry" which is related to the genesis and subsequent evolution of popular culture.

The trans-infusional poise is not just relevant in our consideration of the genre. Instead, it is also relevant in context of an exhaustive research into the material base of the novel. By material base I refer to the intimations and influences that have had a profuse impact on the birth of the novel. A research into the historicality of the novel highlights that both the novel and the sleuth is a curious case of trans-infusion where the fictive is not a purely imagined and hence self-referential category. Instead, it exists in a relation with the material-historical and the real. Sherlock Holmes himself was not a pure invention of the mind of Doyle. Instead, he was built perceptively on such well-liked and famous real-life personalities as the Scottish surgeon and *University of Edinburgh Medical School*-faculty-member Joseph Bell (1837-1911), the Scottish forensic-scientist Henry D. Little-John (1826-1914) (Eyles 1986, 11), and the immigrant German 'consulting detective', Walter Scherer, who successfully investigated the 'St. Luke-East-End-German-Baker-Disappearance-Mystery' in 1881 (Dundas 2015, 65), and was inspired by fictional characters like Edgar Allan Poe's 'C. Auguste Dupin', Emile Gaboriau's 'Monsieur Lecoq' (Eyles 1986, 11), and Henry Cauvain's 'Maximilien Heller' (O' Neill 2006, 3). Regarding the 'genesis' of *The Hound of the Baskervilles*, Allen Eyles writes, "In March 1901, Conan Doyle went on a golfing holiday at Cromer, Norfolk, with a friend called Fletcher Robinson who related to him the West Country legend of a spectral dog. This inspired the writing of [...] *The Hound of the Baskervilles*" (Eyles 1986, 40). In fact, Bertram Fletcher Robinson (1870-1907) — who died mysteriously while investigating the case of the 'Unlucky Mummy' (a painted wooden 'mummy-board' or inner-coffin-lid from c. 950 B.C.- Thebes, preserved at the *British Museum*, London) (Card 2018, 165) — was associated with Doyle and *The Hound of the Baskervilles* in more than one way. An enthusiast in tales of the supernatural and crime, Robinson collaborated with Doyle for the plot of *The Hound of the Baskervilles*, and supplied the English writer with reference materials for the supernatural (Weller 41). Doyle had met the junior Robinson, who was then a reporter for *The Daily Express*, for the first time on a passenger ship sailing from Southampton to Cape Town; with him he established a deep friendship which culminated in Robinson's showing different parts of Dartmoor, south-west England, to Doyle. Just before their tour to Dartmoor — Robinson had described to Doyle in details the legends of the ghostly hounds of Devonshire, and how Richard Cabbell (c. 1622-c. 1672), a lecherous squire and the owner of *Brook Hall* of Buckfastleigh in Dartmoor, was killed by some supposedly-supernatural hounds when he was pursuing a woman at night across the marshes[1]. In the character of Cabbell, probably, Doyle found the 'inspiration' for Hugo Baskerville, the owner of the *Baskerville Hall* (Gordon-Bramer 2015, 128) — said to have been hunted down to death on the moors by a monstrous hound while he was trying to capture an abducted woman who had escaped. William S. Baring-Gould seconds this opinion too (Baring-Gould 1967, 10). John O' Connell has cited a 8 December 1906-letter by Robinson from Paris to one 'Mr. W. E. Crimp' of '17, Essex Street, Westminster, London', detailing how he was carrying a part of the manuscript for *The Hound of the Baskervilles* along with him (O' Connell 2011, 9-10), and how he met Doyle on board *S.S. Briton* on 11 July 1900 (Ibid., 11-12). Robinson's influence is also suggested in the fact that Doyle would dedicate the book to him and Baring-Gould is of the opinion that the latter's coachman at his Ipplepen (Teignbridge)-residence, Harry M. Baskerville (d. 1960) supplied the writer with a 'suitable' surname for the 'cursed' family of landlords (Baring-Gould 1967, 38). In this context Richard Cavendish writes,

> "[...] Robinson told Doyle the legend of a ghostly hound on Dartmoor and the two men decided to write what the latter called 'a real creeper' together. Robinson lived at Ipplepen, near Newton Abbot in South Devon, and the two friends went there to investigate Dartmoor. Robinson wrote later that Doyle 'listened eagerly to my stories of the ghost hounds, of the headless riders and of the devils that lurk in the hollows — legends upon which I had

been reared, for my home lay on the borders of the moor.' They stayed at Robinson's home and at *Rowe's Duchy Hotel* at Princetown near the prison, whose governor, deputy governor, chaplain and doctor solemnly came, as Robinson noted, 'to pay a call on Mr Sherlock Holmes', to Doyle's irritation. He and Robinson explored the moor together and appropriated the surname of Robinson's coachman, Harry Baskerville"[2].

Other than Robinson's description of supernatural hounds, Doyle was also deeply affected by the Devon-legends about the 'Yeth Hound' — rumoured to hunt Devonshire- marshes at night making wailing noises (Blackburn *et al.* 2007, 140-41). Researching his setting in 1901, Doyle was aware of Ebenezer Cobham Brewer's *Dictionary of Phrase and Fable* (1870) which described the 'Yeth Hound' as 'a headless spirit' — the 'apparition of an un- baptised child': as Tiffany Francis-Baker notes in her (e-book) *Dark Skies: A Journey into the Wild Night* (London: Bloomsbury, 2019). The Yorkshire businessman, Michael Denham (1801-59), had also published a number of 'Denham Tracts' between 1846 and 1859, which contained references to spectral dogs of Dartmoor, and probably attracted Doyle's attention.

Further, Carolyne Larrington adds that Doyle was acquainted with the:

> "Baskerville family [who] lived in *Clyro Court*, near Clyro in the Welsh borders. It has now been renamed *Baskerville Hall*, and is run as a hotel. Arthur Conan Doyle is said to have stayed with the family there from time to time; here he would have heard local legends about the Vaughans, who held the land before the Baskervilles built the house in [1839 -] 1845, and who kept packs of black dogs. Black Vaughan, who died in 1469, still rode the countryside, accompanied by a pack of howling, red-eyed black beasts" (Larrington 2015, 93).

In the novel, after James Mortimer leaves — having had discussed with Holmes and Watson several incidents preceding the arrival of Henry Baskerville to take over the possession of the *Baskerville Hall* — Holmes procures a large map of Dartmoor (Sidney Paget, 1860-1908, who was the official illustrator for most of the Sherlock Holmes-stories, had drawn a very complicated structure for the same for *The Strand Magazine*, September 1901-issue), and Doyle gives readers an idea about the location of the 'Baskerville Hall'. Correcting Doyle's "Stamford's" for "[Edward] Stanfort", who "was the sole agent for Ordnance and geological survey maps of England and Wales" (Baring-Gould 1967, 18), Baring-Gould adds, as parts of annotations:

> "No map of Dartmoor—not even a 'very large'-scale map—will show us Grimpen. If we look closely, however, we will have little difficulty in picking out a hamlet called 'Widecombe-in-the-Moor', which we suggest was 'Grimpen'. Widecombe was once famous for 'Widecombe Fair' [...]. No 'Lafter Hall' appears on our map, but there is a 'Laughter Tor', and it seems fair to assume that Laughter ('Lafter') Hall stood somewhere in its vicinity. [...] again, there is no 'High Tor' on our map; Holmes perhaps referred to 'Higher Tor' or to 'higher White Tor' [...]. 'Foulmire' [is probably] 'Fox Tor Mire' [...]" (Ibid.).

There are several manor-houses or large, ruined halls in Dartmoor which several critics and literary historians have shortlisted as possible models for Doyle's *Baskerville Hall*. Soon after his arrival at the *Baskerville Hall*, Watson encounters the murderous lepidopterist 'Stapleton' on the moors (Doyle 1989, 467). The setting and *locale* of the novel are important—especially in light of Kuiper *et al.*'s observation that *The Hound of the Baskervilles* 'uncharacteristically emphasises the eerie setting and mysterious atmosphere rather than the [detective] hero's deductive ingenuity' (Kuiper 1995, 560). Naturally and cautiously, Baring-Gould points out that Watson's description of 'the Great Grimpen Mire' tallies with that of the real-life *Grimspound Bog*, 4.8 kilometres north-west of Widecombe-in-the-Moor. (Baring-Gould 1967, 47)

The first 'model' for the *Baskerville Hall* was *Clyro Court* – built by Thomas Mynors Baskerville (1790-1864) on his fourteenth century property in 1839. An official-website of the British Government thus describes the country house:

> "[The *Clyro Court*] is a Jacobean-Renaissance style house at the centre of the Baskerville estate, comprising a 19th-century three-storey house with Flemish gables and Jacobean finials, also featuring a classical porch with an arcade of three arches. [The *Clyro Court* was] [b]uilt in 1839, in imposing Neo-Jacobean style for Thomas Baskerville Mynors Baskerville by the architect E. Haycock of Shrewsbury. Arthur Conan Doyle was reputedly inspired to write *The Hound of the Baskervilles* whilst staying here. After the Second World War, 1939-45, the house was sold to Radnorshire District Council and became a school; it was sold again in 1976 and converted to hotel. [It is a] large square plan house with a lower service range to north-west. Built of

ashlar stonework with pronounced vermiculated quoins, string courses, and ornate gables with ball finials, all with a pitched slate roof. There is a colonnaded porch to north-east front and stone balconies with bulbous balusters to south elevation. The windows are drop cill sashes, with some tripartite windows in shallow bays"[3].

If Ian Ousby et al. note in Doyle's Sherlock Holmes-stories the writer's "strong feeling for the atmosphere of late Victorian and Edwardian London [and, in extension, of England]", and a "subtle sense of the macabre" (Ousby 1992, 850), such manor-houses as *Clyro Court* and *Fowelscombe House* undoubtedly helped the writer to express his feelings thoroughly.

The *Fowlescombe House*, an early-15th-century manor-house presently existing in ruins at Ugborough in Devon, is another possible model for Doyle's 'Baskerville Hall' — at least according to Philip Weller in *The Hound of the Baskervilles: Hunting the Dartmoor Legend* (2001)[4]. It was the residence of the Fowell-baronets, especially from 1661 to 1692. In 1890, Gordon Walters, a clergyman, had purchased the whole estate, only to sell it in parts in 1919. According to Dartmoor-legends, *Fowelscombe House*-kennels lodged a pack of hounds for many years, and they were deliberately underfed by the kennel-master. On one night the kennel-master himself was devoured to death by the hungry hounds[5] — something hideous enough to appeal to the imagination of Arthur Conan Doyle. The English barrister John Locke's *The Game Laws* — with the third edition published in 1849 — also attests to the presence of hounds and kennels at Fowlescombe House (Locke 1849, 137).

The Gothic-style country-house, *Cromer Hall*, in the county of Norfolk could also have served as one of Doyle's models for the *Baskerville Hall* (Pugh and Spiring 2008, 52). Built in 1829 by the Swaffham-born English architect William J. Donthorn (1799-1859), the Tudor- Gothic-style building was constructed in flint, with stone dressings, and slate roofs. When Doyle, suffering from acute typhoid, returned to England from South Africa in 1901, he was taken to northern Norfolk for a change by his acquaintance, B.F. Robinson. Finding temporary residence at *Royal Links Hotel*, Cromer (187 kilometres north-east of London), Doyle and Robinson would sometimes visit the nearby *Cromer Hall*. As Hugh Madgin

(*Cromer through Time*, Stroud: Amberley Publishing Limited, 2011), Lorna Talbott (*Secret Cromer and Sheringham*, Stroud: Amberley Publishing Limited, 2019), and Christopher Winn (*I never knew that about coastal England*, London: Random House, 2019) write in their respective e-books, during a 1901-dinner at *Cromer Hall* — which had been sold to the English politician and barrister, Benjamin Bond-Cabbell (1782-1874), in 1852 — Doyle learnt about the hound-caused-death of Richard Cabbell from the illustrious owner of the mansion. The writer and his accomplice also learnt from the local people details about the East Anglian apparitional-hound 'Black Shuck', described at various times by writers like Abraham Fleming (1577), E.S. Taylor (1850), Walter Rye (1877), and W. A. Dutt (1901). Also, the Brandon Creek-born folklorist Walter Henry Barrett (1891-1974), in his *Tales from the Fens* (edited by Enid Porter for *Routledge and Kegan Paul* in 1963), mentions the Cambridgeshire-legend of a fourteenth century A.D. black-hound hunting different portions of south-eastern England at night after being killed while rescuing a local woman from a lecherous clergyman. Doyle (and, most probably, B.F. Robinson too) were mentionably attracted to this legend (Croft 2014, 80). One cannot miss the resemblance of *Cromer Hall* to the description of *Baskerville Hall* that Watson gives after reaching there:

> "The lodge was a ruin of black granite and bared ribs of rafters, but facing it was a new building, half-constructed, the firstfruit of Sir Charles [Baskerville's] South African gold. [.] The avenue opened into a broad expanse of turf, and the house
> lay before us. In the fading light [.] [one] could see that the centre was a heavy
> block of building from which a porch projected. The whole front was draped in ivy, with a patch clipped bare here and there where a window or a coat-of-arms broke through the dark veil. From this central block rose the twin towers, ancient, crenellated, and pierced with many loopholes. To right and left of the turrets were more modern wings of black granite. A dull light shone through heavy mullioned windows, and from the high chimneys which rose from the steep, high-angled roof there sprang a single black column of smoke" (Doyle 1989, 463-64).

Readers can also not easily miss the colonial connotation that Doyle, so much a supporter of British imperialism, imparts to the gradual construction of *Baskerville Hall*.

As Mary Dearborn (Dearborn 2004, 87) and David Stuart Davies (Davies 2007, xii) write, two other English country- houses have been also identified as the possible 'inspirations' for *Baskerville Hall*: the fourteenth century *Hayford Hall*, near the town of Buckfastleigh (off *Dartmoor National Park*), which was also owned by John King (d. 1861) of Fowelscombe, and the *Brook Manor House*, located approximately 3.2 kilometres east of Hayford (Devonshire), which was the actual residence of Richard Cabbell. The three-storied, stone-built *Brook Manor House* was completed in 1656, and an English government-website detailing the history of the Manor House states,

> "Richard Cabbell was Lord of the Manor of Brook. He was a man of very ill-repute, and the subject of a local legend. It is said that on the night of his death (allegedly in 1677) black hounds, breathing fire and smoke, raced over Dartmoor and surrounded *Brook Manor House*, howling. He is buried at Holy Trinity Church, Church Hill, Buckfastleigh Teignbridge District, and his tomb in the churchyard was designed to imprison his remains and prevent his haunting the neighbourhood. Arthur Conan Doyle based *The Hounds of the Baskervilles* on this legend"[6].

About *Hayford Hall*, Julie Sampson writes how after the temporary residing of the writer- and-owner Mary W.S. Hawkins in 1888, the Hall was rented by the American art-collector and socialite Marguerite 'Peggy' Guggenheim (1898-1979) and her English lover and literary-critic, John Ferrar Holms (1897-1934), for approximately one year (1932-33)[7]. After her arrival, Guggenheim found that the surroundings of the manor house was somewhat 'haunted', writing in her 1979-memoir *Out of this Century*,

> "[T]his place was still part of the moor. At nightfall thousands of rabbits scurried over the ground in all directions. [...] The moor is hard to describe; it was so varied and so vast. It was hundreds of miles square and completely uninhabited except by wild ponies. The ground was strewn with bones and skeletons. The only plants that grew were bracken and heather. [...] The moor was covered with streams and enormous boulders" (qtd. in Podnieks and Chait 2005, 2).

In this 'ghostly' and 'desolate' atmosphere, Doyle—long before the arrival of Guggenheim and Holms—had probably found the perfect setting for the *Baskerville Hall* – a view that has been supported by critics like Philip Weller and Howard Brody. Connecting the American writer Djuna Barnes's *Nightwood* (1936) to her repeated visits to Guggenheim and Holms at *Hayford Hall*, Julie Sampson writes,

> "Remembered now as one of the first fictional texts to depict explicit homosexuality, [...] the bizarre and brilliant novel [,] [*Nightwood* by Djuna Barnes] [,] [...] does [not] [...] complement Dartmoor's reputation as a place of bewitching inspirational beauty. However, in tune with moor's gamut of dark forces—its headless horseman, its 'spectral hounds', its 'large black dogs' and its 'Devil'—the novel could have more in common with the territory than at first seems possible. Barnes may have been directly inspired by the legendary maleficence of the landscape. It has been suggested that *Hayford* was possibly the site chosen by Arthur Conan Doyle as model for *Baskerville Hall*, and Peggy Guggenheim and John F. Holms must have known *The Hound of the Baskervilles* (which was published in 1902), and probably would have found out the connection between place and book before their arrival. It is possible, attracted by its atmosphere of eerie spectrality, they chose Hayford for that very link"[8].

Malcolm Dunstan adds that after John King died in the saddle following the Hunt on Dartmoor in 1861, rumours of his 'apparitional presence' began to circulate around the regions of Buckfastleigh. He writes, "[I]t is rumoured that his ghost rides from Hawson Court to Hayford on midsummer's night" (Podnieks and Chait 2005, 24).

Such material contexts and crises are often obliterated in the canonisation and the phenomenal transformation of the novel as a specimen of Popular Literature. While the unmatched popularity of the novel has profoundly contributed to its deconstructionist afterlife and has enhanced the possibilities of re-reading the novel, through the fertile repertoire of translations, trans-creations and adaptations, it has also jeopardised the topicality of the context. The reading of the novel is often enacted in withdrawal from and disavowal of the materialities that are associated with historicality of the text. Prodosh Bhattacharya hints at this disavowal of the context and the consequent crisis of authenticity that pervades the afterlife (which is accorded to the text through translation, trans-creation, adaptation) of the text as he analyses two Bengali adaptations of *The Hound of the Baskervilles*. For Bhattacharya "the problem is that a gigantic, infernal dog, while perfectly acceptable as a monstrous creature anywhere, belongs specifically to Western mythology and folk-culture, with Cereberus and the Hound of Hell." (Bhattacharya 3) Bhattacharya argues that this topicality of context is often negotiated by a strategic elimination of the culture and context specific to the text to cater to a more trans-cultural readership/ viewership. Hence, in Ajay Kar's thriller film *Jighangsha* the "footprints of a gigantic hound" are replaced by "the footprints of a huge man-shaped monster." (Ibid.) Such transformations undoubtedly contribute to the popularity of the text and consolidate the status of the already acquired reputation of being a literary chartbuster. However, they simultaneously suggest a mono-dimensional ethics of reading 'Popular literature'. Suspending the considerations of context and the topical, such ethics of reading presupposes the popular as an uncritical corpus that can be freely considered for appreciation outside the limits of the material-historical. An absolute suspension and ignorance of the latter, as the paper has argued, only eclipses the possibility of considering the intricate poetics of representation which renders the material into a timeless piece of fiction that is unbound by the immanence of context. It is only through a reading in context that the finesse of literary imagination and representation can be comprehended in its absolute depth and vigor. Doyle's detective is transcultural and lives beyond the topicality of Victorian England. Yet, to comprehend the transmutation of the same, it is perhaps worthwhile to revisit the topical. Such re-visitations do not necessarily tyrannise the fictive and the trans-real through the conditions of immanence. Instead, through an evaluation of the historic, it renders relevant and foregrounds the liminal poetics of a fertile order of representation which is able to transform the material into the fictive, the context into text.

Notes:

1. "In the Footprints of a gigantic Hound". *The Telegraph – Travel* 9 March 2002. https://www.telegraph.co.uk/travel/723674/Dartmoor-In-the-footprints-of-a-gigantic-hound.html. Accessed on 16th March, 2020.
2. Cavendish, Richard. "Publication of The Hound of the Baskervilles". *History Today* 3. March 2002. https://www.historytoday.com/archive/publication-hound-baskervilles. Accessed on 16th March, 2020.
3. "Clyro Court". Coflein. https://coflein.gov.uk/en/site/81112/details/clyro-court. Accessed on 16th March, 2020.
4. "In the Footprints of a gigantic Hound". *The Telegraph – Travel*.
5. "The Legend of Fowelscombe Manor". Murrey and Blue. https://murreyandblue.wordpress.com/2020/02/28/the-legend-of-fowlescombemanor/. Accessed on 16th March, 2020.
6. "Brook Manor House". Historic England. https://historicengland.org.uk/listing/the-list/list-entry/1168435. Accessed on 21st March, 2020.
7. Sampson, Julie. "Women writing on the Devon Land: The Lost Story of Devon Women Authors up to circa 1965". New Devon Books. https://newdevonbookfindsaway.blogspot.com/p/moor-mire-extract.html. Accessed on 21st March, 2020.
8. Ibid.

Bibliography:

Allan, Janice M. 2019. "Gothic Returns: The Hound of the Baskervilles". In *The Cambridge Companion to Sherlock Holmes*, edited by Janice M. Allan and Christopher Pittard, 168-182. Cambridge: Cambridge University Press.

Anderson, Poula. 1989 "The Archetypal Holmes". In *Sherlock Homes By Gas-Lamp: Highlights from the First Four Decades of The Baker Street Journal*, edited by Philip A. Shreffler, 135-141. New York: Fordham University Press.

Armstrong, Jeniffer Keishin. 2016. "How Sherlock Holmes Changed the World". BBC, https://www.bbc.com/culture/article/20160106-how-sherlock-holmes-changed-the-world. Accessed on 12th August, 2020.

Baring-Gould, William S. (ed.). 1967. *The Annotated Sherlock Holmes*, Vol. II. New York: Clarkson N. Potter.

Bhattacharya, Prodosh. "Two Bengali Transformations of Sherlock Holmes". Retrieved from https://www.nplh.co.uk/uploads/7/3/3/6/7336521/two-bengali-transformations-of-sherlock-holmes.pdf. 1-8. Accessed on 23rd April, 2020.

Blackburn, Jolly, *et al.* (eds.) 2007. *Hacklopedia Field Manual*. Waukegan: Kenzer and Company.

Card, Jeb. 2018. *Spooky Archaeology: Myth and the Science of the Past*. Albuquerque: University of New Mexico Press.

Croft, Malcolm. 2014. *Super Dogs: Heart-warming Adventures of the World's greatest Dogs*. Chichester: Summersdale Publishers.

Davies, David Stuart (ed.). 2007. *Sir Arthur Conan Doyle's 'Memories and Adventures': An Autobiography*. Ware-Hertfordshire: Wordsworth Editions Limited.

Dearborn, Mary. 2004. *Mistress of Modernism: The Life of Peggy Guggenheim*. Boston: Houghton Mifflin Company.

Doyle, Arthur Conan. 1989. *The Complete Illustrated Sherlock Holmes*. New Delhi: Rupa and Company.

Dundas, Zach. 2015. *The Great Detective: The Amazing Rise and Immortal Life of Sherlock Holmes*. Boston: Houghton Mifflin Harcourt Publishing Company.

Eyles, Allen. 1986. *Sherlock Holmes: A Centenary Celebration*. London: John Murray.

Frank, Lawrence. 1996. "Dreaming the Medusa: Imperialism, Primitivism, and Sexuality in Arthur Conan Doyle's "The Sign of Four"". *Signs*, Vol. 22, no. 1 (Autumn): 52-85. JSTOR. http://www.jstor.com/stable/3175041. Accessed on 9th April, 2020.

Gordon-Bramer, Julia. 2015. *Fixed Stars govern a Life: Decoding Sylvia Plath*, Vol. I. Nacogdoches: Stephen F. Austin University Press.

Irwin, John T. 1986. "Mysteries We Reread, Mysteries of Rereading: Poe, Borges, and the Analytic Detective Story; Also Lacan, Derrida, and Johnson". 1986. *MLN: Comparative Literature*, Vol. 101, no. 5 (December): 1168-1215. JSTOR. http://www.jstor.com/stable/2905715. Accessed on 14th April, 2020.

Knight, Stephen. 1998. "Enter the Detective". In *The Art of Murder: New Essays on Detective Fiction*, edited by H. Gustav Klaus and Stephen Knight, 10-26. Tübingen: Stauffenburg.

Kuiper, Kathleen. 1995. "Entry". In *Merriam-Webster's Encyclopaedia of Literature*. Springfield: Merriam-Webster.

Larrington, Carolyne. 2015. *The Land of the Green Man: A Journey through the supernatural Landscapes of the British Isles*. London: I.B. Tauris and Company.

Locke, John. 1849. *The Game Laws*. 3rd edn. London: Shaw and Sons (digitised on *Google Books*).

Miller, J. Hillis. 2016. "Introduction Continued: The Idiosyncrasy of the Literary Text". In *Thinking Literature Across Continents*, Ranjan Ghosh and J. Hillis Miller, 9-24. Durham: Duke University Press.

O' Connell, John. 2011. *Baskerville: The Mysterious Tale of Sherlock's Return*. New York: Marble Arch Press.

O'Neill, Peter. 2006. *Henry Cauvain's 'Maximilien Heller: The Misanthrope Detective'* (ed. and trans.). London: Glen Segell.

Ousby, Ian. 1992. *The Wordsworth Companion to Literature in English* (ed.). Ware-Hertfordshire: Wordsworth Editions Limited.

Podnieks, Elizabeth, and Sandra Chait (eds.). 2005. *Hayford Hall: Hangovers, Erotics, and Modern Aesthetics*. Carbondale: South Illinois University Press.

Pugh, Brian, and Paul Spiring. 2008. *On the Trail of Arthur Conan Doyle: An Illustrated Devon Tour*. Abingdon: Book Guild Publishing Limited.

Smith, Edgar W. 1989. "The Implicit Holmes". In *Sherlock Homes By Gas-Lamp: Highlights from the First Four Decades of The Baker Street Journal*, edited by Philip A. Shreffler, 15-16. New York: Fordham University Press.

Weller, Philip. *The Dartmoor of 'The Hound of the Baskervilles'*. London: Sherlock Publications, 1991.

Worthington, Heather. 2005. *The Rise of the Detective in Early Nineteenth-Century Popular Fiction*. New York: Palgrave Macmillan.

"Our mysterious neighbour, Mr. Poirot": Locating the 'Other' Detective in *The Murder of Roger Ackroyd*

Mandika Sinha

Crime has been the central focus and foundation of an entire genre of literature for centuries, readying itself for the important place that it now holds in literary studies. Much has been written about this highly innovative genre for the pleasure it brings to its readers as well as the seriousness of themes it focuses on. Approaches to crime fiction is varied as the variety of sub genres under the nomenclature of 'crime fiction' but the one constant attitude towards this genre is its popularity which has led critics to delve into its compelling nature and its overall history in search for answers. A simplistic definition of crime fiction especially those produced in the Golden age of British Detection is—'a novel that combines two forms of suspense: the desire to know 'whodunit' along with that suspense derived by the fear that whoever it was might repeat his/her crime' (Gregoriou 2007, 37). This question of "Whodunnit" is a question that a mystery novel tries to answer which in turn emphasises the role of the detective in a detective novel.

Any consideration of the history of crime fiction and the figure of the detective starts with the American author Edgar Allan Poe who extracted the mystery element from gothic romance novels and made it the core of his stories beginning with "The Murders in the Rue Morgue" in 1941. The four tales which were published thereafter laid down the general principles of the detective story. Poe called his stories 'tales of ratiocination' emphasising on the idea of intellect and reasoning which is central to his stories and his famous detective—C. Auguste Dupin who in turn influenced many later fictional detectives. Even though his collection of five tales are different in their tone and structure, the mix of imagination with intellect creates for the first time a character unique and influential as well as introduces certain stock devices like the locked room mystery with the presence of an eccentric detective which has remained central to the detective stories.

Likewise, when Arthur Conan Doyle published *A Study in Scarlet* in 1887 he had created an icon- a detective who could employ scientific methods rather than rely on the stupidity of the criminal remaining fixed in the public imagination. He is described as "a detective who is highly intelligent, essentially moral, somewhat elitist, all knowing, disciplinary in knowledge and skills, energetic, yet also in touch with the ordinary people who populate the stories" (Knight 2010, 55). Industrialisation and commercialisation meant that the old order was rapidly fading. At the face of numerous changes that society was undergoing during these troubled times, the figure of the detective became the voice of reason. In face of disorder, the presence of the detective became an embodiment of rationality. At the incidence of any threat the detective became a force who would restore peace and order. The figure of the detective is thus, an integral part of detective fiction. This is best exemplified in the popularity of detectives like Sherlock Holmes and Hercule Poirot. The numerous books featuring these detectives and the public uproar caused by their fictional deaths is an example of their lasting effects on the public imagination. The iconic deerstalker hat of Holmes and the peculiar moustache of Poirot remains etched in public memory.

The other side of the Atlantic was experiencing a development of this genre too. The hard-boiled tradition which dealt with darker themes introduced a knight-like detective who was fighting against the moral injustices in society. The term 'hard boiled' meant a hero who was tough which became a prototype for the private detective in a genre that developed in the United States. Following the effects of the Two World Wars and the chaos that followed, the detective of the hard-boiled tradition manifested into a morally upright man who would rid the streets of corruption. Raymond Chandler has given a definition of the figure of the detective in his essay "The Simple Art of Murder":

> "Down these mean streets a man must go who is not himself mean, who is neither tarnished nor afraid. The detective must be such a man. He is the

hero, he is everything. He must be a complete man and a common man and yet an unusual man. He must be, to use a rather weathered phrase, a man of honour, by instinct, by inevitability, without thought of it, and certainly without saying it. He must be the best man in his world and a good enough man for any world. He will take no man's money dishonestly and no man's insolence without a due and dispassionate revenge. He is a lonely man and his pride is that you will treat him as a proud man or be very sorry you ever saw him." (Chandler 1988, 18)

This provides a map for the development of the central protagonist of a detective novel. The eccentric detective of the Golden Age is interested in the mystery to provide a puzzle for their mind to be unraveled by their superior deductive reasoning with little or no violent action. On the other hand, the American hard boiled private eye is rooted against organised crime which forces him to resort to violence and often take justice into their own hands. Both these lines of depictions of ideal detectives focus on the idea of male 'hero' who is rational, logical and physically strong. It also presents the detective as a knight in shining armor or a detective who is like savior for the society. Both these images are strongly grounded on the notion of masculinity since studies in gender reveal how both the areas of science and rationality are considered to be the domain of the man whereas women are limited to the emotional and hence intuitive. Detective in hardboiled tradition became hyper masculine while their British counterpart continued to be models of male authority. Consequently, the detective as well as the genre developed along these definite lines of masculinity.

While the basic elements of the detective fiction were being standardised, the rise in the literacy rates during the world wars also provided an apt platform for the popularity of crime fiction. Many authors of crime fiction emerged in the 1920's and their success can be attributed to the rise of the publishing industry as well. The advent of paperback to cater to the growing demands of the reading public did contribute to the overall growth of crime fiction. The Golden age of detective fiction saw an overwhelming number of novelists who tried their hand in writing detective novels probably interested by the set formula of this form, intrigued by the challenge of the narrative. The set of rules laid down by Ronald

Knox provided a further boost to this challenge. Ronald Knox laid down a set of rules that this form of writing should follow —

> "The criminal must be mentioned in the early part of the narrative but must not be anyone whose thoughts the reader has been allowed to follow. All supernatural agencies are ruled out. There must not be more than one secret room or passage. No undiscovered poisons should be used or, indeed, any appliance which needs a long scientific explanation. No china man must figure in the story. No accident must help the detective, nor is he allowed unaccountable intuition. The detective himself must not commit the crime. The Watson-like figure should be slightly less intelligent than the average reader and his thoughts should not be concealed. Finally, twin brothers and doubles must not appear unless the reader is prepared for them." (James 2019, 18)

Had the writers followed this rigid set of rules, the popularity of this form would have diminished by now. However, this set of rules proved to be a challenge to the writers- the question being how much of it they could strictly adhere to and how much of it they could break? An arch breaker of rules is Agatha Christie who has been given the title of 'Queen of crime', the 'Mistress of mystery' and even the 'Duchess of death' at various times. In a career spanning over fifty years, Agatha Christie transformed detective fiction by creating memorable characters like Hercule Poirot and Miss Marple and in her hands the mystery novel found its most popular proponent. Evidence of her popularity rests in the fact that worldwide her books are outsold only by the Bible and Shakespeare.

Among the many books that Agatha Christie wrote *The Murder of Roger Ackroyd* remains a bench mark in any study of detective fiction. *The Murder of Roger Ackroyd* was published in 1926 and is a landmark publication in the history of detective fiction which had a lasting impact on the genre. It is regarded as Agatha Christie's most well-known and controversial novels. It has enthralled aficionados and critics alike with its puzzle like feature and its ingenious concluding plot twist. Hence, much has been written about this book, be it on the presence of the unreliable narrator or the subtle connection this work has with Dickens' *Nicolas Nickleby*. The lasting popularity of the detective fiction lies in the cat and mouse game between the writer and the reader. While this means that the genre must adhere to the formulaic traditions, it also means that there is a need for constant reworking of these formulas to keep the genre alive. *The Murder of Roger Ackroyd* manages to do just this not only in the narrative structure but through clever reworking of characters setting and conclusion. It was a challenge to the rules that made detective fiction and paved the way for later detectives who were more postmodernist in their approach.

Agatha Christie started writing mystery novels in response to a challenge by her sister and she created Hercule Poirot—her fussy Belgian detective in 1916 in her novel *The Mysterious Affair at Styles*. He would go on to be the second most famous detective in the world outranked only by the iconic Sherlock Holmes. Contemporary reports of the reading public capture their acceptance of the Belgian detective which noted—'the exuberant personality of M. Poirot who is a very welcome variation on the "detective" of romance' (Curran 2011, 22). Like his predecessor, Hercule Poirot is a man of extraordinary intelligence. This intelligence which is above ordinary is a characteristic of most detectives of the golden age whose source of inspiration can be traced back to Poe's Auguste Dupin.

In him we find some basic features which became a standard for the detective of the golden age. Dupin is an amateur who often looks at the police force with contempt as his skills exceed that of the police. He is an eccentric person who enjoys taking walks at night at Paris. He does not have any family or any personal life. This makes him a unidimensional character as he does not grow as a human being in the stories that feature him. The focus remains solely on his outstanding knowledge and detecting skills. In spite of this, Dupin in not useful when it comes to practical day to day life. He lives only to unravel some absurd mysteries which he looks upon as puzzles that need to be solved. Poe introduces Dupin as a man who is extremely detached from everything—'this detachment from the ordinary world is a sign of the detective's eccentricity and decadence and of his particular analytic brilliance and insight, which above all takes the form of an ability to read the hidden motives of men' (Cawelti 1976, 81) These features have remained characteristics of most classical detectives like Mr. Campion, Lord Peter Wimsey and Hercule Poirot.

Like her co crime writers Ngaio Marsh, Dorothy L.Sayers and Mary Allingham, Agatha Christie has modeled her detective after her predecessors. Hercule Poirot is described in *The Mysterious Affair at Styles* as —

> "an extraordinary man. He was hardly more than five feet four inches, but carried himself with great dignity. His head was exactly the shape of an egg,[…] His moustache was very stiff and military.[…he] had been in his time one of the most celebrated members of the Belgian police. As a detective, his flair had been extraordinary, and he had achieved triumphs by unraveling some of the most baffling cases of the day." (Christie 2012, 35)

His reasons for pursuing cases on the surface seem similar to Holmes and Dupin who does for the sake of unraveling the puzzle. There is no mention of his family and his eccentric nature places Poirot in the tradition of the great detective of the golden age.

Yet, a study of the writings of Agatha Christie reveals that she was an arch breaker of rules. Much to the shock of her readers, she even broke the rule of presenting the narrator as a murderer in *The Murder of Roger Ackroyd*. While this created a wave of criticism, it also bought the writer much accolade for presenting such an ingenious plot. But Christie's reworking of the genre is not limited to breaking obvious rules. She has subtly reworked characterisation, especially when it came to the figure of the detective. Her work is replete with questioning of stereotypes which informs her work with new possibilities and interpretations. While any study of *The Murder of Roger Ackroyd* is focused on the plot and narrative structure, Poirot's characterisation and his act of detection is something which can lead to interesting deductions and conclusions. The character of the central detective is based on a stereotype but Christie leaves subtle clues for her readers to reconstruct him in unexpected ways. Hence, her innovative contribution to the detective figure cannot be overlooked.

In her notebooks, Agatha Christie writes about the creation of her famous detective — 'What kind of a man […] should he be? A little man perhaps, with a somewhat grandiloquent name. Hercule

Poirot — yes that would do. What else about him? He should be very neat — very orderly' (Curran 2011, 250). While we can see a clear influence of his predecessors and his contemporaries Curran notes how Christie also "endowed him with an overweening vanity and a neurotic precision, as well as magnificent moustaches and his famous little grey cells [...] and, thanks to the brilliant television portrayal by David Suchet, is now firmly fixed in the public consciousness and affection for all time" (Christie 2011(a), 13). Christie also based her creation on a Belgian refugee patient, hence making him a literal outsider in the social settings that she portrays.

A look into the history of detective reveals how Poirot is 'feminine' — 'he is a parody of the male myth; his name implies his satirical status: he is a shortened Hercules, and a Poirot — a clown' (Munt 1994, 8). This is also emphasised in his effeminate way of walking best exemplified in Suchet's portrayal of the detective in film version of *The Murder of Roger Ackroyd* and his dandified clothing. Many a times Poirot is able to solve a crime based on his observations of the domestic space, a chair being moved in the drawing room or the location of a particular object on the mantelpiece. Though Poirot is presented as relying on his little grey cells, his detecting skills are based on far simpler methods of acute observation which are stereotypically a feminine domain. This is manifested in the contemporary opinion of — "H. Douglas Thomson [who] had complained about the 'lowbrow' likes of Christie [who] were 'feminising' Doyle's 'highbrow' (i.e., masculine) school of detective fiction by including domestic details and emotion" (Brenthal 2016, 39). By undermining the traditional role of the detective Christie mocks the genre's need for a manly hero.

Poirot is a reinvention, a combination of inspiration as well as innovation of the figure of the great detective of the golden age but more importantly he is a renegotiation of the essential masculinity of the genre. Brenthal credits this change to — "the First World War (1914-18) [which] meant gender stereotypes were sometimes radically rethought as, with men in combat, women took on traditionally masculine jobs; famously in public transport, medical care and munitions factories" (Ibid., 35). When we meet Poirot in *The Murder of Roger Ackroyd*, he is presented as an unassuming man living a retired life. There is nothing grand about him unlike his contemporary Lord Peter Wimsey, an aristocrat who takes up investigation as a hobby. Created by Dorothy L. Sayers, Lord Peter Wimsey is 'an upper-class detective (in Albert Campion) — so grand, apparently, that the name of his mother can only be whispered' (James 2009, 35). Similarly, Albert Campion created by Margery Allingham first appears in *The Crime at Black Dudley* in 1929 and is described as "a fey, insightful figure [who] is mysteriously, and playfully, aristocratic or even royal in origin." (Knight 2010, 102). Poirot lives such a mundane life that even Caroline who is privy to all gossips at Kings Abbot and who surprisingly draws correct inferences throughout the narrative decidedly remarks — 'there's no doubt at all about what the man's profession has been. He's a retired hairdresser. Look at that moustache of his" (Christie 2011(b), 17). Poirot's concern when it comes to his appearance has been remarked over the course of the series of novels featuring him. Later through the course of the narrative, Dr. Sheppard observes Poirot's concern with his clothing — "I looked at him inquiringly, but he began to fuss about a few microscopic drops of water on his coat sleeve. The man reminded me in some ways of a cat. His green eyes and his finicking habits" (Ibid., 83). Dr. Sheppard's comparison of Poirot to a cat recalls a feline quality associated with the feminine. This overt distress when it comes to appearances not only dispels the reader's image of a stereotypical detective but also functions to conceal an important clue.

While the great detectives of the previous era like Holmes and Dupin are always regarded with respect (even though grudgingly given at times), Poirot's appearance often gives a mistaken impression to people around him. His small stature, his egg shaped head and his 'finicky habits' project a non-threatening impression — 'why should this little upstart of a foreigner make a fuss? A most ridiculous-looking creature he is too — just like a comic Frenchman in a revue." (Ibid., 117). While this is similar to G. K Chesterton's detective Father Brown who exudes a non-threatening appearance, Poirot's repeated reference to his vanity stands opposite to Father Brown's world of spirituality and morality. But this empathy that Father Brown displays is present in Poirot too. There is a sense of protectiveness in the character of Poirot. While this is a personality trait in case of Father Brown which goes hand in hand with his role of a cleric, it is part of his method of detection in Poirot. Poirot frequently refers to his powers of detection as — "the study of human nature" (Ibid., 19). His detecting skills are therefore, not based on studying fingerprints and shoeprints like the police force though he has knowledge of it. Instead, he relies on his knowledge of human psychology and his keen powers of observation. He also presents himself as a figure who is willing to listen to any kinds of confession without fear of judgment — "it is Papa Poirot who asks you this. The old Papa Poirot who has much knowledge and much experience. I would not seek to entrap you, mademoiselle" (Ibid., 106). Poirot projects an image of a father figure by referring to himself as a 'papa'. It also makes him an approachable character who gives the impression of being kind. This departure from any method followed by Holmes reflects a breaking down of the traditional roles played by the detective hero. Moreover, Holmes and the detectives that followed his footsteps are eccentric creatures who certainly are not approachable to most company. This focus on empathy and human compassion in the character of Poirot emphasises the feminine which is a departure from the focus on rationality celebrated by readers.

When the readers meet Poirot in *The Murder of Roger Ackroyd*, he is an unassuming neighbour who apparently has taken to growing vegetable marrows. This retired life of anonymity is a deliberate choice on the part of Poirot. Upon learning about his former profession, Flora requests him to look into the murder in order to save Ralph Paton, the prime suspect. Here, Christie raises the question of motive in case of Poirot too. What is the reason behind Poirot taking a case? A look into the history of detective fiction reveals that detectives of the Holmesian tradition took up cases for the pleasure of it. The act of ratiocination was an exercise for the mind which is evident in case of Dupin. On the other hand, the detectives of the hard-boiled tradition are presented as private investigators for whom detection is a profession. Amidst these dual approaches we find the character of Poirot who chooses to take up the case of the murder of Roger Ackroyd only in pursuit of truth. When Flora approaches him for help, Poirot initially refuses at which point she raises the question of money — 'if it is a question of money'. In response to this Poirot clearly states — "not that, I beg you, mademoiselle. Not that I do not care for money. [...] no, if I go into this, you must understand one thing clearly. I shall go through with it to the end. The god dog, does not leave the scent remember! You may wish that, after all, you had left it to the local police" (Ibid., 58). He eventually takes up the case only when Flora agrees that she is willing to accept 'all the truth' that would be uncovered through the course of the investigation. Likewise, when the police are wary of his presence in the case he smooths things over — "I never intended to take up a case again. Above all things, I have a horror of publicity. I must beg, that in case of my being able to contribute something to the solution of the mystery, my name may not be mentioned" (Ibid., 60). This not only shows supreme tact on the part of Poirot who realises that the police in question does not like the idea of sharing the limelight. It is also a reiteration of his quest for truth which remains the sole reason behind his investigation. By rejecting both money and fame, Poirot takes an anti-capitalistic stance when it comes to detection.

Unlike his predecessors, Hercule Poirot does not have a definite theoretical method when it comes to solving his cases. Holmes describes himself as a consulting detective who solves crimes through 'the science of Deduction' elaborated in *A Study in Scarlet*. This, in turn, is based on observation of all the details and coming to the most logical conclusion. While this seems nothing out of the ordinary, it is complex and involves considerable knowledge of various subjects like geology and chemistry. The one subject that Holmes does not take into account or hold his interest is human psychology. This is where we find a diverging path from the traditional methods of detection. Poirot relies on his intelligence but he goes beyond that — "the little grey cells of the brain',[...]then there is the psychology of a crime. One must study that" (Ibid., 71). This can be elaborated as examination of different human personalities and a study of relationships at personal and communal level which is born out of many years of experience. This study of human nature is explained by Susan Rowland; she writes that by psychology he—'means an empathy with the passions of both victim and suspects in the close-knit village of Kings Abbot'(Rowland 2001, 28).

This reliance on emotions is diametrically opposite to the masculine methods of the great detectives. Shedding light on the act of detection, Agatha Christie writes—'method and order still meant much to him—but not nearly so much as before. In *The Murder of Roger Ackroyd* he is at his best investigating a crime in a quiet country village and using his knowledge of human nature to get at the truth' (Curran 2011, 250). Poirot elucidates further as he explains the skill of observation—'they invent haphazard—and by miracle they are right. Not that it is that really. Women observe subconsciously a thousand little details, without knowing that they are doing so. Their subconscious mind adds these little things together—and they call the result intuition. Me I am very skilled in psychology. I know these things' (Christie 2011 (b), 111). By praising and celebrating the observation skills of women, Poirot aligns himself with the feminine and gives it a rational basis by naming it psychology. Agatha Christie has also used the character of Caroline to elaborate on this feminisation of detecting skills. Caroline is presented as a village busy body who keeps track of all the gossip. She has an uncanny ability to extract information from everyone including her brother, Dr. Sheppard who describes her thus—"As I say, there is no need for Caroline to go out to get information. She sits at home and it comes to her." (Ibid., 8). From the onset of the novel, we see a friendly rivalry among the siblings which reflects the larger dichotomy between the feminine sister who is gossipy in nature and her brother James who is a doctor firmly rooted in scientific rationality. Interestingly, Caroline has rightly deduced her brother as well as she comments—"you are weak, James [...] I'm eight years older than you are [...]. And I've always considered it my duty to look after you. With a bad bringing up, Heaven knows what mischief you might have got into by now" (Ibid., 148). These observations eventually fall into place when we reach the conclusion of the novel.

As mentioned earlier, Poirot manages to gain information by asking apparently simplistic questions like the colour of Ralph Paton's boots. He also manages to ask the right question to the right person which is elucidated by his method of enquiry about the fire in the fireplace where he has a conversation with Dr. Sheppard — "one must always proceed with method [...] to each man his own knowledge. You could tell me the details of the patient's appearance — nothing there would escape you. If I wanted information about the papers on that desk, Mr. Raymond would have noticed anything there was to see. To find out about the fire, I must ask the man whose business it is to observe such things" (Ibid., 64). Thereafter, he proceeds to question Parker who is the butler of the Fernly Park household who provides him with the required information.

He also makes his suspects feel comfortable enough for them to voluntarily part with important information. He plays upon the human subconscious and on human beings' natural instinct for curiosity and also their need to unburden their secrets. The reaction of Ursula is a reflection of that — "for a moment or two the girl looked mutely at Poirot. Then, her reserve breaking down completely, she nodded her head once, and burst into an outburst of sobs" (Ibid., 179). Throughout the narrative of *The Murder of Roger Ackroyd*, Poirot proclaims that each of the suspects is hiding something and as the narrative unfolds, we realise how each character from Flora to Parker have all committed crimes of various levels. Poirot cleverly breaks down each of their defenses to finally extract the truth. Christie also leaves a vital clue for the readers when each of the characters reaches out to Poirot to finally reveal their personal secrets except for Dr. Sheppard who remains self-assured of his rationality.

The initial masculinity that is reflected in the character of Dr. Sheppard in relation to his sister can be extended to Poirot too. Dr. Sheppard is convinced of Poirot's failure as he sees himself in a more masculine and hence superior place. Christie hints at this masculine vs. feminine divide at the choice of drinks offered when Dr. Sheppard visits Poirot for dinner — "he had placed a bottle of Irish whiskey [...] on the small table with a soda water siphon and a glass. He himself was engaged in brewing hot chocolate. It was a favourite beverage of his, I discovered later" (Ibid., 110). Here, the drink of whiskey and chocolate furthers the stereotyped image of man vs. woman, and hence, masculinity vs. femininity. By making hot chocolate the favourite beverage of Poirot, Agatha Christie clearly subverts the expectations we have from a great detective.

Like Holmes or even Thorndyke, Poirot searches for physical clues in the summerhouse—"I was startled to observe my new friend. He dropped to his hands and knees and was crawling about the floor. Every now and then he shook his head as though not satisfied" (Ibid., 75). He finds a quill and a piece of cloth but it is his knowledge of laundry which helps him to understand the clue. Perhaps the most obvious clue that Poirot rightly dwells on is a chair that has been moved from its usual location. Poirot has been described as a finicky person who abhors any kind of disorder. It is a moved vase which leads Poirot to solve the mystery in *The Mysterious Affair at Styles*. Likewise, Poirot gives a serious consideration to the fact that a chair has been moved in the room where the murder took place. While this is something which neither the police nor any other character ponders on, Poirot comments—"it is completely unimportant [...] that is why it is so interesting" (Ibid., 65). By focusing on this clue which lies within a stereotypical domestic space, Christie has feminised the method of deduction. Poirot is also presented in a role beyond that of a detective. His friendship with Hastings throughout the series featuring him is an example of this. Poirot is a keen observer of human nature and hence observes the undercurrents of human emotions. His friendly advice to Major Blunt regarding his feelings for Flora reaches a happy conclusion. Here, Poirot is presented not just as a detective but as a figure of guidance.

The detective was an embodiment of the best of men following a strong moral code and a bearer of traditional values. Poirot embodies this traditional male role by playing the detective yet everything about him encourages the reader to navigate our perceptions of feminine and domestic. Poirot is a manifestation of Christie's understanding of masculine and feminine which reflects a changing time where traditional views were being questioned. By bordering on the playful, Christie destabilises all expectations from a detective story, especially by breaking down stereotypes and by doing so offers her readers a chance to dispel their own prejudices. In the words of Susan Rowland —

> "In learning not to dismiss the gossipy buffoonery of Poirot, the feminine intelligence network of the spinsters with their intuitive grasp of social interaction, the 'trivial' domestic clues in the Ackroyd house and learning to distrust the confident narrative of the professional male, the reader is alerted to feminine modes of knowledge traditionally marginalized by law" (Rowland 2001, 28).

Bibliography:

Brenthal, J. C. 2016. *Queering Agatha Christie: Revisiting the Golden Age of Detective Fiction*. Switzerland: Palgrave Macmillan.

Christie, Agatha. 2011. *Clues to Christie: An Introductory Guide to Miss Marple, Hercule Poirot, Tommy & Tuppence and All of Agatha Christie's Mysteries*. London: HarperCollins. (a)

…2011. *The Murder of Roger Ackroyd*. London: Harper. (b)

…2012. *The Mysterious Affair at Styles*. London: Harper.

Cawelti, John G. 1976. 'The formula of the Classical Detective Story'. In *Adventure, Mystery, and Romance: Formula stories as Art and Popular culture*, 80-105. Chicago: Chicago University Press.

Curran, John. 2011. *Agatha Christie's complete secret notebooks*. London: Harper Collins.

Chandler, Raymond. 1988. *The Simple Art of Murder*. New York: Vintage Crime.

Doyle, Arthur Conan. 2001. (1887). *A Study in Scarlet*. India: Penguin books.

Gregoriou, Christiana. 2007. *Deviance in Contemporary Crime Fiction*. New York: Palgrave Macmillan.

James, P.D. 2009. *Talking About Detective Fiction*. Oxford: Faber.

Knight, Stephen. 2010. *Crime Fiction since 1800: Detection, Death, Diversity*. New York: Palgrave.

Munt, Sally R. 1994. *Murder by the Book? Feminism and the crime novel*. London: Routledge.

Rowland, Susan. 2001. *From Agatha Christie to Ruth Rendell: British Women Writers in Detective and Crime Fiction*. New York: Palgrave.

Scaggs, John. 2005. *Crime Fiction*. London: Routledge.

The Murder of Roger Ackroyd. Dir. Andrew Grieve. ITV 2000. TV Series.

"What Shall I see in my dreams tonight?": Reading the Repressed in Wilkie Collins's *The Woman in White*

Shubham Dey and Rupayan Mukherjee

Wilkie Collins's *The Woman in White* has provoked distinct critical contentions owing to its multifarious thematic tendencies. It is also for this reason that the novel refutes an unproblematic categorisation. For many critics, the novel is an exemplary sensational novel, for some, it is a mystery novel and for a handful few like Robert P. Ashley, the novel can be typified as an early detective novel. Ashley claims that the novel has "sufficiently strong" (Ashley 1951, 51) resemblances with the detective genre and argues that the protagonist Walter Hartright performs "some capable detective work" (Ibid.) to unravel the mystery that is the driving force of the novel. Hence, although not a typical whodunnit, *Woman in White* can be arguably placed in the generic category of Detective Fiction.

The present chapter does not intend to re-read the novel as a detective fiction. Instead, it proposes to consider the aspect of the repressed in the novel. It is worth mentioning at the very outset that the repressed shall be considered in this discussion beyond its psychoanalytic connotations. The consideration of the repressed will be made in a larger perspective, also focusing on the thematisation of the repressed through the motifs of Gothic and madness. It will be further argued that unfollowing the standardised pattern of classical detective fiction, the repressed in the novel serves not just as a withheld secret which is born into existence only in exposition/ revelation. Instead, it also functions as a premonition that, to quote Ann Cvetkovich, "installs a hermeneutics of suspicion" (Cevetkovich 1989, 25) and tempts the sleuth-protagonist to pursue detection.

Walter Hartright is a young art teacher in the novel who encounters a "solitary woman" (Collins 2012, 23) and soon discovers a resemblance between her and his student turned beloved Laura.

However, Laura is betrothed to the Baronet Sir Percival Glyde and ultimately, against her will, marries him. Her marriage places her amidst a series of conspiracies which increasingly put her identity at stake. As she is duped and admitted to the asylum, Laura is (forcibly) made to live the socio-institutional identity of Anne, the mysterious woman who appears at the very opening of the novel. For the world, Laura is dead and buried while in reality, it is Anne who has died of heart disease. Through the intervention of Hartright, Laura's lost identity is restituted to her, but only after a secret has been revealed and thereby the repressed has been exposed.

As it is, the repressed has an elemental function in the novel. It is that entropy which, once unleashed, alters the course of events. Identities are regained, images are unmade and the question of reality is profoundly problematised once the repressed is granted exposition. This subversive capacity of the repressed to disturb the verisimilitude of the status quo is repeatedly implied and thematised in the novel. For instance, one can consider Hartright's first encounter with Anne. In the novel, Anne is a socially repressed woman who has been "cruelly used and cruelly wronged" (Ibid., 27). She has been denied recognition in intimate familial circles and has been subjected to intensely coercive institutions of repression like the asylum. Her agency has been formulated within the either-or conditions of denial or subjection and she is an unambiguous and undeniable embodiment of the repressed in the novel. Hence, her encounter with Hartright, a representative (masculine) subject of the London-bred middle class, causes in the latter a sense of unease. The normative order of the status quo is suddenly breached for the latter who retrospectively acknowledges "It was like a dream". (Ibid., 25). Very soon, the familiar is de-familiarised for Hartwood who apprehensively self-reflects:

> "Was I Walter Hartright? Was this the well-known, uneventful road, where holiday people strolled on Sundays?... I was too bewildered..." (Ibid., 25-26)

An encounter with the socially repressed 'bewilders' the normative and problematises the conventional rationale of sense making.

Anne's embodiment of the repressed is also operative at a more personal and intimate level if we consider her impact on

Walter Hartright. The protagonist discovers an "ominous likeness" (Ibid., 60) between Anne and Laura, his pupil whom he has started to desire. Initially, the desire and love for Laura is mystified as a love at first sight. Yet, the sudden return of the memory of Anne at the enthralling romantic hour when Hartright is gazing at Miss Fairlie basking in moonlight is significant. It problematises the economy of desire and the typically middle-class consciousness of Hartright is clearly disconcerted by such a return.

> ""I see it—more unwillingly than I can say. To associate that forlorn, friendless, lost woman, even by an accidental likeness only, with Miss Fairlie, seems like casting a shadow on the future of the bright creature who stands looking at us now. Let me lose the impression again as soon as possible." (Ibid.)

One can barely forget that the very opening encounter between Hartright and Anne has been affective in nature and has been considerably dependent on the semiotics of touch. Touch and corporeal contact have served as a potent medium to materialise dialogue. Anne has been "obliged to...touch you (Hartright)" (Ibid., 24) and has very soon "laid her hand, with a sudden gentle stealthiness, on my (Hartright's) bosom..." (Ibid.,25) Hartright is initially apprehensive, though clearly not apathetic, of the "thin hand; a cold hand" (Ibid.) but he is quick to recall that he "...was young" and "...that the hand which touched me (him) was a woman's." (Ibid.) The consciousness of the woman by youth is often a consciousness of the desire and the erotic undertone of the exchange becomes a perfect semiotic design through which the desire is signified. Cvetkovich observes that it is rather strange that Hartright does not fall in love with Anne in the novel. She points out that Anne does not just precede Laura sequentially but also has a presence formidable enough to inhabit, from the very beginning, Hartright's desire of Laura.

In his studies on Repression, Sigmund Freud observes that repression is a strategic means to control and govern impulses which are potentially precarious in nature. For Freud the "essence of repression lies simply in turning something away, and keeping it at a distance, from the conscious". (Freud 1957, 147). Freud argues that repression has a two-phase progress, namely: Primal Repression and Repression Proper. The first is the elementary phase of Repression which "consists in the psychical representative of the instinct being denied into the conscious" (Ibid., 148) while the latter "affects mental derivatives of the repressed representative, or such trains of thought as, originating elsewhere, have come into associative connection with it." (Ibid.) Freud deciphers an associative economy in the second stage whereby what was primally repressed exercises an "attraction...upon everything with which it can establish a connection". (Ibid.) Freud argues that the conscious does not exist in an absolute separation from "all the derivatives of what was primally repressed". (Ibid., 149). Rather, "they have free access to the conscious" (Ibid.).

It is not irrelevant to argue that Anne acquires the status of the Primal repressed in Hartright's psyche. For Hartright, Anne (or to be precise, her idea) is the psychical representative of the instinct of desire/ instinctual representative of desire that is, as discussed before, symptomatically revealed in the erotic design of the exchange. However, the instinct of desire is quickly negated by the information he derives from the verbal exchange between the agents of two authoritarian institutions, the police and psychiatry. Hartright is repelled by the knowledge that Anne has escaped from the asylum and is intimidated by the realisation that he has been involved in an exchange with "absolute insanity". (Collins 2012, 30). What follows is a terrible sense of unpleasure (as Freud argues, unpleasure is a prominent motive behind repression) and guilt which consequently drives a repulsive-reaction mechanism that is inclined to disown the traces of the exchange and deny them an entry or presence in the conscious. Such a repulsive mechanism is well expressed in Hartright's desperate attempt to stay awake and keep away the thoughts of the woman in white by engaging in active psychic activities like drawing or reading a book, which cannot be accomplished without an aware conscious, in the immediate aftermath of his first encounter with Anne. Yet, the repressed keeps returning and exercises "...a continuous pressure in the direction of the conscious" (Freud 1957, 151) and Hartright confesses that "...the woman in white got between me and the pencil, between me and my book." (Collins 2012, 30) Freud recounts that the continuous tension of repression "finds expression in the psychical characteristics of the state of sleep…" (Freud 1957, 151) and claims that dreams are often outcomes of this agonised encounter between the repressed and the conscious. Elsewhere, Freud also observes that "a dream is a (disguised) fulfilment of a (suppressed or repressed) wish" (Freud 1955, 183) and it is only fitting that before falling asleep in his first night at the Limmeridge House, Hartright wonders "What shall I see in my dreams tonight?" (Collins 2012, 31) and is considerably considerate about the possibility of dreaming about the woman in white. Such a consideration provides substantial ground to argue that Anne considerably constitutes the repressed of Hartright's consciousness. Her presence in Hartright's psyche is so overwhelming that even when he "seemed to burst into a new life and a new set of thoughts…" (Ibid., 33), Hartright confesses that, although fading gradually, "…the woman in white was still in my mind" (Ibid.).

It is little surprising that Hartright is barely able to develop an interest for Marian Halcombe who bears no similarity with the woman in white. Anne had a "…youthful face, meagre and sharp to look at about the cheeks and chin" (Ibid., 23), Marian has "a large, firm, masculine mouth and jaw" (Ibid., 36). Anne had "large, grave, wistfully attentive eyes" (Ibid., 23), Marian has "prominent, piercing, resolute brown eyes" (Ibid., 36). Anne had appeared to be nervous and "…a little touched by suspicion" (Ibid., 23); Marian, on the contrary, was "bright, frank…" and "appeared…altogether wanting in those feminine attractions of gentleness and pliability, without which the beauty of the handsomest woman alive is beauty incomplete." (Ibid., 34). On the contrary, Laura, for whom Hartright develops an immediate desire, smiles in a "nervous contraction" (Ibid., 50), has "…large and tender and quietly thoughtful eyes" (Ibid.) and a face "that is delicately refined towards the chin." (Ibid.). It is perhaps not irrelevant but unnecessary to highlight the resemblance in the physical and behavioural attributes of Laura and Anne because, as mentioned before, Hartright himself soon becomes conscious of the resemblance. Instead, one can engage in a reading of the immediate effect that Laura's first appearance has on Hartright to comprehend the intimations of the repressed.

> "Think of her as you thought of the first woman who quickened the pulses within you that the rest of her sex had no art to stir. Let the kind, candid blue eyes meet yours, as they met mine, with the one matchless look which we both remember so well...Let her footstep, as she comes and goes, in these pages, be like that other footstep to whose airy fall your own heart once beat time." (Ibid., 51)

With the foreknowledge that soon Hartright is going to decipher an "ominous likeness" (Ibid., 75) between Anne and Laura, the significance of these lines change. We, as readers, are tempted to comprehend Anne as the first woman who did indeed affect Hartright enough to realise that she was a 'woman' and he was 'young', who had affectively kissed his hand and to whom Hartright had specifically mentioned as 'woman'. The possibilities of such a reading are further strengthened by Hartright's confession that among the flurry of sensations which the first impression of Laura had provoked, there "was one that troubled and perplexed me." (Ibid., 51). The elementary intimation of the repressed, as Freud states, is perplexing for it surfaces only in/ through an agonised exchange with the conscious. That there is a constant intimation of a precedence in words and phrases like 'remember', 'other footstep' without an outright mention of a determinable precedent is suggestive of a reference to the repressed, which ironically the self is often unconscious of.

However, the repressed in the novel does not merely function within the limits of Hartright's consciousness. Neither can its pertinence in the novel be discussed through a strategic reading that considers Anne as a repressed subject in a narrowed sense. Instead, any reading of the repressed in the novel is possibly incomplete without an engagement with the motif of madness. The asylum occupies a position of prominence in the novel. It is the dreaded space where the dominant forces of patriarchy confine hapless dominated women; it is the inexplorable labyrinth where faces and traces of terrible conspiracies are 'safely' (emphasis is mine) locked and repressed. One can barely fail to notice that the social history of late-eighteenth and early nineteenth century England is strewn with incidents of false incarceration. Individuals were often accused of lunacy by their family or spouses, often with the intention of depriving them from ancestral wealth and property. Such rampant cases of false charges of lunacy had prompted the licensing of madhouses from 1774 by the Regulation of Madhouses Act, "following public concern that some non-lunatics were being unlawfully detained at the whim of their spouses or families" (Historic England, n.d.). Madness was strategically used to disenfranchise individuals and asylums emerged as perfect repressive means to accomplish this design.

What is more interesting is that these asylums were notorious for repressing without repression. Michel Foucault's genealogical study of the institutionalisation of madness depicts that the nineteenth century asylum, owing to the intervention of philanthropists like Tuke and Pinel, underwent a significant change in the mode and nature of repression and the methods of cure. Foucault argues that with the liberalisation of the asylum there was a significant reduction in physical torture. Instead, responsibility emerged as an effective mode of repression. The madman was made to live in a close proximity of the rational order of being and was systematically encouraged to practice self-restraint. As such, he was subjected to the "stifling anguish of responsibility" (Foucault 1988, 247) whereby he "…must feel morally responsible for everything within him that may disturb morality and society, and must hold no one but himself responsible for the punishment he receives." (Ibid., 246). Under such circumstances, self-repression became the only means for the marked insane to escape repression. The result was twofold: while the madman engaged in a consistent self-fashioning that would try to repress all that was diagnosed as excess by the sensibilities of reason, he would also simultaneously (compellingly) interiorise his own identity as the lunatic. Once diagnosed with madness and admitted into the asylum, the madman was compelled to accept his madman identity and subsequently engage in a practice of self-censorship and self-repression. This consistent self-repression resulted in the production of a perpetually repressed agency.

Anne and Laura, the two women who have been forced to spend a substantial period of their life within the disciplining atmosphere of the asylum, exemplify rampant instances of self-repression throughout the novel. Hartright in his first encounter with Anne cannot help noticing that the woman "spoke with unnecessary earnestness and agitation and shrank back from me (him) several paces." (Collins 2012, 24). The performance of earnestness and the unmeditated 'physical' withdrawal is a reflection of an overconscious consciousness which is consistently trying to project a normative ideal of selfhood through an unfailing self-censorship and self-repression. It is significant that Anne is unnaturally concerned about the impression she creates on the other and chronically seeks the Other's response for self-validation:

> "You don't suspect me of doing anything wrong, do you? I have done nothing wrong...Why do you suspect me of doing wrong?" (Ibid., 24)

Anne's chronic tendency of depending on the Other for self-validation recurs throughout the novel. At a later point in the novel when Hartright meets her at the churchyard and asks her about the address of the asylum, she immediately responds "You don't think I ought to be taken back, do you?" (Ibid., 97). Such persistent self-apprehensions signify that Anne has interiorised her identity of/ as the insane and is deeply dependent on the Other to decide if she is revealing symptoms of mental illness. What it also suggests is a great force of self-repression that is functional beneath the projected personality of Anne.

Such self-repressions repress deeper conspiracies in an obtuse manner. Anne is immensely disturbed even at the slightest mention of "the person who put you (her) in the Asylum..." (Ibid., 101) and desperately intreats Hartright to "Talk of something else" (Ibid.). She is worried that she will "lose myself (herself)" (Ibid.) if the discussion about her perpetrator persists. The possibility of losing her calm and behaving abnormally haunts her so persistently that she prefers to repress greater truths about the conspiracy. This is because Anne is aware that her natural reaction and response to these truths will raise questions on her sanity and she might end up being identified as the insane subject, susceptible to further subjections, yet again, by great repressive institutes like asylum. For Anne, self-repression is the only possible means through which she can convince the other of her normativity. Hence, she is unconditionally dedicated to practice the same, even when that amounts to the repression of unjust conspiracies that have victimised her. Hartright has to depend on his intuitions and sensibilities to realise the hidden truths about the conspirator and the conspiracy.

While Anne considerably engages in a conscious act of self-repression, it is difficult to arrive at any such determinable conclusion regarding Laura. Instead, Laura's self-repression is possibly a combined outcome of her refusal to speak and the greater systemic forces of coercion which refuse to listen to her. We are unsure about her possible response to the curious situation when she is forced to live in the asylum as Anne Catherick. As she remonstrates the incident to her sister, there are little evidences for the reader to conclude that she had protested to the imposition of Anne's identity upon her. The text narrates in a matter-of-fact manner that Laura was made to wear Anne Catherick's clothes and was advised by the nurse to not "worry us (them) all any more about being Lady Glyde." (Ibid., 402). Such a narration seemingly suggests that Laura had unproblematically accepted her new identity as Anne Catherick. Even the Proprietor of the asylum confides to Halcombe (Laura's cousin) that although he had noticed "certain differences between his patient before she had escaped (i.e., Anne) and since she had been brought back (i.e., Laura)", "those differences were too minute to be described." (Ibid., 395).

On the contrary, one must not forget that it is only natural for the proprietor of a classical nineteenth century asylum to be myopic towards the 'differences' and ignore them without elaborating, under the pretext of being 'minute'. None but Michel Foucault observes that a typical feature of the nineteenth century asylum was its absolute denial to acknowledge delirium as language (Foucault 1988, 262) and its persistent refusal to listen, until Freud, to the language of the insane. Hence, it is very possible that the authorities of the asylum, much like the classical nineteenth century asylum which refused to find in the madman's rambling any possible substance or truth, had dismissed Laura's initial refusals (if any) to accept the thrust-upon identity of Anne as signs of delirium which can never be relied upon. The case is even strongly made as the proprietor of the asylum in the novel admits that he did notice a "modification in the form of Anne Catherick's delusion" (Collins 2012, 395) but had considered them as mere discontinuities, typically characteristic to insanity. In such confessions, the text betrays symptoms of a forced repression of identity to which Laura had been unwillingly subjected to.

These symptoms of repression are, interestingly and rather ironically, conveyed in the novel through the Gothic, a prominent literary motif that is associated with the Repressed. Gothic strains in the novel have been a matter of chronic critical interest and there have been multifarious readings (all equally relevant) of the nature and function of the Gothic in the novel. Among others, Stephen Bernstein considers the relationship between the setting and the Gothic in the novel. Although a substantial section of Bernstein's argument focuses on the textual and thematic strategies through which Blackwater Park, "the ancient and interesting seat... of Sir Percival Glyde, Bart" is organised to host the motif of the Gothic, yet he is also equally interested in depicting that the "...numerous settings of the novel are closely linked". (Bernstein 1993, 301). Bernstein argues that the various settings, in the novel, resemble each other in their "oppressive claustral" (Ibid.) design and their ability to estrange and defamiliarise the individual by evolving as "...suffocating sites of anxiety". (Ibid.). Even the familiar and otherwise natural cityscape of London is no exception as, resembling the Dickensian tradition, it has the possibility of transforming into "one great Gothic mansion." (Ibid.).

This uncanniness of the everyday serve greater purposes beyond the obvious function of estrangement. It is that affective medium through which the repressed is able to appeal to the intuitive sensibilities of the normative subject. The very "primal scene" (D.A. Miller 1986, 110) of the novel perfectly exemplifies such a case. As Walter Hartright journeys through the otherwise familiar roads of London, he cannot help noticing the "stillness of the scene, and admiring the soft alterations of light and shade as they followed each other..." (Collins 2012, 22) The Gothic nocturnal stereotypes of "a moon full and broad, in the dark blue starless sky, and the broken ground of the heath" (Ibid.) prepare Hartright for his founding encounter with Anne. The mysterious and suddenly appearing woman in white, with her equally uncanny behaviour, affects and informs Hartright's intuition to the intimations of a mystery. Although Walter is not initially concerned about the whereabouts of the mysterious woman, she does exert a formidable influence on his consciousness. In time, this influence develops into curiosity, thereby making possible the resolution of the mystery and resurfacing of repressed realities. Similarly, the Gothicity of Blackwater Park and the mysterious design of "the ancient and interesting seat" (Ibid., 188) intuitively awakens in Marian a sense of unease. Marian's fundamental problem with the landscape and the house seems to be its impenetrably concealing nature which is unwelcoming and with which one can only engage in estrangement. Marian's exploration of the house makes her sense that "dirty 'good old times'" (Ibid., 195) are locked in the unused rooms and closets; her further exploration of the estate makes her develop a growing intuition that all is not well between Sir Percival and Mrs. Catherick.

It is worth noting that detection in the novel is considerably premised on intuition. Inferences to mysteries are often reached through intuition. Hartright intuitively infers that Anne's mother is guiltless and Sir Percival Glyde is responsible for her misery; Marian Halcombe intuitively sees a "sad torpor" (Ibid., 192) of her sister Laura although in the letters that Laura sends her, there is "...no undertone of complaint to warn me (her, i.e., Marian) that she (Laura) is absolutely unhappy in her married life." (Ibid.). Further conspiracies which evolve are also intuitively suspected by the sleuth consciousness of both Marian and Hartright. In fact, one cannot deny that to an extent Hartright's over-intuitive consciousness appropriates the narrative design. It "raises the possibility that, Walter, far from being objective, is in fact manipulating the narrative for his own ends." (Perkins and Donaghy 1990, 392). Rachel Ablow points out that Hartright's instant recognition of Laura, whom the world has accepted as Anne, is founded on nothing but a sensation that is anything but rational. (Ablow 164). Instead, when considered in lights of John Locke, the sensation reveals itself to be pure intuition. John Locke argues that intuitive knowledge is often "clearest" in nature and is often arrived at without any "...room for hesitation, doubt, or examination." (Locke 1999, 521). Hartright's unhesitant and unproblematic recognition of the veiled woman as Laura, contrary to the established and accepted regimes of truth which claim her to be dead and even validate it in form of a concrete tombstone, is a sheerly intuitive claim.

The Gothic appeals to this predominant intuitive design of truth determination that is prevalent in the novel. Andrew Smith observes that one of the characteristic features of the Gothic is "its analysis of the limits of rationality" (Smith 2000, 1) and the Gothic motif in the novel constantly jeopardises the rational design of reality through an intimation of the repressed. Such intimations, by suggesting other realities which remain repressed, problematise the status-quo's claim to an undisputable truth. They are traces through which an-other world can be conceptualised and subsequently born out of investigation. In that other world, Anne is not an embodiment of absolute insanity but is rather a victim of conspiracy. In that other world, Percival Glyde is not a chivalrous aristocratic 'man of manners' (emphasis mine) but a parasite who seeks to survive on Laura's fortune and dupe her into non-existence. In that other world, Anne and Laura share a common scandalous origin. This repressed world can only be detected if the intuitive modes of detection are relied upon. It is thus that the repressed in the novel ceases to be a secret that is born only after exposition. Rather, it is very much functional as a possible intimation which affects the intuitive sensibilities of the detecting agency, thereby making detection possible.

Works Cited:

Ablow, Rachel. 2003-2004. "The Sensationalization of Masculinity in "The Woman in White"". *NOVEL: A Forum on Fiction*, Vol. 37, no. 1/2 (Fall-Spring): 158-180. JSTOR. https://www.jstor.org/stable/30038534. Accessed on 3rd March, 2021.

Ashley, Robert P. 1951. "Wilkie Collins and the Detective Story". *Nineteenth-Century Fiction*, Vol. 6, no. 1 (June): 47-60. JSTOR. https://www.jstor.org/stable/3044284. Accessed on 29th February, 2021.

Bernstein, Stephen. 1993. "READING BLACKWATER PARK: GOTHI-CISM, NARRATIVE, AND IDEOLOGY IN "THE WOMAN IN WHITE"". *Studies in the Novel*, Vol. 25, no. 3 (fall): 291-305. JSTOR. https://www.jstor.org/stable/29532954. Accessed on 23rd February, 2021.

Collins, Wilkie. 2012. *The Woman in White*. New Delhi: Rupa Publications.

Cvetkovich, Ann. 1989. "Ghostlier Determinations: The Economy of Sensation and "The Woman in White"". *NOVEL: A Forum on Fiction*, Vol. 23, no. 1 (Autumn): 24-43. JSTOR. https://www.jstor.org/stable/1345577. Accessed on 12th March, 2021.

Foucault, Michel. 1988. *Madness and Civilization: A History of Insanity in the Age of Reason*. Translated by Richard Howard. New York: Vintage Books.

Freud, Sigmund. 1955. *The Interpretation of Dreams*. Translated by James Strachey. New York: Basic Books.

...1957. *The Standard Edition of the Complete Psychological Works of SIGMUND FREUD: Vol XIV (1914-1916)*. Translated under the General Editorship of James Strachey. London: The Hogarth Press.

Historic England. n.d. "The Age of the MadHouse—Home of the Well-Attired Ploughman". https://historicengland.org.uk/research/inclusive-heritage/disability-history/1660-1832/the-age-of-the-madhouse/. Accessed on 5th March, 2021.

Locke, John. 1999. *Essay Concerning Human Understanding*. Pennsylvania: Pennsylvania State University.

Miller, D. A. 1986. "Cage Aux Folles: Sensation and Gender in Wilkie Collins's The Woman in White". *Representations*, no. 14 (Spring): 107-136. JSTOR. https://www.jstor.org/stable/2928437. Accessed on 23rd February, 2021.

Perkins, Pamela and Mary Donaghy. 1990. "A MAN'S RESOLUTION: NARRATIVE STRATEGIES IN WILKIE COLLINS' "THE WOMAN IN WHITE"". *Studies in the Novel*, Vol. 22, no. 4 (Winter): 392-402. JSTOR. https://www.jstor.org/stable/29532745. Accessed on 13th February, 2021.

Smith, Andrew. 2000. *Gothic Radicalism: Literature, Philosophy and Psychoanalysis in the Nineteenth Century*. London: Macmillan Press Ltd.

Section IV
Romance

Trauma as Calamity or Capital?: The Aporia of Representation and the Ethics of Reading in Anne Frank's *The Diary of a Young Girl*

Puja Chakraborty

The debate, whether 'popular fiction' and 'literary fiction' stand poles apart on the scale of literary merit, has been the centre of discord for many literary critics/scholars for the last few decades; yet the proliferation of this particular form of writing indicates that popular narratives not just concoct a sheer form of fantasy and romantic escapade but has left an indelible imprint on the collective psyche of its readers. However, such stratification of literary importance based on its aesthetic value, constraining its genealogical and teleological evolution, often overlooks the imbricate structure of the socio-political economy that functions at the backdrop of the texts. The field of 'high' (emphasis is mine) literature is frequently distinguished with an elite position, exceptionally available for scholarly interventions, whereas, popular literature is fundamentally democratic in nature, therefore, atrociously labelled as uncritical, leisurely and ephemeral. Clive Bloom (2002) has convincingly remarked that "Best-selling fiction gives us an insight into the modes and methods of literary production [...] and perceptual history [...]; it provides a unique insight into the imaginative history of a nation over a one-hundred period" (Bloom 2002, 4). In order to gain proper cognition of the domain of 'literary production', Pierre Bourdieu's theoretical contemplation on the strategies of 'marketization' seems insightful as it locates the possible rift between the category of 'industrial literature' that follows "successful formulas" against 'literature without conventions' that is grounded upon the stakes of 'originality and independence'. Bourdieu (1993) distinguishes highbrow cultural production as 'autonomous', indifferent and often contemptuous of the market values of profit/loss or even the readers' response, from the commercial cultural production which he referred to as 'heteronomous' because it is essentially caught up with the language of industry and mercenary success. Trauma as a popular literary canon has gained perspectives from a diverse range of historical occurrences namely the World Wars, the Holocaust, 9/11, just to mention a few. However, the incentive role of media and television in the public projection of traumatic experiences has been one of the constitutive agents of what is now known as popular trauma culture. The nascent engrossment of general audience in the life and experiences of trauma survivors, in the forms of memoir, film and opera, by infusing with the pain of others, undergoing the historical and political pastness of their present, has invoked a host of discursive issues — if/how the neurotic experience of trauma can be easily explicable for mass consumption, what kind of the politics of representation is active behind such narratives of suffering-and-redemption through physical mortification, or what sort of 'latent voyeuristic kitsch' (Rothe 2011) encodes the dominant mode of reception, and whether the polysemic nature of the subjective self can be held authentic enough to profess the flow of a traumatic history. For these critical inspections, this article aims to focus on Anne Frank's *The Diary of a Young Girl*, a highly popular memoir written by a Dutch teenager of Jewish heritage, bearing a supposedly faithful transcription of the Holocaust, which first appeared in 1947 (in Dutch) and afterwards has successfully maintained its best-seller position in over sixty-two languages. Therefore, this study will further excavate the dynamic matrix behind the irreducible appeal of the text along with a nuanced understanding of the narrative voice and will attempt to interrogate the marketability of trauma as a symbol of capital within the ever-growing milieu of cultural commodification and consumption.

Reading Popular Fiction: In Theory and Practice

A genealogical study of Popular fiction traces back to a larger historical backdrop of its emergence in the late nineteenth century, mostly in the form of Science fiction and Detective fiction. The word 'popular' (emphasis is mine) invokes a generative ground for contemplation and articulation as it reflects the ever-shifting paradigms of cultural dimensions. Today, the fictions that come under the rubric of popular literature are produced, marketed and consumed generically, providing logic for easy identification and hence, disparagingly marked as formulaic, cheap and disposable. However, it is this heterogeneous nature of popular fiction that facilitates an understanding of 'the construction of modern self' (McCracken 1998). In his reading of pulp fiction, Scott McCracken contends:

> ...(it) refers to two things. One is the fiction, which... can be moulded to our fantasies, and desires. The other is the self, which appears to be equally squashy and shapeless, but equally and for that reason, can take up a multitude of new forms. If popular fiction turns mind to mush, then mush is also the fertile compost for growth. (Ibid., 14)

Foregrounding this 'fertile' aspect, that interlinks the (post)modern subject(s) with the (post)industrial socio-cultural practices, Walter Benjamin in his seminal essay *The Work of Art in the Age of Mechanical Reproduction* (1973, originally published in 1936) observed a hopeful and productive engagement with the 'mass culture'[1] as he considered the individual, not as a passive recipient of the authoritarian-capitalist market, but an active agent who is able to appropriate the mechanisms of the 'culture industry' for personal as well as potentially political subversive ends. The massive transformation brought in by mass literacy and advanced technology has greatly affected the flow of artistic creation and its reception; thereby, in his words, "Quantity has been transmuted into quality. The greatly increased mass of participants has produced a change in the mode of participation" (Benjamin 1973, 241). Insofar as it can be ascertained, the dawn of postmodernist era has vastly impacted the imperative forms of popular culture, with a diverse range of representational structure, the negation of meta-narratives, media-saturated social economy and a visceral celebration of populist relativism. In this context, Pierre Bourdieu's formulative study of cultural preference which signifies the form of acquired knowledge gained from various socio-cultural apparatus (family, educational institution, religious organisations etc.) and its relationship with social class, remains significant. In *Distinction: A Social Critique of the Judgment of Taste* (1999), Bourdieu outlined the multiple roles of social factors that construct the aesthetic and cultural taste of the individual—"taste classifies, and it classifies the classifier"(Bourdieu 1999, 6). Therefore, this dialogic relationship between the capitalist market and the social class exponentially gives space for newer literary genres to flourish, essentially functioning as incisive pointers to decipher the codes of commodification vis-a-vis consumption. This further unfolds the urgency to relocate the plurality of production histories, the structural deconstruction/reconstruction of cultural forms, the social characteristics of receiving audience and the symbolic expression of 'knowledge as power' that determine the prevailing realm of popular culture/literature.

However, the dynamic, and therefore, volatile matrices of cultural populism into the field of popular culture often destabilise/subterfuge the critical apprehension of the former. Jim McGuigan (1992) has presciently suggested:

> a discernable narrowing of vision in cultural studies, exemplified by the drift into an uncritical populist mode of interpretation. I support the wish to understand and value everyday meanings, but, alone, such a wish produces inadequate explanations of the material life situations and power relations that shape the mediated experiences of ordinary people. (McGuigan 1992, 244)

Populist theory underscores that popular culture cannot be governed by the imposition of capitalist hegemony, by the interest of a bourgeois class, or by the dictates of a universal structure of class struggle, upon the ideological formation of people's expression; rather it intervenes more or less with a genuine impression of their thoughts and actions. This, according to McGuigan, is what is precisely wrong with it as it unintentionally endorses a homogenised dissection of popular belief. His main contestation concerns the neglect of 'the macro-processes of political economy'(Ibid.,172) as well as the failure of accountability for "both ordinary people's everyday culture and its material construction by powerful forces beyond the immediate comprehension and control of ordinary people" (Ibid., 175). Put simply, an empirical study of popular culture demands a more sociological-historical understanding of the society rather than just a re-examination of the 'signs of stress' in textual analysis, without which the visionary aspect of popular literature as alternative historiography of civilisational progress would appear to be nothing more than an inconsequential record of triviality (Strinati 2004, 252).

Trauma Culture and its Vicissitudes

Trauma narrative gains its literary as well as cultural currency in the West mostly through a series of stimulating representation and interpretation of the Holocaust, re-contextualising the psychological intricacies of ficto-historical accounts of the survivors/victims of that cataclysmic devastation. Such narratives constitute an intriguing cultural paradigm, as Roger Luckhurst points out the permeating effect of trauma in the present time, suggesting that "it (trauma) has been turned into a repertoire of compelling stories about the enigmas of identity, memory and selfhood that have saturated Western cultural life" (Luckhurst 2008, 80). In fact, the concept of trauma has been consistently prevalent in the contemporary study of history and its "all-inclusive" (Caruth 1995) magnitude has compulsively attracted both the critics and the curious readers simultaneously. Michael Rothberg convincingly discusses the co-temporality of trauma as an ever-evolving phenomenon, in the light of the Holocaust: "exploring the recent fascination with the Holocaust means exploring a more general contemporary fascination with trauma catastrophe, the fragility of memory, and the persistence of ethnic identity" (Rothberg 2000, 3). However, the epistemological debate over the subject of trauma being a generative ground for mass consumption through a vicarious experience of "the pain of others", to use Susan Sontag's phrase (2003), heavily depends upon the unhindered facilitation of media representation. The trial of Adolf Eichmann, which began on April 11, 1961,[2] was widely disseminated through radio, newspaper and the newly emerged television, possibly, marked the first entry of the unprecedented horror of the Holocaust into the popular culture. It infused the public consciousness with the dramatic display of raw emotions of the survivors followed by their personal narrations of the ghetto-life and the subsequent process of the Jewish massacre, directly addressed the triumph of social justice over the complicated judicial and historical accounts of Eichmann's part in the "Final Solution" (Rothe, 2011). The Western culture has witnessed more such popular manifestations of the genocide, for instance, in Roberto Benigni's critically acclaimed film *Life is Beautiful* (1998), Steven Spielberg's extraordinary blockbuster *Schindler's List* (1993), Roman Polanski's *The Pianist* (2003), to mention a few. More recent film adaptations of the trauma bestselling novels include Stephen Daldry's *The Reader* (2008), based on the German law Professor and crime author Bernhard Schlink's *Der Vorleser* (1995), Mark Herman's *The Boy in the Striped Pajamas* (2008) adapted from John Boyne's (2006) children's novel of the same name and many others that have gradually changed the modes of reception of Holocaust as a historically specified event and transformed it into a commercial site for critical as well as a popular medium of consumption.

The proliferation of popular trauma culture, centering around the irrefutable stipulation of traumatic experience, unwittingly triggers some imperative questions: in what possible way the idiosyncrasies of individual traumatic expression, frequently resulting in psycho-somatic disorder, can be inferred into linear, comprehensible language? Or what could be the ethics of reading trauma which is essentially represented through the economy-oriented, media-saturated social apparatus? Any speculation would lead to the liminality of cognitive faculty that could explicate the effect of trauma in its entirety. Dominick LaCapra points out a "tendency in modern culture" to compare trauma with "occasion" of sublimity:

> In the sublime, the excess of trauma becomes an uncanny source of elation or ecstasy. Even extremely destructive or disorienting events, such as the Holocaust or the dropping of atomic bombs on Hiroshima and Nagasaki, may be occasions of negative sublimity or displaced sacralization. (LaCapra 2001, 23)

Therefore, both trauma and sublime imply incoherency, disruption, pain, incommensurability and terror, marking the limits of reason and resisting undemanding representation. LaCapra further suggests the method of being "responsive" to such "disruptive experience that disarticulates the self and creates holes in existence" (Ibid., 41), which he has termed as "empathetic unsettlement" – that implicates a close link between trauma and ethics by posing "a barrier to closure in discourse and places in jeopardy harmonizing or spiritually uplifting accounts of extreme events" (Ibid.).

Another significant trope that eternalises the glory of historical trauma from which the cultural industry derives vicarious pleasure as well as moral values, is the act of mythification. Roland Barthes (1972) has postulated the elementary function of myth in social belief that "abolishes the complexity of human act" and "gives them the simplicity of essence" as it "organizes a world which is without contradictions" (Barthes 1972, 143), suppressing any sort of counter-narrative. Barthes has characterised myth as the "language of the oppressor", thus, being inherently hegemonic in nature. LaCapra traces the founding role of trauma back in the "myths of origin" (LaCapra 2001, xiii). Through a genealogical study of human history, he expatiates the legacy of loss and exile in the Old Testament, proceeding to the suffering and sacrifice of Christ in the New Testament which, in modern times, culminates into the corporeality of the Holocaust and other subsequent manmade disasters. The prefiguration of trauma kitsch, thus, continues to generate the suffering-and-redemption chronicle, re-establishing the grand narrative of a benevolent universal humanism over the dichotomous representation of evil versus goodness. Therefore, it can be argued that the 'superstructure' of such strategic mythification imperviously attempts to connect the ruptures created by the inexplicable narratives of trauma and transvalues it more into a capitalist commodity for consumption than a historical crisis.

Anne Frank's *Diary* as Symbolic Capital

The contemporary popularity of misery memoirs, singularly ascribing to the experiences of extremity within a specific socio-political framework, has become a unique phenomenon considering the recent revival of interest in 'critical memory studies'. Akin to the process of public symbol making, Anne Frank's canonisation also involved a diverse range of contested social constructions along with a rosy-representation of her journal, assigning her the position of a martyr who died in the face of extreme severity in the Nazi concentration camp in Bergen-Belsen. Since the publication of the English translation of her *Diary* in 1952, Frank has been metonymised as the symbol of hope and universal benevolence. One of her most enshrined quotations—"... in spite of everything, I still believe that people are good at heart"(July 15, 1944, 288) may seem to epitomise her unshakable faith in humanity, but this is also the most misrepresented line from her diary that tends to sum up the multiplicity of her complicated situation while hiding from the Nazi persecution in the "Annex". However, the metamorphosis of Anne Frank from a teenage girl who mainly depicted the anticipation of the Holocaust persecution along with a vivid awareness of the 'Final Solution' to an iconic optimistic figure has been promoted essentially through the 1955 Broadway play by Goodrich Hackett and Albert Hackett and then again the cinematic projection in *The Diary of Anne Frank* (1959) by George Stevens. According to Nora Nunn, both the versions of the *Diary* contentiously represented the journey of Frank and her family within the popular trope of victimisation, enticing a sentimentalised, commercial depiction which diverted the attention from more "inconvenient truths, such as the fact that, due to bureaucratic "red tape" and "national security concerns", the Frank family had been unable to enter the U.S. as refugees" (Nun 2020, 65), thus, eventually delineating the picture of a "rose-coloured genocide". One of the most vocal critics of the commercialisation of Frank's *Diary* was Cythia Ozick (1997) whose rueful indictment aptly presented the underlying capitalist structure:

> The story of Anne Frank in the fifty years since "The Diary of a Young Girl" was first published has been bowdlerized, distorted, transmuted, traduced, reduced; it has been infantilized, Americanized, homogenized, sentimentalized, falsified, kitschified, and in fact, blatantly and arrogantly denied. (Ozick 78)

Although it was not just this morally uplifting "harmonizing narrative" (LaCapra 2001), typical of American popular culture of that time, resonating the virtue of tolerance and the value of progress, that gives the text the unprecedented popularity; readers, as well as viewers, unwittingly identify with the rebellious zeal of Frank, her self-criticism, her adolescent romance with Peter van Pels, her shifting idealisms, her emotional turmoil with her parents, especially her mother and her constant acknowledgement of the unequivocal terror of captivation and the probable death. Marouf Hasian contends the "polysemic and polyvalent nature" (Hasian 2001, 362) of the Holocaust memoirs that overwhelmed the post-war decades in terms of popular read, especially the *Diary* of Anne Frank which, nonetheless, received much more attention from both the readers and the critics because,

> (t)his was obviously the type of genre that appealed to many audiences who were not going to read the works of writers like Gerald Reitlinger or Raul Hilberg. The *Diary* at least gave them some exposure to the Holocaust that might serve as a catalyst for inquiring minds who could learn more about the Judeocide on their own (Ibid., 363).

Precisely this is how *The Diary of a Young Girl* obtains the status of what Bourdieu has termed—'symbolic capital'. In his essay *The Forms of Capital* (2006), Bourdieu proposes to extend the sense of the term 'capital' by employing it in a wider network of exchange e.g. social, cultural, linguistic, rather than just a narrow inscription of the mercantile interchange. According to him, capital is i) *objectified*, ii) *embodied* and iii) *institutionalized*; therefore, the diverse system of cultural capital extensively depends upon its dialogic relationship with various forms of consciousness in terms of different social class or *habitus*, comprising of education, cultural taste, class, creed and other constitutive bodies. The precondition of symbolic capital is an accumulation of "well-constructed habitus", a sort of specialisation to understand the underlying formation of the symbolic structure so that eventually it can acquire a preponderant space in the market economy. The memory of trauma, as presented in the *Diary* of Anne Frank, has been objectified, embodied and institutionalised in the collective consciousness; its diachronic, as well as synchronic interpretations, have been the locus of many contested ideas, but at the same time, the text also anticipates assimilation of common interests, namely—the existential crisis of historical horror, the feeling of uncertainty and disorientation, the conflicts of hope and disappointment, all of which together make it a vivid testimony of what we understand as popular trauma culture.

Conclusion

In its attempt to contribute an argument against the homogenised tropes of the 'zeitgeist' of trauma culture, this essay presents an analytical endeavour to situate the problematics of 'authentic representation' of the Holocaust through the Americanised version of Anne Frank's *The Diary of a Young Girl*. In search of a faithful rendition of historical accuracy, the narratives of trauma, the inexplicable sufferings of the victims have been instrumentalised as cultural artefacts through the vigorous consumption of—misery memoirs, Television shows and operas, documentaries and films and more interestingly trauma-tourism or "dark tourism" (John Lennon and Foley 2004) which acts much like a modern-day pilgrimage to the 'spots' of history; a sort of vicarious participation in the grand historical experiences. Primo Levi (2012), a Holocaust survivor, ruminatively said, "one single Anne Frank moves us more than the countless others who suffered just as she did but whose faces remain in the shadows" (Levi 312). The monopoly of capitalism along with a thriving ascendency of the "culture of confession" (Atlas 1996), provides a generative site for popular trauma narratives, entailing the dual purpose of knowledge producer as well as commercial entertainment. The popular reception of the *Diary* indeed resembles the role of "truamatropism" (LaCapra 2001) which signifies the transformation of trauma from a banal psychosis into a quasi-religious phenomenon that produces a pattern, a meaning to the everyday-struggle for existence, but the erroneous act of valorising Anne Frank, the character, over her memoir, would inadvertently lead to a singular understanding of the process of her evolution from a mere observer of the Holocaust to a survivor, a believer in the true force of life. By attempting to universalise the discursiveness of her diary into a generic mould, stripping it from its essential individualism, the populist theory of interpretation, thus, perpetuates the complacency of a depoliticised version of the genocide, leading to cultural amnesia.

Notes:

1. Both the terms 'mass culture' and 'culture industry' have been used by the Adorno and Horkheimer in their seminal book *Dialectics of Enlightenment* (1973, originally published in 1947), to signify the commodity fetishism of the capitalist culture. The Frankfurt School evaluates the culture industry as ensuring and creating a false need and satisfaction through the projection of mass consumption. However, Walter Benjamin, whose intellectual activities were resonating with the ideals of the school for a while, but his cultural analyses, later, appears to differ from that of Adorno's. Benjamin has clearly seen more potential into the expansion of mass literacy along with a growing consonance of technology. His stimulating essay *The Work of Art in the Age of Mechanical Reproduction* (1973) provides an insightful study of this argument.
2. Both the terms 'mass culture' and 'culture industry' have been used by the Adorno and Horkheimer in their seminal book *Dialectics of Enlightenment* (1973, originally published in 1947), to signify the commodity fetishism of the capitalist culture. The Frankfurt School evaluates the culture industry as ensuring and creating a false need and satisfaction through the projection of mass consumption. However, Walter Benjamin, whose intellectual activities were resonating with the ideals of the school for a while, but his cultural analyses, later, appears to differ from that of Adorno's. Benjamin has clearly seen more potential into the expansion of mass literacy along with a growing consonance of technology. His stimulating essay *The Work of Art in the Age of Mechanical Reproduction* (1973) provides an insightful study of this argument.

Bibliography:

Adorno, Theodor. 1991. *The Culture Industry*. London: Routledge.

Atlas, James. 1996. "Confessing for Voyeurs: The Age of the Literary Memoir is Now." *The New York Times*. May 12, Sunday, Late Edition, Section 6; Page 25; Column 1.

Barthes, Roland. 1972. *Mythologies*. New York: Hill and Wang.

Benjamin, Walter. 1973. 'The Work of Art in the Age of Mechanical Reproduction'. In *Illuminations*. London: Fontana [1936].

Bloom, Clive (ed.). 2002. *Bestsellers: Popular Fiction Since 1900*, New York: Palgrave Macmillan.

Bourdieu, Pierre. 1993. *The Field of Cultural Production*. Cambridge: Polity Press.

... 1999. *Distinction: A Social Critique on the Judgement of Taste*, London: Routledge.

... "The Forms of Capital". 2006. In *Education, Globalisation and Social Change*, edited by H. Lauder, P. Brown, J.-A. Dillabough and A. H. Halsey. Oxford: Oxford University Press.

Caruth, Cathy (ed.). 1995. "Introduction." In *Trauma: Explorations in Memory*, Baltimore: The Johns Hopkins University Press.

Frank, Anne. 1997. *The Diary of A Young Girl: The Definitive Edition*. Frank, H. Otto and Pressler, Mirjam (ed.), Massotty, Susan (translated). Doubleday: Bentham Books.

Gilmore, Leigh (ed.). 2001. *The Limits of Autobiography: Trauma and Testimony*, USA: Cornell University Press.

Grenfell, Michael (ed.). 2008. *Pierre Bourdieu: Key Concepts*. Stocksfield Hall: Acumen.

Hasian, Marouf. 2001. "Anne Frank, Bergen-Belsen, and the Polysemic Nature of Holocaust Memories". *Rhetoric and Public Affairs*, Vol. 4, no. 3 (Fall): 349-374.

LaCapra, Dominick (ed.). 2001. *Writing History, Writing Trauma*. London: Johns Hopkins University Press.

Lennon, John and Foley, Malcolm (ed.). 2004. *Dark Tourism: The Attraction of Death and Disaster*. Andover, UK: Thomson Learning.

Levi, Primo. 2012. quoted in Barbara Kirshenblatt-Gimblett and Jeffrey Shandler, eds., *Anne Frank Unbound: Media, Imagination, Memory*, Bloomington: Indiana University Press, 2012, 312.

Luckhurst, Roger (ed.). 2008. *The Trauma Question*. London and New York: Routledge.

McCraken, Scott (ed.). 1998. *Pulp: Reading Popular Fiction*, New York: Manchester University Press.

McGuigan, Jim. 1992. *Cultural Populism*. London: Routledge.

Murphy, M. Bernice (ed.). 2017. *Key Concepts in Contemporary Popular Fiction*, Edinburgh: Edinburgh University Press.

Nadal, Maria and Calvo, Monica (ed.). 2014. "Introduction" in *Trauma in Contemporary Literature: Narrative and Representation*. New York: Routledge.

Nunn, Nora. 2020. "Rose-Colored Genocide: Hollywood, Harmonizing Narratives, and the Cinematic Legacy of Anne Frank's Diary in the United States". *Genocide Studies and Prevention: An International Journal*, Vol. 14, iss. 2: 65-89.

Onega, Susana and Ganteau, Jean-Michel (ed.). 2014. "Introduction" in *Contemporary Trauma Narratives: Liminality and The Ethics of Form*. New York: Routledge.

Ozick, Cynthia. "The Misuse of Anne Frank's Diary." *The New Yorker*, September 29, 1997. https://www.newyorker.com/magazine/1997/10/06/who-owns-annefrank. Accessed on 29th August, 2020.

Rothberg, Michael (ed.). 2000. *Traumatic Realism: The Demands of Holocaust Representation*. Minneapolis: University of Minnesota Press.

Rothe, Anne (ed.). 2011. *Popular Trauma Culture: Selling the Pain of Others in the Mass Media*, London: Rutgers University Press.

Sagan, Alex. 1995. "An Optimistic Icon: Anne Frank's Canonization in Postwar Culture". *German Politics & Society*, Vol. 13, no. 3 (36): 95-107.

Sontag, Susan (ed.). 2003. *Regarding the Pain of Others*. New York: Picador.

Storey, John (ed.). 2009. "The Frankfurt School". In *Cultural Theory and Popular Culture: An Introduction*. London: Pearson and Longman.

Strinati, Dominic (ed.). 2004. *An Introduction to Theories of Popular Culture*, London: Routledge, 2004.

Phantasmagoria of the Hegemonic Cultural Structure: Interrogating the Indian Urban Facade in Chetan Bhagat's *Half Girlfriend*

Jaya Sarkar and Goutam Karmakar

Popular fiction provides us with a temporary sense of the self and also a structure within which our lives can be understood. Popular fiction has emerged to be a 'craft,' which not many can write successfully, but those who do earn great reputations. This genre of fiction includes production, output, deadlines, sequels, which makes it much more difficult than other genres. This form of high cultural production has achieved its popularity over the years by breaking the myth of dealing with trivial issues that can be spared any serious literary discussions and dialogues.[1] Most of the readers at stations, airports, or those who require to pass some time pick up a popular fiction since it is "unencumbered by educational apparatuses and pedagogical pressures, free from workplace stress. It is also true that readers of popular fiction read faster" (Gelder 2004, 37). Chetan Bhagat has established himself as a prominent popular fiction writer who is incredibly prolific, and churns out novels at regular intervals, maintaining the creative output over a long period. Besides performing the roles of any other popular fiction such as providing leisure, making the facts believable, and reading fast, Bhagat's novels also make the readers *think*. More often than not, he highlights those issues which we come across every day but never consider their seriousness. From issues such as financial conflicts, inter-caste marriages, Indian politics, to the portrayal of the difficulty of Indian students while speaking fluent English, Bhagat has covered a wide range.

Half Girlfriend, Bhagat's sixth novel published in 2014, deals with the issue of semantic-cultural hegemony of the English language in the urban Indian society. Dedicated to the *"non-English types*" (emphasis is mine), the novel demonstrates how the English language as the medium of instruction and communication has crept into the Indian education system and resulted in academic capitalism. Bhagat interprets this also as a class conflict between the English and non-English speakers of the country. This becomes instantly relevant in a country where a large part of the population still struggles to speak English. The interrogation into the class structure and class struggle is also represented through Madhav Jha's linguistic struggle and his love interest for a high-class girl, Riya Somani. Madhav comes from Dumraon, Bihar and arrives to the courtyard of St. Stephen's College in Delhi on the merit of his sports quota and with high hopes and big dreams. As soon as he arrives, he realises his struggle to speak fluent English will be a marker for his merit, proficiency, and social inclusion. He falls in love with Riya, a fellow sports quota holder but one who speaks fluent English and belongs to the high-class society of Delhi. Madhav proposes Riya to be his 'half girlfriend' which further problematises their relationship and re-intensifies the class difference and class consciousness, prohibiting Riya to be Madhav's 'full girlfriend.'

Educational Institution as an ISA and a Panopticon

In his "Ideology and Ideological State Apparatuses (Notes towards an Investigation)" (1971), Louis Althusser asserts that the chief function of the state is to exercise its hegemony and mediate capitalist interests within democratic contexts through different state apparatuses.[2] People under the state, engages with its different apparatuses such as religious and educational institutions, family, cultural and political groups, media outlets, etc. through which knowledge is imparted to them on how to be proper subjects. Each of these state apparatuses influences the individual's daily activities and makes their notion of a free subject an illusion. This transformation from an individual to a subject is done through ideology by a process of interpellation. As such, subjecthood is materialised only through the mediation of certain structures and practices and "these practices are governed by the rituals in which these practices are inscribed, within the material existence of an ideological apparatus" (Althusser 1971, 168). The ideology of the capitalist class controls the state apparatuses through the reproduction of conditions of production and reproduction of relations of production. Hegemony thus relies on these Ideological State Apparatuses (ISAs) to inculcate ideology in all subjects. The education system is a crucial state apparatus that reproduces the values of the dominant class, and promotes corporatisation. Its function is complex, since it is the stake as well as the site of class struggle. Althusser believes that the educational institution is the core of ideological state apparatuses: it produces subjects and teaches them the proper conduct of behaviour, morals and ethics. This way the educational institution has replaced the Church by taking over the role of the reproduction of the relations of production. The educational institution as an ISA takes over the dominant role in the capitalist society and conceals the ruling class ideology behind its liberating qualities of creativity and freedom, so as to keep their agendas inconspicuous. This false consciousness provokes the subjects to behave in a certain way, and adopt certain practices which conform to the ideology of the state.

In the habitation of St. Stephen's, English-speaking is the norm and is established as a principle of coercion with the illusion of a standardised education for all. For people like Madhav and the villagers of Dumraon, English-speaking people indicate status and privilege. This level of affiliation makes it easier to normalise the speaking of the language but simultaneously it also plays a part in hierarchisation and classification. For Madhav, being able to speak fluently in English would make him a better fit in his college. This is the brilliance of educational institutions like St. Stephen's as ISA since they carry out the hegemony through their willing subjects. The subjects surrender to the domination and the ISA imposes concrete control over them. From the time of his interview, Madhav was made to realise that not being able to speak fluent English is a disadvantage and it is unacceptable at St. Stephen's college. While this realisation remains on the level of ideology, the bureaucratisation of students leads to the complete loss of liberty. Those who are not able to speak fluent English are not recognised as worthy, capable, or responsible in any way. From the moment Madhav enters the interview-room, he becomes a subject of ridicule for the interview panel consisting of some of the distinguished teachers of the country. Even for those teachers, being able to speak fluent English is the sole marker of the student's worth. From this moment, Madhav realises that this is how the urban society will treat him if he does not learn proper English: "Without English, I felt naked. I started thinking about my return trip to Bihar. I didn't belong here—these English-speaking monsters would eat me alive" (Bhagat 2014, 19). For Madhav, learning English is also synonymous with achieving Riya's love and later on earning the grant from the Gates Foundation. He is webbed in the requirements of the capitalist society and never gets the opportunity to love the language, for it has always been a necessity for him. However, the same ISA does not apply for a foreigner like Phil who visits India and is unaware of the language of the country. For him, being unable to speak any Indian language is justified and adds to his charm: "'Namaste,' Phil addressed the audience. That one word in Hindi made the audience swoon in ecstasy. This is how we Indians are. If white guys speak even a tiny bit of Hindi, we love them" (Ibid., 204). The state apparatus controlling Madhav has no control over Phil, since he is not an inhabitant of the state, but is an important contributor to the economy of the capitalist society.

The unquestioned adherence to the ISA and the illusion of the capitalist ideology as a natural and harmonious force, restricts the students to question the dominant capitalist narratives. To pay a little attention to the mechanisation of St. Stephen's, it should also be considered that they are training their students to be a good corporate worker or a bureaucrat. This training of social efficiency is marketed to the students and they accept their own exploitation. So, they become willing subjects of the state apparatus while chasing ideas like increased intelligence, establishing themselves, and a bright future. It is in this way ideology "represents the imaginary relationship of individuals to their real conditions of existence" (Althusser 1971, 162). The students are coerced into a condition of passive acceptance and the exploitation seems to be legitimate. As an ISA, St. Stephen's guarantees the reproduction of existing capitalistic means of production: "All ideological State apparatuses, whatever they are, contribute to the same result: the reproduction of the relations of production, i.e., of capitalist relations of exploitation" (Ibid., 154). The English-speaking hegemony of St. Stephen's as an ISA aims at preparing the students to capitulate to the reproduction of existing forms of the economic society, rather than preparing them to participate as emancipated and liberated agents in the society.

St. Stephen's becomes a sort of Panopticon, a blockaded space for Madhav where normal rules are suspended: "This enclosed, segmented space, observed at every point, in which the individuals are inserted in a fixed place, in which the slightest movements are supervised, in which all events are recorded" (Foucault 1995, 197). Madhav is constantly examined and supervised in the college and its surroundings. In Madhav's mind, there is always an assumed gaze that induces in him a state of consciousness. Foucault argues that Marxism and liberalism operate together since discipline is intricately connected with the production and the division of labour. St. Stephen's as an ISA produces labour and hence, it imposes its surveillance power on its students by creating an illusioned elitist environment to which everyone must adhere to. St. Stephen's with its modern power advances its disciplines for the production of docile bodies rather than individuals.[3] It creates a standard of appearance and behaviour for its subjects. The docile bodies are shaped by the state apparatuses so that they are easy to manage and control:

> The human body was entering a machinery of power that explores it, breaks it down and rearranges it. A 'political anatomy', which was also a 'mechanics of power', was being born; it defined how one may have a hold over others' bodies, not only so that they may do what one wishes, but so that they may operate as one wishes, with the techniques, the speed and the efficiency that one determines. Thus discipline produces subjected and practised bodies, 'docile' bodies. (Ibid., 138)

The more subjects conform to this norm, the more powerful the norm becomes. Madhav posits little or no resistance at all to this norm, and willingly surrenders to it. The fear of social disapproval is powerful and this prevents any resistance from the subjects. This is how such power structures of the society operate by instilling the fear in the subjects. Besides the norm of speaking fluent English, St. Stephen's also normalises a certain fashion and way of life. For instance, expensive cars, hearing English music, attending elitist events, parties become part of the social norms. These norms make Madhav constantly practice self-surveillance and self-correction which results in his transformation into a 'docile' body. The constant need of 'improving' himself in order to fit into the dictates of the capitalist society demonstrates how Madhav conforms to the established norms and becomes obedient to the rules of the capitalist society. In this way, St. Stephen's no longer remains "a place where the cognitive processes can freely develop," but a place that governs and controls the movements of docile bodies (Bánovčanová and Masaryková 2014, 257).

In India, the dominant ideology is applied through classes. The caste system in India is another ISA with consequent socio-economic and political connotations. The higher castes enjoy a sort of upward mobility and social status, and maintain their hegemony over the lower castes. This hegemony of the caste system serves both as the ideology and also instigates violence upon the oppressed classes to sustain its own being and also to control the socio-political relations. This capitulation of the students to the economist society works in two ways. Firstly, the students believe it is their own choice to be a part of this society. Socially privileged students like Riya even after dropping out, manages to find a prospective job that guarantees financial security. But for students like Madhav, Ashu, Raman and Shailesh, who attend the college, despite their day-to-day humiliation due to their inability to speak fluent English, their individuality dissipates and they believe that this is how "the real world" functions:

> All four of us came front Bihar or Jharkhand, and none of us were the 'classy' types you find in Stephen's. For instance, nobody in Stephen's would say they watched Bhojpuri movies. We loved them. We liked Hindi music, from Mohammed Rafi in the sixties to Pritam in the here and now. We didn't understand English music beyond one song by Michael Jackson — 'Beat it'. Of course, we never admitted all this to the rest of our classmates. We nodded our heads every time someone mentioned a great English movie or brought a rock CD to class. 'Yeah, yeah, cool,' we said. (Bhagat 2014, 56)

Rather than being satisfied with their present status, the students embark on a journey of a competency collection and desires for higher levels of achievements. Deleuze argues that in a "society of control one is never finished with anything" (Deleuze 1992, 5). Even when Madhav successfully graduates and gets a job offer from a private bank, he still struggles with his English-speaking abilities to further his career. In his attempt to convince the Bill Gates Foundation for donating some money for his school, Madhav once again struggles with his speech in English. Despite his achievements, English remains a marker for recognising his worth. In a helpless attempt Madhav comes up with a speech to communicate the hardships faced by the students of his school:

> 'Good morning, Mr Bill Gates, Miss Samantha and guests. I, Madhav, welcoming you all to the Bihar, My school doing excellent coaching of children, farmer's children, poor children, small children...' I couldn't think of what to say next so I referred to various kinds of children, I continued, '...boy children, girl children, and many, many children,'
> I heard my mother snigger.
> 'What?' I said,
> 'Who are all these children?' I scratched my head.
> 'Anyway,' I continued. 'My school needing toilet as nobody able to toileting when toilet time coming,'
> My mother burst out laughing. (Bhagat 2014, 141-142)

It was with his perseverance and Riya's help that Madhav accomplishes the task and successfully delivers a speech in fluent English which results in the securing of the grant money for his school.

Fetishisation of the City and the Subsequent Exclusion

Half Girlfriend depicts in clear terms how an exclusion of a group of city residents is carried out throughout the novel. This exclusion is two-fold: first, Madhav and his friends are excluded from access to all that St. Stephen's and Delhi has to offer based on their class, caste and their inability to speak fluent English; second, Riya is excluded in Dumraon based on her being a city-girl and her elitist upbringing:

> 'How come she's already married and divorced?'
> 'That surprised me too. I ran into her in Patna by chance.'
> 'And she latched on to you,' Ma said.
> 'Not true. I can't study English all the time, Ma. I need friends there. Besides, she helps me practise. Her English is excellent. She is from a high-class society.'
> 'I can see the class,' my mother said. (Bhagat 2014, 179)

When a metropolitan person like Riya is placed in a small town, she feels barriers around her which were not there as long as she existed in her natural habitat. For her, Dumraon becomes an enforcer of restrictions and her boundaries as an individual also dissolves. Her conduct of life and outlook are questioned as soon as she is put out of the metropolis. Both for Madhav and Riya the exclusion is cultural, where "the group members are marginalised from the symbols, meanings, rituals, and discourses of the dominant culture" (Madanipour 2011, 186). This cultural exclusion revolves around the denial of access to resources and common narratives. The more restricted these resources are, the more restricted are the social and spatial options. Having a wide range of social options allows one to go to places for work and entertainment. For someone like Madhav, access to "Agni at the Park" is not possible because of his cultural exclusion.

Besides the urban space, there is also the concept of mental space or one's own perceptions of space. This is regulated through signs which individuals perceive themselves and prevents them from entering some spaces:

> Capitalist society tends to separate its own conditions from each other. The effect of separation is inherent to this society, to its efficiency; it is based, practically, on the division of labor pushed to the extreme by the analytic intellect. By projecting them onto the background, by making them perceptible, the separation reveals the internal contradictions of society that are generally inaccessible to the senses. (Lefebvre 2000, 119)

Social exclusion leads one to be hesitant to enter elitist surroundings even when there are no other real barriers. The public-private boundaries are a result of a combination of informal signs, fears and hesitance for the limitations of an individual's cultural exclusion. Madanipour writes in "Social Exclusion and Space" that the hegemonic capitalist society promotes socio-spatial segregation through market forces. The large-scale housing estates create an urban fabric and ensure the segregation among social classes. The capitalist society expects its commodities to be safe and hence guards their space against intrusion. In "The Right to the City," David Harvey writes: "Cities become more ghettoized as the rich seal themselves off for protection while the poor become ghettoized by default" (Harvey 2003, 940). The class division along with the caste and ethnic divisions results in the monopoly of the power of the dominant class. The marginalised groups willingly surrender their rights to the city once they experience the social exclusion. In Bhagat's novel, when Madhav goes to attend Riya's birthday party, Aurangzeb Road with its massive mansions seems like an enchanted place to him. This particular urban space is not accessible to those who do not belong to the dominant class of the society. The fragmented and gated neighbourhood of 100, Aurangzeb Road is always under heavy private surveillance and restricts any form of intrusion by the socially excluded groups. Hence, when Madhav requests entry to Riya's house, the surveillance is many-fold:

> In college I underwent no layers of security to meet Riya. I felt awkward standing and waiting so I made conversation with the guard.
> 'Are you from Bihar?' I said.
> 'Yes, from Munger. You?'
> 'Dumraon.'
> 'And you are Riya madam's friend?' he said. I heard the condescension in his voice. A low-class can smell another low-class. (Bhagat 2014, 60)

This condescending behaviour is followed by other instances of cultural and social exclusion at the party (Mr. Somani's shift in attitude when he learns that Madhav hails from Bihar, judging Madhav based on his English proficiency by Riya's friends, keeping Madhav aloof from Rohan's plan of attending another party). These instances depict how those belonging to the urban space assert their dominance and keep the segregation in check, when their space is accessed by the marginalised groups.

In "Poverty and the 'City'," Susan Parnell argues that urban poverty is quite different from its rural counterpart. In cities, being unable to participate in social life because of poverty, leads to the exclusion. Regardless of being rich or poor, "'the city' is the material, operational and ideological scale that mediates contemporary humans' identity, economy and investment" (Parnell 2015, 22). Decentralisation and privatisation of the material resources of the city are solely controlled by its local elites. Hence, Madhav who is already subjected to social exclusion, gets further segregated from the material resources which the city has to offer. Similar to the material resources, social welfare is also controlled by the patriarchal elites in capitalist societies. Gender is another factor that plays a role in the unequal distribution of resources. In Bhagat's novel, we find Riya and her mother, both being victims of urban poverty, since their lives are completely dependent on the elites of the likes of Mr. Somani and Rohan. Riya is subjected to physical and mental violence by both her father and her husband. When she decides to marry Rohan, she is enchanted by the promise of an adventurous and a luxurious life in a foreign country. As soon as that capitalist illusion comes to an end, Riya realises how the dynamics of power operated in the city and her household. When she leaves Rohan and comes back to Delhi, she again steps into her urban household, where possessing and keeping a hold on to the prestige is crucial, whether it's materialistic or elitist dignity:

> 'Women have to learn to adjust, beta,' my mother said.
> 'Adjust? How does one adjust to violence?'
> I lifted my left hand to show her the swelling. Rohan had pushed me and I had broken my wrist.
> 'What will people say?' Mom blurted out. (Bhagat 2014, 223)

"Two sets of reactions to the diversity in the city can be identified: there are those who have tried to impose an order onto it so that it becomes understandable and manageable and those who promote a celebration of diversity", observes Madanipour (2011, 190). We see both of these sets of reactions in *Half Girlfriend*. The first set of reaction includes the interview panel at St. Stephen's, Riya's family and friends who try to impose the dominant language and culture on everyone residing in the city. The second set of reaction would be from Riya herself, who tells Madhav in very clear terms: "What you say matters, not the language" (Bhagat 2014, 33). This shows how the city is situated at an interface of 'near order' and 'far order.' Riya, Piyush Yadav, Madhav's friends and Samantha might be considered as those relations of Madhav who support him and comprise the 'near order.' The 'far order' of the society is regulated by the large and powerful institution of the dominant culture which imposes its power, although appearing as "abstract, formal, suprasensible and transcending in appearances" (Lefebvre 2000, 101). However, the 'far order' always tries to project itself on the 'near order,' and tries to subordinate it using their ideologies. By this act of subordination, the city maintains its relations of production and property. We witness through the course of the novel, how Riya and Shailesh are subjected to subordination by the 'far order' of the city. Both of them become a part of the production of relations of power and become active agents through which the domination is carried out. For Shailesh, he becomes a part of the bourgeois class:

> Shailesh had done an MBA from Harvard after Stephen's. He had joined Goldman Sachs, a top Wall Street investment bank. He shared the apartment with his girlfriend, Jyoti, whom he had met at Harvard. Jyoti worked at Morgan Stanley, another Wall Street investment bank. The size of the apartment told me the banks paid them well. Dark circles under Shailesh's eyes told me they also made him work hard. (Bhagat 2014, 238-239)

Similarly, Riya decides to marry Rohan based on his class, the privileges it promises, and for the desire of claiming a right to the city of London.

The urban networks such as 100 Aurangzeb Road and the Chandak household in the two cities are largely hidden and opaque from public view. This contributes to the tense relationships and the power mechanisms operating in those spaces. The phantasmagoria of and the fascination with St. Stephen's and Aurangzeb Road, with their roles as ideological apparatuses and also objects of admiration and desire, suggests their transformation into fetishised products for Madhav.[4] Both of these urban networks "enshrined an instrumentality in terms of reifying social relations" (Kaika and Swyngedouw 2000, 130). The fascinations with these networks mask the underlying power relations. The display keeps the phantasmagoric character alive and it infuses with a utopian dream of possessing the objects of desire:

> Phantasmagoria is thus a fantastic illusion, but a necessary one, without which the texture of 'reality' would disintegrate (Andreotti and Lahiji 2017, 10).[5]

However, the fetishised objects of desire strip themselves off from their ideology and reveal the exploitation of the labour involved in the process of the production of relations of power. St. Stephen's, 100 Aurangzeb Road and the city of Delhi lose their fascination for Madhav and he becomes disenchanted with his utopian dream. The city had appeared as an 'exhibition of the world' for Madhav, when he arrived in Delhi, but he soon witnessed the unfolding of the phantasmagoria of the capitalist society masking behind its glamour.

Madhav's biggest challenge during his stay in Delhi and New York, was to preserve his individuality amidst overwhelming social forces of two external cultures. The metropolis creates psychological conditions where "the sharp discontinuity in the grasp of a single glance, and the unexpectedness of onrushing impressions" becomes lasting impressions (Simmel 2010, 104). This was the reason why Madhav fell in love in the first sight of Riya. His mind became stimulated with the momentary impression of Riya at the basketball court, and he held on to that throughout the course of three years in Delhi and even later on when he went back to his native place. That one momentary impression became rooted in the unconscious layers of Madhav's psyche. Even after repeated rejections, Madhav becomes indifferent to his individuality because his reactions and feelings could not be exhausted with logical operations. For Riya and Rohan, their matter-of-fact attitude was intimately related to their dominant class in the metropolis. However, Madhav was never one of them and so he couldn't get over his feelings with the same matter-of-fact attitude.

However, the metropolitan person is not always 'free' in a refined sense, and are more often than not victims of the same pettiness and prejudices to which they subject the small-town person. In London, within the Chandak household, Riya suffers from an exclusion more so because of her gender rather than her social status. Her dressing style, her freedom, and choice of profession are constantly scrutinised and she is even subjected to force and violence when she refuses to participate in the metropolis culture. This is an instance of what Simmel argues that "one nowhere feels as lonely and lost as in the metropolitan crowd" (Ibid.). The narrowness of the space results in the mental distance which grips Riya all her life. She is subjected to violence in the households of both metropolitan cities of Delhi and London, and yet her suffering goes unnoticed even by the members of the same households. The immediate size and area of the metropolis are always in contrast to the extent of freedom one experiences in it.

Conclusion

Half Girlfriend, as a popular fiction, succeeds in portraying the many complexities behind the cumbersome urban life which is both a site and an initiator of class struggle. Throughout the course of this chapter, it is highlighted that Madhav's linguistic abilities problematically determine his social status and literacy, despite his many achievements. Using English as the primary medium of instruction, St. Stephen's and the semantic cultural hegemonic society of Delhi try to mechanise Madhav into a domination with consent. However, Madhav resists as much as he can, through his rejection of the job offer. It was the fantasy of attaining Riya's love that makes Madhav a docile body in St. Stephen's, but once, he goes back to Dumraon, he regains some of the individuality that he lost in Delhi. Once Madhav successfully crosses the barrier of linguistic restrictions, he becomes confident about Riya being his 'full girlfriend.' At this juncture, the cultural exclusion which Riya suffers in Dumraon further hinders their relationship. Once Madhav and Riya put aside the different exclusions they have been subjected to by the city, the household, and the hegemonic culture, they forge a strong relationship which results in marriage. This popular fiction, thus, manages to bring to the forefront the many serious and complex issues of capitalist hegemony and disenchantment through which the Indian urban socio-cultural structure operates.

Notes:

1. Ken Gelder associates popular fiction with two keywords: industry and entertainment, which results in making the field of popular culture a 'culture industry.'
2. The state apparatus is composed of various institutions which coalesce into governmental, coercive, administrative, and ideological groups. Expanding on Marx's state structure, Althusser argues that the state apparatus has an economic base and a superstructure which includes ideological state apparatus.
3. Foucault refers to 'docile bodies' as those bodies which are closely related to the discipline imposed by social organisations, using the techniques of enclosure, partitioning, and functional sites. These techniques put individuals in their own separate place and then monitors those places. A 'rank' is assigned to each individual and they are expected to behave according to that particular role and place.
4. Marx uses the term 'phantasmagoria' to refer to the fetish role played by the commodities in the market. Walter Benjamin uses the same term to refer to the scene of urban modernity. He argues that the hyper-mediated city witnesses a new reality in which "the totalization of earlier trends generates extreme and paradoxical levels of concentration, disintegration, dispersal — new kinds of sensory bombardment, and new forms of control that must be examined and theorized" (Andreotti and Lahiji 2).
5. Phantasmagoria from its very origin has been instruments to produce illusions and hallucinations in horror shows. In the contemporary moment, it is used in parallel with Baudrillard's concept of hyperreality. Phantasmagoria thus becomes a 'fantasy structure' which governs the specters of a city.

Bibliography:

Althusser, Louis. 1971. "Ideology and Ideological State Apparatuses (Notes towards an Investigation)." In *Lenin and Philosophy and Other Essays*, 127-186. New York: Monthly Review Press.

Andreotti, Libero, and Nadir Lahiji. 2017. *The Architecture of Phantasmagoria: Specters of the City*. London: Routledge.

Bánovčanová, Zuzana, and Dana Masaryková. 2014. "The Docile Body- Reflecting the School." *Journal of Pedagogy*, Vol. 5, no. 2: 251-264. doi: 10.2478/jped-2014-0012.

Bhagat, Chetan. 2014. *Half Girlfriend*. Delhi: Rupa Publications.

Deleuze, Gilles. 1992. "Postscript on the Societies of Control." *October*, Vol. 59: 3-7. JSTOR. www.jstor.org/stable/778828. Accessed on 3rd March, 2021.

Foucault, Michel. 1995. *Discipline & Punish: The Birth of the Prison*. Translated by Alan Sheridan. New York: Vintage Books.

Gelder, Ken. 2004. *Popular Fiction: The Logics and Practices of a Literary Field*. London: Routledge.

Harvey, David. 2003. "The Right to the City." *International Journal of Urban and Regional Research*, Vol. 27, no. 4: 939-941.

Kaika, Maria, and Erik Swyngedouw. "Fetishizing the Modern City: The Phantasmagoria of Urban Technological Networks." 2000. *International Journal of Urban and Regional Research*, Vol. 24, no. 1: 120-138.

Lefebvre, Henri. 2000. "The Specificity of the City." In *Writing on Cities: Henri Lefebvre*, edited by Eleonore Kofman and Elizabeth Lebas, 100-103. Oxford: Blackwell Publishers Ltd.

...2016. *Marxist Thought and the City*. Translated by Robert Bononno. Minneapolis: University of Minnesota Press.

Madanipour, Ali. 2011. "Social Exclusion and Space." In *Social Exclusion in European Cities: Processes, Experiences, and Responses*, edited by Ali Madanipour, Goran Cars, and Judith Allen, 186-194. London: Routledge.

Parnell, Susan. 2015. "Poverty and 'the City'." In *The City in Urban Poverty*, edited by Charlotte Lemanski and Colin Marx, 16-38. London: Palgrave Macmillan.

Simmel, Georg. 2010. "The Metropolis and Mental Life." In *The Blackwell City Reader*, edited by Gary Bridge and Sophie Watson, 103-110. Oxford: Blackwell Publishing Ltd.

Relocating the Classic as Popular: Reading *Jane Eyre* as a Romance

Madhuparna Mitra Guha and Rupayan Mukherjee

To claim *Jane Eyre* is a popular literary text can be an arguable assertion or proposition. But to argue that *Jane Eyre* can be canonised as Popular Literature is possibly blasphemous. It is likely to enrage highbrow scholars who revere the canon as an unquestionable, sacrosanct, prelapsarian, 'pure' truth. It is likely to annoy the reactionary safeguards of culture who believe in water-tight distinctions between high and profane culture, elite and popular literature, classics and best-sellers and are perpetually apprehensive of any possible overlaps. It is likely to discomfort the English reader of the postcolonial Nation state who has interiorised the fabricated truth, owing to the legacy of a colonial ideological apparatus, that popular Victorian novelists were/ are prophets and their works were/ are not meant to be read for leisure but with the deeper motive of learning the lessons of civilisation. Even the reigning regime of Postcolonialism fails to convince the diligent third-world reader to read *Jane Eyre* as Popular Literature. The possibility of such a radical engagement with the novel is clearly not permitted by the prevalent popular ethics of reading.

Yet, esoteric readings, or what Hillis Miller calls "good reading" (Miller 1987, 189), have tried to respond to the novel outside the characteristic response of reverence. In doing so, these readings have tried to dissect the novel to explore the contentions of class, race, gender in the novel. Whether such readings have managed to profanise the text or strengthen its position as a Classic within the literary canon of Literature is debatable and is difficult to answer. But what does stand out is a relatively autonomous mode of reading that attempts to approach the text in a non-ritualised manner, free from any pre-discursive inhibition. Such readings have considerably contextualised the novel and in doing so, have tried to negate the universalistic strains that are often typically identified with the English literary canon. Thus, for instance, Chris R. Vanden Bossche argues that the novel has dominant symptoms of class consciousness and "...deploys the language of class in order to confront a series of social situations". (Bossche 2005, 47) For Gayatri Spivak, *Jane Eyre*, like any nineteenth century British literary text, cannot be possibly read without "...remembering that imperialism...was a crucial part of the cultural representation of England to the English". (Spivak 1985, 243) Spivak is critical of the "high feminist norm" (Ibid.) that an isolationist reading of the novel propagates and thereby ignores the tropes of individualism that is dominant in the text, which makes Jane an accomplice in the project of English imperialism. Spivak argues that it is "...the active ideology of imperialism..." (Ibid. 247) and the "unquestioned ideology of imperialist axiomatics...that conditions Jane's move from the counter-family set to the set of the family-in-law" (Ibid. 248)

The present chapter follows such reading tendencies and argues that the novel can be considered as an ideal case of Popular turned classic. The chapter reads the novel as a Romance and, through a close reading of the text, further reflects upon the possibility of considering the novel as an "ideal Romance" (Radway 1984, 119). For this purpose, the chapter initially engages in a historical reading of the material conditions of production and reception of the novel to argue that the motive of popularity was an important consideration for the novelist. The chapter then traces the features of an ideal Romance in the novel only to argue that the novel is not a Romance but a more than Romance.

That *Jane Eyre* was a popular literary text in its own time is a relatively undisputable assertion. Elizabeth Rigby's derogatory review of the novel, published in *The Quarterly Review*, observed that the book has enjoyed a "great popularity" (Rigby 1848) and held the book's ability to combine "genuine power with horrid taste" (ibid.) as the principal reason behind its unfailing success. Another review published in *The Christian Remembrancer* stated that "...the public taste seems to have outstripped its guides in appreciating the remarkable power which the book displays" (*Christian Remembrancer* 1848, 396). Such apparently unappreciative reviews had a silver lining for the aspirant writer writing under the *nom de plume* of Currer Bell and writing "because I (she) cannot help it" (Brontë 1836 (a), 407). They were validations of the novel's substantial success among mass readership and oblique encouragements to the woman writer who had lifelong aspired to be an author.

Charlotte Brontë had aspired to pursue writing professionally since a very early age. In 1836, a twenty-year old Brontë had enclosed a set of poems with her letter to Robert Southey, the then poet-laureate of England, firmly stating that she aspired to be "forever known" as a poetess (Brontë 1836 (b), xix-xx). Although Southee's infamous (or rather, infamously interpreted) response "Literature cannot be the business of a woman's life, and it ought not to be" (Southey 1837, 166) had apparently prompted a disillusioned Charlotte to state that "...I (she) shall never more feel ambitious to see my name in print..." (Brontë 1837, 9), yet the disillusionment, thankfully, did not last long. In 1840, Charlotte posted her prose tale, a "demi-semi novelette" (Brontë 1840, 27) to Hartley Coleridge (which was rejected again), in 1847, after having already refused by six publishers, she submitted her manuscript of *The Professor* to Messrs Smith, Elder & Co. and only a few months later, on being rejected again for the seventh time, she tried to convince the publisher that the work "...might be published without serious risk if its appearance were speedily followed up by another work from the same pen of a more striking and exciting character." (Brontë 1847 (a), 85) Brontë's perseverance yielded fruits and the later work of a 'more striking and exciting character' was finally published as *Jane Eyre*.

The short historical background to Charlotte Brontë's literary career has not been attempted in the present chapter to highlight or emphasise the exceptionally enormous obstacles which often impeded and denied the woman writer's path to fame and success in the high Victorian age. Such impediments and denials were perhaps natural to an epoch or age that was notoriously infamous for foreunderstanding the woman as one who lacked 'a mind of her own'[1] and had complacently locked her up within the ideological dungeon of the angel in the house. What we have rather tried to suggest is the unfailing determination of Charlotte Brontë to pursue writing as a profession and thereby earn for herself the institutional identity of the author. In the "Roe Head Journal", a compilation of the semi-autobiographical narratives written during her early-life as a Governess at Roe Head, Charlotte Brontë is rather unequivocal about her distaste for the life of a governess and her longing desire to write. The helpless sighs of an aspirant author, who is caught up miserably within her material reality as a governess and cannot concentrate on her writing, is evident in the following entry from The Roe Head Journal:

> "...am I to spend all the best part of my life in this wretched bondage, forcibly suppressing my rage at the idleness, the apathy and the hyperbolical and the most asinine stupidity of those fatheaded oafs, and on compulsion assuming an air of kindness, patience and assiduity? Must I from day to day sit chained to chair prisoned within these four bare walls, while these glorious summer suns are burning in heaven and the year is revolving in its richest glow and declaring at the close of every summer day the time I am losing will never come again? ... I longed to write. The spirit of all Verdopolis, of all the mountainous North, of all the Woodland West, of all the river-watered East came crowding into my mind. If I had time to indulge it, I felt that the vague sensations of that moment would have settled down into some narrative better at least than anything I ever produced before. But just then a dolt came up with a lesson. I thought I should have vomited." (Brontë n.d., 403-404)

Virginia Woolf's immaculately pragmatist assertion "...a woman must have money and a room of her own if she is to write fiction..." (Woolf 1992, 50) seems impossibly appropriate when considered in the lights of the context described above. The ailing health of Mr. Brontë had prompted him to "seek to provide for his daughters" (Winnifrith 1988, 40) and in anticipation of an impending financial crisis, Charlotte Brontë had sought employment as a teacher and subsequently as a governess[2]. Biographer Tom Winnifrith points out that Charlotte was not a happy teacher and had, in all possibilities, "found teaching difficult". (Ibid. 42) However, keeping the more imminent and material concerns of the family in consideration (which, apart from Mr. Brontë's ailing health, also included the Anne's (Charlotte's sister) school fees and Branwell's (Charlotte's brother) failed career as a poet and painter) Charlotte pursued professions that were of little interest to her. In a letter to her sister Emile, Charlotte laments:

> "…a private Governess has no existence, is not considered as a living and rational being, is not considered as a living and rational being except as connected with the wearisome duties she has to fulfill. While she is teaching the children, working for them, amusing them, it is all right. If she steals a moment for herself she is a nuisance." (Brontë 1839, 12-13)

Charlotte's distaste for her profession laid not in the "oceans of needlework" (Ibid. 12) which preoccupied her but in her profound realisation that the Governess lacked a room (in the most irreducible sense of the word) of her own. While she earned a salary "…not really more than £16" (Brontë 1841, 29) at the Upperwood House (it can be assumed that her salary at the Sidgewick house was no better[3]), her chief concern was the lack of leisure that would let her give room to her creative preoccupations. In a letter to W.S. Williams, Charlotte Brontë expresses her discontent at the lack of leisure in the life of a Victorian woman and claims that no social reform can satisfactorily engage with the 'condition of the woman' question without contemplating a remedy to this naturalised ideal of womanhood where "…a woman has little family to rear and educate and a household to conduct, her hands are full, her vocation is evident—when her destiny isolates her—…she must do what she can—live as she can—complain as little—bear as much—work as well as possible" (Brontë 1848 (a), 108) Brontë's explicit critique of the patriarchally conditioned ideal of womanhood also implicitly points out that the woman, caught up in her "proper duties" (Gaskell 2005, 166), has no room of her own.

Virginia Woolf considers this lack of a room, in a broader perspective, as the underlying motive behind the nineteenth century women writers' preference for novel as a genre of practice. For Woolf, the unconducive exposed space of the general sitting room, which was the only available room which the middle-class woman writer could use to pursue her craft, lacked the seclusion that was necessary for the practice and production of thoughtful genres like poetry and play. It could, at best, host the creation of novels—a genre which, in Woolf's opinion, required "less concentration". (Woolf 1992, 96) However, for the Victorian middle-class woman writer, who was in search of "…any corner where I (she) could really be alone" (Brontë 1848(b), 114), the desired room was not merely an architectural category. Rather, it was a synecdochical symbol of the much-desired leisure that would allow her to indulge her creative talents. Many Victorian novelists lacked the room to write or retrospect their art. Their pressing material concerns had thrust upon them the *grander* project of homemaking, either as married wives or as employed governesses. Charlotte Brontë was no exception; chained by the shackles of her material reality, she was desperately striving for a fairy tale denouement whereby she would find a room to pursue her craft and let her craft sustain the room. This would only be possible if she could earn for herself the socio-economic status of the author.

It is worth mentioning in this context that Charlotte Brontë's career as an author was not smooth. As mentioned before, many of her early writings were rejected by publishers and reputed litterateurs had discouraged her to pursue her creative interests. Tom Winnifrith reminds us that until *Jane Eyre*, Charlotte Brontë's literary ventures had failed (Winnifrith 1988, 74). Such consistent failures had been instrumental in planting within Charlotte's consciousness the seeds of self-doubt and apprehension. Elizabeth Gaskell notes that the ""stringent" letter" of Southee, previously referred to, had convinced a young Charlotte Brontë to "...put aside, for a time, all idea of literary enterprise" (Gaskell 2005, 169). When she had finally acquired the courage to pursue her literary aspirations meaningfully and had sent the manuscript of her poems, along with her sisters', to various publishers, she was prepared to realise that "...neither we nor our poems were at all wanted..." (Brontë 1850, 272) In her preface to the 1850 edition of "Wuthering Heights and Agnes Grey" Charlotte revealed that all the three sisters' decision of publishing under Christian masculine names were outcomes of their "...vague impression that authoresses are (were) liable to be looked on with prejudice..." (Ibid. 271) Elizabeth Gaskell notes that even after the profound success of Jane Eyre, the author, "...unaccustomed to adopt a sanguine view of any subject..." had "timidly" reacted to "...the idea of success." (Gaskell 2005, 304) She further remonstrates that in context of the immediate success and popularity of the novel, Charlotte Brontë had confessed to her that she had "...hardly expected that a book by an unknown author could find readers." (Ibid. 307)

Hence, it is rather intriguing to decipher Charlotte Brontë's untimely hope about the novel's success among its readers, even before the publication of the work. That she had bargained with her publishers is evident from her letter to Smith Elder & Co. dated September 12, 1847. In this letter, Brontë remarks that she had consented to the "conditions" of the publisher only after she had felt "...convinced that in case the ultimate result of my (her) efforts should prove more successful than you now anticipate, you would make some proportionate addition to the remuneration you at present offer." (Brontë 1847 (b), 86-87) This perceivable note of confidence in an author who has been so long seasoned in rejections is unprecedent and worth a critical examination. What had, all of a sudden, made Charlotte Brontë anticipate success while her lived reality as an author had so long been steeped in failure and disillusionment? Was it an arbitrary reflection of her Robert Bruce like will (Gaskell 2005, 288) that had ever refused to surrender to the perennial climate of adversities? Or, was it a more rational hope, formed out of the author's foreknowledge that the work will be popular among readership, for she has deliberately crafted it so?

It ought not to come as a surprise to us that a woman writer (writing under the masculine *nom de plume* Currer Bell) — desperate to secure a career as an author against extreme personal and systemic adversities, would aim to produce a text with the pre-consideration of readership in mind. "Business reasons" (Gaskell 2005, 299) had been elementary in Messers. Smith and Elder's rejection of the manuscript of her first novel *The Professor* and the author was now considerate of an extra-literary consideration called acceptability. Her correspondences with her publisher during the process of publication of *Jane Eyre* foreground her intent and unfailing motive to "suit the public taste better" (Brontë 1847 (b), 86); in the immediate after-period of publication the correspondences highlight her intense concern for "a brisk sale" (Brontë 1847 (c), 305) of the novel. In response to G.H. Lewes's cautionary advice "beware of melodrama"[4] (Brontë 1847 (d), 312), she is quick to point out that her previous work, i.e. the manuscript of *The Professor*, had been rejected because the publisher felt that "such a work would not sell" (Ibid.) and subsequently six other publishers, who had all refused to accept the work, had unanimously agreed that "...it (the manuscript) was deficient in 'startling incident' and 'thrilling excitement'". (Ibid.) Although in the same letter Charlotte Brontë claims that *Jane Eyre* had met with similar criticisms but was later accepted, thereby implying that she had not followed the publishers' advice and not compromised with realism, nevertheless the latter half of her letter seems to suggest otherwise. In this section, Brontë is critical of Lewes's understanding of realism and one cannot miss the strains of a guarded caustic cynicism in her ardent endeavour to "...direct your (Lewes's) attention to certain literary evils" (Ibid.) and requesting him to "...bestow a few words of enlightenment on the public who support the circulating libraries..." (Ibid.). The cynicism is all the more prominent when considered in lights of her later confession in a letter to G.H. Lewes, "...You were a stranger to me. I did not particularly respect you. I did not feel that your praise or blame would have any special weight." (Brontë 1847 (e), 315) Katie Kapurch has rightly pointed out that as a writer, Charlotte Brontë was not aversive to melodrama and sensationalism and her "...investment in Romantic epics, evident in her Angria tales...reveal a penchant for the sensational that stretched back to her childhood." (Kapurch 2016, 12) Neither is the novel *Jane Eyre*, contrary to its author's claim, free from sensationalist and melodramatic strains. Rather, the author had "...invested much of the importance of the novel (i.e., Jane Eyre) in those sensational moments, legitimizing their narrative vitality." (Ibid.)

Lewes's letters to Charlotte Brontë have not managed to survive. However, his review published on December, 1847 in the *Fraser's Magazine* restates his concern over "...too much melodrama..." (Lewes 1847, 692) in *Jane Eyre*, a concern which he had (presumably) already conveyed to Charlotte Brontë in form of a personal letter. Along with this, Lewis is also mildly critical of the "improbability" quotient in the novel, which he identifies as typical to the "circulating library" culture. (Ibid.)

Such critical commentaries and authorial confessions convincingly question the popular presumption that unproblematically valorise *Jane Eyre* as a classic. They are able to re-historicise the novel as a popular literary work and problematise the canonical status currently accorded to the novel. A basic acquaintance with the plot makes one aware of the diverse stylistic and thematic strategies undertaken by the author to secure acceptability among readership. Besides the melodramatic and the sensational, there are recurrent overtones of the romantic, the Gothic and a free will-ed subjectivity. Above all, the novel follows the typical pattern of a nineteenth-century romance in its strategic use of the motif of marriage to accomplish the desired denouement of a female bildungsroman and to signify the female protagonist's successful initiation into a pragmatic ideal of life. Pamela Ragis's definition of the Romance emphasises the trope of "betrothal" (Ragis 2003, 17) as the objective of the narrative design of a romance[5] and identifies it as an exclusive mark of distinction and the denouement of Brontë's *Jane Eyre* begins with the famous, contented assertion of the authoritative first-person voice "Reader, I married him." (Brontë 1971, 382) Marriage seems to be the long-awaited station where the protagonist Jane Eyre's carriage of life has finally arrived.

In fact, the endeavor to read Jane Eyre as romance is anything but novel. Critics like Helen Moglen have observed that "the form and structure of Jane Eyre approximate the form and structure of romance which Northrop Frye describes". (Moglen 1976, 108) Gill Frith holds a deeper conviction in asserting that "Brontë's novel is also a romance, the mother-text of all those novels—written, and read, primarily by women—in which innocent heroine meets brooding hero and lives happily ever after." (Frith 1993, 172) What is more, the disenfranchised female subject's journey towards enfranchisement against vital socio-economic adversities replicate the form of the Classical Romance. Gilbert and Gubar observe that *Jane Eyre* borrows "the mythic quest-plot…of Bunyan's male *Pilgrim's Progress*…" to consider the "…female realities within her and around her: confinement, orphanhood, starvation, rage even to madness." (Gilbert and Gubar 2000, 477) While such considerations on the *condition of women* definitely accord an element of social realism to the novel, yet, such strains of realism are not extraneous to the genre of the Romance. Romance, although duly associated with the notion of fancy or wish fulfillment, is not necessarily devoid of reality. On the contrary, as Janice Radway points out, "elementary realism" (Radway 1984, 197) is often a characteristic feature of Romance as it allows the woman reader to easily decode the narrative. Brontë's thematisation of the "female realities within her and around her" allows the Victorian woman reader to easily decode Jane's world as a representation of her own material reality. This in turn enhances her possibility to unproblematically and impartially identify with Jane. Such identification produces and ensues in the woman reader that febrile sensation of 'wish fulfillment' (Ibid., 151) which is often the characteristic effect of a romance. Hence, the *condition of women* trope in the novel does not compromise the novel's generic identity as a romance but rather complements it.

In fact, there are numerous other characteristics and traits in the novel which can arguably qualify it as an "ideal romance" (Radway 1984, 119). Janice Radway's field study of the reading habits of a small group of Romance readers (all women and living in a midwestern US town called Smithton) enables her to decipher certain common characteristics (which she calls "crucial generative matrix" (Ibid. 120)) in all the Romances which her research participants identify as ""excellent" or "favorite" examples of the genre" (Ibid.). Subsequently, on the basis of these characteristics, Radway proceeds to elaborate her hypothesis of the ideal romance.

Radway's understanding of the ideal romance is too elaborate to define in a nutshell. There are paradoxical assertions and characteristic nuances which cannot be complicitly contained within the constricted design of a definition. Neither does the present chapter aim to do so. Instead, in its endeavour to consider the possibilities of reading *Jane Eyre* as a romance, the chapter only highlights the characteristics of an ideal romance that are locatable in the novel. It should be mentioned beforehand that Brontë's *Jane Eyre* is not mentioned by any of the research participants in Radway's survey as a reading preference. However, that should not be an impediment to our evaluation of the resemblances that the novel bears with an ideal Romance. Aristotle's elaboration on tragedy, although typically constrained to his contemporary repertoire of Greek theatre, has been endlessly used by literary critics worldwide to determine whether a play qualifies as a tragedy. Likewise, one can afford to use Radway's hypothesis on ideal Romance to consider if a literary text does qualify as a Romance, without really being concerned if the same text had been considered by Radway while proposing her hypothesis.

A considerable number of features of the ideal romance can be traced in *Jane Eyre*. The eponymous protagonist, resonating Radway's contention, is initially *unwomanly* (emphasis mine) in nature and possesses an "...early rebelliousness against parental strictures" (Ibid. 123). Her cruel guardian Mrs. Reeds finds her disregardful towards her elders and Bessie's maid Abbot retorts that "I (she) never saw a girl of her age with so much cover." (Brontë 1971, 10) Also, her voracious reading habit and her violent reaction to the physical brutality of John Reeds makes her resemble the Radwayian heroine of an ideal romance who is "differentiated from her more ordinary counterparts in other romance novels by unusual intelligence or by an extraordinary fiery disposition" (Radway 1984, 123). Radway remarks that ideal romances often "...begin by expressing ambivalent feelings about female gender by associating the heroine's personality or activities with traits and behaviour usually identified with men." (Ibid. 123-124) Jane's unwomanly countenance and the initial lack of typically feminine qualities in her, that is revealed in the very opening chapters of the novel, leaves a remarkable impression in the reader's mind. Eizabeth Rigby, an early reviewer of *Jane Eyre*, observed that one can "neither fondle nor love" (Rigby 1848) little Jane for she possesses a "...hardness in her infantile earnestness, and a spiteful precocity in her reasoning..." and "...is of a nature to dwell upon and treasure up every slight and unkindness, real or fancied..." (Ibid.) Another review published in The Christian Remembrancer on January 1848 had emphasised the "unfeminine" tone of the novel and had noted the abundance of "...masculine power...combined with masculine hardness, coarseness, and freedom of expression" (Christian Remembrancer, 1848) in the novel.

However, the character of Jane is not the only premise which can support the proposition that *Jane Eyre* is an ideal Romance. Instead, there are other characteristics of an ideal romance in the novel. For instance, the character of Mr. Edward Fairfax Rochester. Radway observes that the "hero of the romantic fantasy is always characterized by spectacular masculinity" (Radway 1984, 128) where "almost everything about him is hard, angular and dark" and the reader is overtly and repeatedly made aware "…that every aspect of his being, whether his body, his face, or his general demeanor, is informed by the purity of his maleness". (Ibid.) The very introduction of Mr. Rochester in the narrative action bears an overpowering mark of maleness and it is possibly worthwhile to revisit the celebrated passage which renders, in a subjective voice, the protagonist heroine's firsthand impression of the hero:

> "His figure was enveloped in a riding cloak, fur collared, and steel clasped; its details were not apparent, but I traced the general points of middle height, and considerable breadth of chest. He had a dark face, with stern features and a heavy brow; his eyes and gathered eyebrows looked ireful and thwarted just now…" (Brontë 1971, 96)

Such overtly descriptive emphases on masculine physical attributes and manly attire prominently establish the trope of dark masculinity in the novel, which is reflected further in the reserved countenance of the hero. Radway claims that ideal Romances often emphasise on the "hero's reserve, indifference, and even cruelty when he is first confronted by the heroine." (Radway 1984, 129) One cannot probably miss the disinterestedness that the hero in *Jane Eyre*, i.e., Rochester depicts in his first encounter with the heroine:

> "'Can I do anything?' I asked again.
> 'You must just stand on one side,' he answered as he rose, first to his knees, and then to his feet.
> … 'If you are hurt, and want help, sir, I can fetch some one either from Thornfield Hall or from Hay.'
> 'Thank you; I shall do: I have no broken bones—only a sprain;' and again he stood up and tried his foot, but the result extorted an involuntary 'Ugh!'" (Brontë 1971, 96)

Jane Eyre is honest to admit that she would have quit the place easily but for "the frown, the roughness of the traveller" (Ibid. 97) and quickly informs the reader that the fallen stranger "had hardly turned his eyes" (Ibid.) towards her, i.e., noticed her, until she had expressed her resolve to stay by him till he was "fit to mount your (his) horse". (Ibid.)

However, Rochester's resemblance with the perfect hero of an ideal Romance exceeds his dark masculinity and his outwardly indifferent and impolite attitude. He also resembles the ideal Romantic hero in his confession that he had once "...a kind of rude tenderness of heart" (Ibid. 113) which, due to the unfortunate touch of ill fortune, had given way to a nature that is "hard and tough as an Indian rubber-ball." (Ibid.) Rochester's hope for humanisation — a "final re-transformation from India-rubber back to flesh" (Ibid.) and Jane's significant role in making the transformation possible are typical to the plot of an ideal Romance. Radway points out that very often the romantic hero in an ideal Romance, otherwise depicting an exemplary masculinity, always bears in him an intimation of a "softness" (Radway 1984, 128) that is generously nurtured and nourished by the heroine to "magically remake a man incapable of expressing emotions..." (Ibid. 127) into an ideal figure who possesses both masculine power and prestige and an empathic consciousness of the woman.

Hence, it is perhaps not impossible to read *Jane Eyre* as an example of ideal Romance and perfectly possible to read it as a Romance. Yet, it is striking that not only the research participants of Smithton but also most of the Romance readers till date do not even consider the novel as a Romance, let alone list it as their favourite. The reason perhaps is due considerably to the unexplainably problematic policies of canon formulation. However, there are also salient traits in the text which situate the novel in distinction from the generic tradition of a Romance. For instance, unlike the stereotyped Romance, there are no contending rivals in the novel who can threaten the happy unison of the hero and the heroine. Bertha Mason is too disenfranchised to arouse any form sexual jealousy in Jane; John Rivers is too incestuously personal (as is revealed in due course, he is Jane's adopted brother) and too "cold" (Brontë 1971, 351) to be a substitute for Rochester. Although a temporary crisis disrupts Jane's idyllic marriage to Rochester yet there is an essential lack of "...a true villain, who actually attempts to abduct the heroine from the arms of the hero." (Radway 1984, 133) Such villains, as

Radway contends, are indispensable to the narrative design of an ideal Romance. Also, one could argue that Jane's marriage to Rochester is not the most Romantic and fantastic marriage. Unlike other marriages in conventional Romances, it is founded not on a love that is flamed by desire but by sympathy. Most importantly, marriage for Jane is not the only means of agency acquisition, as is often the case with Romance. Jane acquires her agency independently; the balance of power is apparently inverted in this unconventional marriage where the woman has a considerable upper hand and marries not to find a means to emancipation but to emancipate the disenfranchised and marginalised masculine subject. Indeed, marriage in the novel, is the last hope of enfranchisement for Rochester. Of course, one could further contend that such a marriage, in which the woman possesses a definite superiority over the man, is the absolute fantasy of a Victorian woman reader and thereby stress that the novel is not just an ideal but a sublime Romance. Such ambiguities and paradoxes exist as irreducible aporias in the novel.

The novel, owing to such irreducible aporias and ambiguous approaches to the form of the Romance, is perhaps a 'more than Romance'. It has definite traits of a Romance and only a brief historical reading of the material conditions of the production and the reception of the text clearly suggest that the novel was intended to be popular. The Romance had been an exceedingly popular literary genre in the Victorian age and Charlotte Brontë was perhaps consciously trying to re-produce certain generic traits of the romance to ensure a brisk popularisation of her work. However, like her sister Emily, she was also simultaneously trying to interrogate the limits of the genre by accomplishing her own modulations and moderations. It is perhaps these faithful interrogations that have contributed to the birth of a text whose popularity has outlived the limits of time and space.

Notes:

1. Virginia Woolf in her essay "Professions for Women" argues that the archetypal Victorian angel in the house was a woman who was born to please masculine sensibilities and was expected to possess no agency of her own that was outside the conditioned ideal of womanhood propagated by Victorian culture.
2. Although M. Jeanne Peterson claims that the mid-nineteenth century usage of the term governess also signified a woman who taught in a school, yet the present chapter has preferred to use the word in its lexical sense. The Oxford dictionary defines the governess as a woman employed to teach the children of a rich family in their home and to live with them.
3. M. Jeanne Peterson claims that Victorian governesses were miserably underpaid, with their average annual salary ranging between £20 and £45 a year. Also see Charlotte Brontë's letter to W.S. Williams dated 12th May, 1848 in Selected Letters of Charlotte Brontë (ed. Margaret Smith)
4. G.H. Lewes had read Jane Eyre and had responded to the novel, in form of a personal letter to the author. Unfortunately, the letter does not survive and we can, following the footprints of other scholars like Franklin Gary, only assume the content of Lewes's letter from Brontë's response to the same, both in form of a letter to Lewes dated Nov. 6th, 1847 and a letter to Williams, written on the same day. Brontë's responses convince us that Lewes had expressed his appreciation while being simultaneously critical of the melodramatic strains in the novel.
5. Note that Ragis defines The Romance novel as a "work of prose fiction that tells the story of the courtship and betrothal of one or more heroines."

Bibliography:

Bossche, Chris R. Vanden. 2005. "What Did "Jane Eyre" Do? Ideology, Agency, Class and the Novel". *Narrative*, Vol. 13, no. 1 (January): 46-66. JSTOR. https://www.jstor.org/stable/20107362. Accessed on 15th April, 2021.

Brontë, Charlotte. 1836 (Approx). "I'm just going to write because I can't help it". In Charlotte Brontë, *Jane Eyre*, edited by Richard J. Dunn. New York: W.W. Norton & Company, 1971. (a)

...Letter to Robert Southey, December 19, 1836. In *Selected Letters of Charlotte Brontë*, edited by Margaret Smith. Oxford: Oxford University Press, 2007. (b)

..."All this day I have been in a dream". n.d. In Charlotte Brontë, *Jane Eyre*, edited by Richard J. Dunn. New York: W.W. Norton & Company, 1971.

...Letter to Robert Southey, March 16, 1837. In *Selected Letters of Charlotte Brontë*, edited by Margaret Smith. Oxford: Oxford University Press, 2007.

...Letter to Emily Jane Brontë, June 8, 1839. In *Selected Letters of Charlotte Brontë*, edited by Margaret Smith. Oxford: Oxford University Press, 2007

...Letter to Hartley Coleridge. December 10, 1840. In *Selected Letters of Charlotte Brontë*, edited by Margaret Smith. Oxford: Oxford University Press, 2007.

...Letter to Ellen Nussey. March 3, 1841. In *Selected Letters of Charlotte Brontë*, edited by Margaret Smith. Oxford: Oxford University Press, 2007.

...Letter to Messrs Smith, Elder & Co. August 7, 1847. In *Selected Letters of Charlotte Brontë*, edited by Margaret Smith. Oxford: Oxford University Press, 2007. (a)

...Letter to Messrs Smith, Elder & Co. September 12, 1847. In *Selected Letters of Charlotte Brontë*, edited by Margaret Smith. Oxford: Oxford University Press, 2007. (b)

...Letter to Messrs Smith, Elder & Co. October 26, 1847. In *The Life of Charlotte Brontë* by Elizabeth Gaskell. New York: Barnes and Noble Classics, 2005. (c)

...Letter to G. H. Lewes, Esq. November 6, 1847. In *The Life of Charlotte Brontë* by Elizabeth Gaskell. New York: Barnes and Noble Classics, 2005. (d)

... Letter to G. H. Lewes, Esq. November 22, 1847. In *The Life of Charlotte Brontë* by Elizabeth Gaskell. New York: Barnes and Noble Classics, 2005. (e)

...Letter to W. S. Williams. May 12, 1848. In *Selected Letters of Charlotte Brontë*, edited by Margaret Smith. Oxford: Oxford University Press, 2007. (a)

…Letter to W. S. Williams. July 31, 1848. In *Selected Letters of Charlotte Brontë*, edited by Margaret Smith. Oxford: Oxford University Press, 2007. (b)

…"Preface to Wuthering Heights and Agnes Grey". 1850. In *The Life of Charlotte Brontë* by Elizabeth Gaskell. New York: Barnes and Noble Classics, 2005.

…1971. *Jane Eyre* edited by Richard J. New York: W.W. Norton & Company.

Christian Remembrancer. 1848. "Art IV.—Jane Eyre: an Autobiography. By Currer Bell. Second Edition. Smith, Elder and Co., Cornhill". Archive.org. https://ia802605.us.archive.org/4/items/nschristianremem15londuoft/nschristianremem15londuoft.pdf. Accessed on 3rd April, 2021.

Frith, Gill. 1993. "Women, Writing, and Language: Making the Silences Speak." In *Thinking Feminist: Key Concepts in Women's Studies*, edited by Diane Richardson and Victoria Robinson, 151-176. New York: Guilford Press.

Gaskell, Elizabeth. 2005. *The Life of Charlotte Brontë*. New York: Barnes and Noble Classics.

Gilbert, Sandra M. and Susan Gubar. 2000. *The Madwoman in the Attic: The Woman Writer and the Nineteenth-Century Literary Imagination*. London: Yale University Press.

Kapurch, Katie. 2016. *Victorian Melodrama in the Twenty-First Century: Jane Eyre, Twilight, and the Mode of Excess in Popular Girl Culture*. New York: Palgrave Macmillan.

Lewes, G.H. 1847. "Recent Novels: French and English". Fraser's Magazine for Town and Country, xxxvi (December): 686—695. https://babel.hathitrust.org/cgi/pt?id=mdp.39015030944956&view=1up&seq=741. Retrieved from HATHITRUST Digital Library on 11th April, 2021.

Miller, J. Hillis. 1987. "The Ethics of Reading". *Style*: Deconstruction, Vol. 21, no. 2 (Summer): 181-191. JSTOR. https://www.jstor.org/stable/42946145. Accessed on 8th April, 2021.

Moglen, Helene. 1976. *Charlotte Brontë: The Self Conceived*. New York: W. W. Norton.

Radway, Janice A. 1984. *Reading the Romance: Women, Patriarchy and Popular Literature*. London: The University of North Carolina Press.

Ragis, Pamela. 2003. *A Natural History of the Romance Novel*. Philadelphia: University of Pennsylvania Press.

Rigby, Elizabeth. 1848. "Vanity Fair—and Jane Eyre". *The Quarterly Review.* Re-posted by Derek Turner on March 23, 2012. http://www.quart erly-review.org/classic-qr-the-original-1848-review-of-jane-eyre/. Accessed on 3rd April, 2021.

Southey, Robert. "Letter to Charlotte Brontë, 12th March, 1837". In *The Life of Charlotte Brontë* by Elizabeth Gaskell. New York: Barnes and Noble Classics, 2005.

Spivak, Gayatri C. 1985. "Three Women's Texts and a Critique of Imperialism". *Critical Enquiry: "Race", Writing and Difference*, Vol. 12, no. 1 (Autumn): 243-261. JSTOR. https://www.jstor.org/stable/1343469. Accessed on 1st April, 2021.

Winnifrith, Tom. 1988. *A New Life of Charlotte Brontë*. London: Macmillan Press.

Woolf, Virginia. 1992. *A Room of One's Own and Three Guineas*. Oxford: Oxford University Press.

Post Script

Why my Children Love Cinderella and I Don't: Negotiations with a Classic-Popular Fairy Tale

Anisha Ghosh

1990's, Elementary school, second standard, the little plump Bengali girl in a school somewhere in the NCR was picked to play a part in one of the most frequently heard fairy tales from her mother — Cinderella. As excited as the girl was for the auditions, the results didn't quite match up to her expectations as she was picked not for the part of Cinderella, but for one of her 'wicked' step sisters! She was disheartened, slightly offended as her fragile moral ego of being a "good girl" in school, the class topper teacher's pet, the face of the school in important events was injured when she was nominated for playing not the "good girl Cinderella" but her tormentor. However, the fear of being excluded was far bigger than her moral ego and hence she accepted whatever part was offered, though with a heavy heart. She always wondered, all through her days in that school, what actually prompted the choice. Was it better acting skills, or simply because the super senior who played Cinderella was taller than her, and slightly fairer and slimmer?

Years went by, and the little girl outgrew the world of stories only to grow up into a student, then teacher of literature. The rational cerebral thirty something that she has turned into now hardly relates to any of the two female parts–one missed and the other imposed — from her childhood world of stories. She refuses to mourn losing out on being able to play Cinderella, as much as she refuses to accept that any person can be as mean or insensitive as the wicked step sister she played. Cinderella now offends her in a different way, not quite because of her injured sense of morality but because of the cripple moral fabric the story upholds.

Our childhood is a time when we are most receptive to stories, heard and passed down by family elders; the legacy is continued by the subsequent generations orally weaving a nexus of stories within the extended family, branching out into other family units when the daughters are married off to other houses. Across different cultures, times and communities, it is women who are seen as the harbingers of stories. Be it the Big mother officiating the moonlight story telling sessions in Nigeria, or the virgin bride of King Shehryar who keeps postponing her execution by telling and withholding the denouement of thousand and one stories to the king every night, or the ubiquitous grandma of the Bengali children's story collection "Thakurmar Jhuli" — women are the puppet masters of the oral tradition of telling stories. Writer Gabriel Garcia Marquez too has admitted that he owes the unique storytelling quality of his writing to his grandmother's tales. The feminists of the second wave too challenged the dominant patriarchal perspective of the metanarrative of history with 'herstory' — history written from women's point of view. Such is the power of storytelling that it can challenge any written word or metanarrative, remould the truisms of the written word by a convincing narration of the unwritten.

An oft narrated story not only leaves a good feeling but also makes an inimitable impact on the consciousness of the child/ audience. The child/ audience is drawn into the make-believe world of the childhood stories so much so that they even buy the logic that the cow jumps over the moon. A very popular Bengali adage encapsulates this whole sense of the unreal being the reality of children's stories — *'golper goru gacchhe othe'* (meaning, the cows can climb trees in tales). Childhood stories are the first discursive space which unsuspectingly initiates the process of socialising and gendering of the child subject through an innocent yet potent tool. Despite the fact that the women control this oral tradition, they are mostly seen as the carriers passing down these tales with slight modifications, but still keeping the patriarchal, heteronormative moral essence intact from generation after generation. Seldom do they give a thought to re-narrating a tale into a more gender-neutral fashion or make the woman characters more empowered, enlightened or gentle to each other. The most popular fairy tales rebuild the myth of a "happily ever after" (emphasis is mine) and reinstate the faith in a perfect and heteronormative marital bliss.

Orality has its own share in building subjectivity, shaping identity and socialising the male and the female child through ubiquities as well as through exceptions if only the child/ subject is receptive enough to see through it. Orality creates a magic spell, a mesh of stories which are accepted as "stories" and hence the authenticity is never tried or tested. So, when Pinocchio tells a lie and his nose becomes longer, we believe that lying is wrong; when the Pied Piper gets the children of Hamelin captive to his tunes, we believe in the power of art and also in a vague sense of justice. Similarly, fairy tales like Snow White and Cinderella serve us the pettiness of a 'stepmother' towards their husband's children from the first marriage. No matter what their social status is — a queen or a middle class housewife — the common trait between the two infamous stepmothers of the two popular fairy tales is cruelty towards those not born of them. However, we come to believe in the concept of 'virtue rewarded' when these tormented girls find themselves the princes who dish out 'the happily ever after' as a reward to their perseverance and 'good conduct'. Can we really truly blame Mr. Samuel Richardson for using this hidden ulterior moral agenda as the blueprint for what we have as the first novel in the history of English Literature, *Pamela* or *Virtue Rewarded* (1740)?

Richardson's Pamela is, in a way, the Cinderella of the 18th century, the only difference is her notion of the happily ever after is fraught with the reformation of her tormentor. She is a house maid protecting her feminine virtue from the indecent sexual advances of her debauch master Mr. B. Then after a series of failed attempts of seduction, several sexual assaults and a period of abduction, Mr. B eventually 'reforms' and makes a marriage proposal to Pamela. To the utter shock of the informed reader, the lady concedes and the next part of the novel is devoted to how she adjusts herself in her new social role of the mistress of the house and the wife of a 'gentleman'. The moral agenda of Richardson is quite pragmatic and materialistic. There is an upward social ascent which comes as the fruit of a virtuous conduct, which, in a way is a commentary on the pragmatic aspect of conventional morality. In the same century, this materialistic aspect of conventional morality was brought under the scanner and satirised by Richardson's contemporary Henry Fielding in two of his novels — *Shamela*, a direct lampoon of *Pamela*, and *Joseph Andrews*, in which he just reverses the gender roles and turns the whole idea of sexual harassment at work (which actually is the problem Pamela should have been more worried about) into a gender role reversed prey predator equation. Fielding's *Joseph Andrews* laughs at the shallowness of conventional morality from the other side of the mouth and critiques the flimsy moral fabric upheld in Richardson's novel.

In *Cinderella*, conventional morality is encoded in a pattern of stereotypes through the characters — a virtuous maiden, her tormentor the evil stepmother, her benefactress the fairy godmother and her reward the Prince with the promise of a coveted 'happily ever after' (emphasis is mine). Cinderella's story too is a narrative of the rags to riches journey of an underdog. This motif has been adapted in different contexts and genres, so much so that the optimistic journey of a protagonist from adversity to affluence is termed as a Cinderella story. The heavyweight boxing champion J. J. Braddock is remembered as the "Cinderella Man", a name given to him by the American paparazzi after his glorious comeback and win against Max Baer in the 1935 heavyweight championship. Braddock hit an all-time low in his career due to a string of unfortunate hand injuries; he was compelled to work at the docks and depend on the welfare system for the sustenance of his family during the great depression, until his fairy tale comeback and success in heavyweight boxing. The biopic *The Cinderella Man* featuring Russell Crowe as J. J. Braddock is a beautiful illustration of the success story and, hence, the Cinderella motif on celluloid. The film is one of the finest instances of the Cinderella story in Hollywood mainstream cinema which avoids the pitfalls of the stereotypical success myth — success is not the product of a fortunate turn of incidents but the outcome of suffering, perseverance, hard work, family's support, self-care and self-healing. Another classic Hollywood instance of the Cinderella story can be found in the 1990 romcom *Pretty Woman* starring Julia Roberts and Richard Gere. Our

Cinderella in this feature film is not a damsel in distress tormented by the circumstances that befell her, but an independent woman who earns her bread by a way that is questionable and offensive to conventional morality of any society. She is a sex worker who reserves her agency in deciding whether or not to accept a client. The prince here is no unflawed righteous prototype of chivalry, but a hot shot man of business who hires her as a companion for a business deal. The uncanny connection develops, they fall in love, they realise the social rift and the impossibility of ever being together. Our Cinderella realises she can be so much more and decides to leave on an odyssey into something more worthy than her current occupation. The story ends in the happy union of the two as the hero acknowledges his feelings and goes back to her and again the choice is hers to take him back or not. She takes him back, and makes no secret of the fact that by doing so she rescued him of his otherwise loveless, joyless, mechanical, materialistic, emotionally challenged life.

In her 1997 book *Ella Enchanted*, Gail Carson Levine also reworks and brings back the question of agency. The Cinderella of the original fairy tale version is a passive recipient of good or bad luck. Her tribulations are brought upon by the doings of her stepmother and her callous father's unwillingness towards his daughter's wellbeing. The fortunate turn of events is brought upon by the fairy godmother who empowers her with a chariot, horses and a fine attire as a rite of passage to enter the royal banquet. The two women represent the two prototypes of womanhood which have always been pitted against each other in literature. Empowered thus, Cinderella imitates a social self which is not her own and happens to win the heart of the prince. The last test of perfection is fitting into the glass slipper she accidentally drops at the ball in her bid to return home before the magic expires. The prince, enamored by the charms of the mystery girl, keeps looking for the feet that fit the slipper and that's how ends up tracing Cinderella. The glass slipper symbolises conventional morality, feminine perfection, approved gender stereotypes, and Cinderella is the right fit! Something disturbingly normal (read normative) about the Cinderella story might have sparked off the imagination of Gail Carson Levine who in her fantasy novel gives the fairy tale a different spin. Ella is a metamorphosed Cinderella, with agency and choices. Ella bears the burden of a curse, that she cannot disobey a command, cast on her by a bewildered fairy at her birth. However, the curse of obedience is turned into a boon every time Ella obeys it. It helps her stand up to the ogres, and finally when she finds strength to refuse the command of Hattie and agrees to marry the Prince, she through her own agency releases herself from the curse. This Cinderella thus beaks the glass ceiling instead of fitting into the glass slipper.

Apart from the Cinderella story motif contributed to the popular culture, the fairy tale of Cinderella has created a psycho-social domino effect, as can be traced in the two popular phenomena in psychology – the Cinderella effect and the Cinderella complex. The Cinderella effect is a phenomenon in evolutionary psychology; it means the incidences of different types of child abuse and maltreatment of children by their step parents. Martin Daly and Margo Wilson in their paper "The 'Cinderella Effect': Elevated Mistreatment of Stepchildren in Comparison to those Living with Genetic Parents" write that step-parental care is an ancient ubiquitous phenomenon among all cultures and species, as taking care of the progeny of a new partner's prior unions is part of the mating practices, especially in species looking for a longer union than that of the period of one breeding season (species like the human). Daly and Wilson write,

Investing pseudo-parental care in a predecessor's offspring can thus be adaptive and favoured by selection. However, a stepchild must rarely have been as valuable to a stepparent's expected fitness as a child of one's own would be, and we may therefore anticipate that stepparents will not, in general, feel such wholehearted, self-sacrificial love for their wards as genetic parents so often do. It is on these grounds that we hypothesized, many years ago, that any and all sorts of abuse and exploitation would be seen to occur at higher rates in step-relationships than in genetic parent-child relationships, and that the differences would persist when possible confounds such as socio-economic status were controlled for (see Daly & Wilson 1998). This hypothesis has since been abundantly supported in our own research and in that of many others.

This differential (mis)treatment is what we refer to as the "Cinderella effect". (Daly and Wilson n.d., 1-2)

The data collected and interpreted by Daly and Wilson in the cases of fatal child battering or non-lethal abuse puts the role of the stepfather or the genetic mother's boyfriend/ male partner as the antagonist of the narrative of Cinderella Effect, which seemingly makes this study lopsided up to this point. However, a disclaimer comes from the authors as they take up the case of the stepmothers, claiming that the instances of small children living with stepmothers are less frequent in the databases captured in their research (done during the 1970's-90 in Canada, England and Wales and also in Australia and the US), hence the estimate of abuse risk from stepmothers is quite unreliable in those studies. Moving further, they cite other studies conducted at different periods to come to the conclusion that the abuse rate of step parents, irrespective of gender, to the children is much more than the abuse rate of genetic parents to their children:

The best evidence on this question comes from large child abuse data bases such as those analysed by Daly & Wilson (1981) and Creighton & Noyes (1989). Both studies included large numbers of stepmother cases and provided evidence that rates of physical abuse in stepmother and stepfather households are roughly similar and far in excess of those in two-genetic-parent households... We have already mentioned the identical abuse rates in stepmother and stepfather households in the Korean study by Kim & Ko (1990). Finally, stepmother households tend to be even more extremely overrepresented than stepfather households among adolescent runaways who aver that they are fleeing abusive families. (Daly and Wilson n.d., 6)

This overrepresentation factor cannot be overlooked when it comes to analysing the archetype of stepmother that is presented to the innocent reader in Cinderella, and throughout canonical English literature for that matter. This also raises the question if the origin of the Cinderella effect is in that portrayal or if that portrayal is too monstrous just because of its gender identity, so much so, that the narrative requires a fairy godmother, a benevolent female, to strike the fine balance. Also, the patriarchal subconscious of the literary text strategises shaping the feminine archetype of the 'good woman' through Cinderella, by pitting these two 'good woman/ bad woman' (emphasis is mine) archetypes against each other. In their feminist interrogation of the history of women in classical literature, Sandra Gilbert and Susan Gubar write about shaping a feminist poetics of literary studies. They draw attention to the ubiquity of the two female archetypes of 'angel' and 'monster' being so pervasive throughout the literature authored by men that these images of female benevolence and female monstrosity have seamlessly permeated in the work of women writers as well. They write:

From Anne Finch's Ardelia, who struggles to escape the male designs in which she feels herself enmeshed, to Sylvia Plath's "Lady Lazarus," who tells "Herr Doktor... Herr Enemy" that "I am your opus,"/"I am your valuable," the woman writer acknowledges with pain, confusion, and anger that what she sees in the mirror is usually a male construct, the "pure gold baby" of male brains, a glittering and wholly artificial child. With Christina Rossetti, moreover, she realizes that the male artist often "feeds" upon his female subject's face "not as she is but as she fills his dreams." (Gilbert and Gubar 2004, 813)

The patriarchal ploy to put female archetypes at cross purposes with each other goes back in time, beginning from a virtuous virgin mother image to the emasculating Dalila (Samson Agonistes), or the curious Eve to 'tempt' Adam into eating the forbidden fruit and bringing mortality to the mankind, a woman is either a nurturing mother or a seductress. In Cinderella the receptacle of the female archetype's cruelty and kindness is yet another woman, or a girl being socialised into womanhood. She has limited options to choose from when it comes to choosing her own role in the gender dynamics—the wicked stepmother or the nurturing fairy godmother. Finally, it is narrowed down to but one 'fit'—her glass slipper returned by the prince.

The glass slipper is fraught with many levels of symbolic significance. For one, it is the accepted normative mould that the collective unconscious of the society deliberately preserves as the positive heteronormative woman image. Cinderella makes three appearances in the ball and every time she has to leave before the vestiges of grandeur, that act as her gate pass, disappear in thin air and she is exposed as the 'misfit'. There is this latent desire to fit in, and a derived sense of empowerment when the 'good mother' bestows her benevolence through magic on her, in a way of directing the younger progeny to fit in and perpetuate the stereotypes. The glass slipper is very much a part of her attire, always already there holding her feet. At a symbolic level, it is an essence of the sex which, according to Judith Butler, is always already gendered. In her *Gender Trouble*, and beyond, Butler has questioned gendered acts as performative with no doer behind the deed. The repeated acts thus performed produce the (gendered) subject as an effect of the performances. Simone de Beauvoir's theory of gender as a social construct, challenging biological essentialism, puts sex before gender. When Beauvoir writes "One is not born but rather becomes a woman", she keeps sex before gender. Anatomy precedes the cultural significance that comes to be attached to the social destiny of this being, in other words 'being' decides the course of 'becoming'. In her essay "Sex and Gender in Simone de Beauvoir's The Second Sex", Judith Butler questions the sex gender divide and proposes the theory that perhaps sex was always already gender: "We never experience or know ourselves as a body pure and simple, i.e. as our 'sex', because we never know our sex outside of its expression as gender. Lived or experienced 'sex' is always already gendered. We become our genders, but we become them from a place which cannot be found and which, strictly speaking, cannot be said to exist" (Butler 1986, 39). Sex does not precede gender, rather sex is always, already gender, and in the present context the glass slipper exemplifies this idea. If the prince's act of returning the slipper to the rightful owner and checking the 'fit' before tying the knot of holy matrimony appears as a process of gendering that decides the social destiny of Cinderella, then a moment should be spared to think that the slipper was always already there, the prince just returns it. This act of 'returning' (emphasis is mine) and checking the fit can be read as what Butler calls the repetitive performative acts which produce the gendered subject as an effect.

This leads to another more serious and lasting impact of *Cinderella* on social psychology, an impact which perhaps every mother, every parent raising a girl child should take into consideration — the Cinderella Complex. If subjectivity/ identity is not essential but a discursive effect, then a critical reexamination of the Cinderella story heavily fraught with archetypes and stereotypes to shape a feminine consciousness should come under serious scrutiny. The Cinderella story is more like what Gilbert and Gubar identify as the "conduct books for ladies [that] proliferated, enjoining young girls to submissiveness, modesty, selflessness; reminding all women that they should be angelic" (Gilbert and Gubar 2004, 819). The Cinderella Complex is the discursive effect of the narrative of this fairy tale; it is a subconscious desire of women to be looked after, and a fear of independence. The term was first used by Agatha Christie in her 1955 novel *Hickory Dickory Dock*. The concept was later developed in the 1981 book *The Cinderella Complex: Women's Hidden Fear of Independence* by Colette Dowling. Cinderella complex is the fear women experience at the prospect of living a life on their own, fending for themselves and being responsible for their social and emotional well-being. Colette traces the roots of this fear in the socialisation of the female child — how they are conditioned since birth to live a life totally dependent on others, especially a male relative or partner. She takes the analogy of Cinderella who cooks, cleans and washes in silence for her abusive stepmother until she is rescued from her misery by the Prince Charming. This lack of agency is celebrated (or rewarded) with the myth of 'happily ever after' (emphasis is mine) as the carrot dangling for perfect feminine conduct in a heteronormative fairy tale universe. Colette describes her experience of discovering her own Cinderella complex in the book, when she gets romantically involved with a man and decides to move in with him. She writes:

> The moment the opportunity to lean on someone presented itself I stopped moving forward — arrived, in fact, at a dead halt. I no longer made decisions, rarely went anywhere on my own, rarely visited with my friends. In six months I had not met one deadline or gone through the friction involved in working out a contract with a publisher. A flight-from-stress had become my unconscious goal. I had slipped back — lounged back, really, as into a large tub of tepid water — because it was easier. Because tending flower beds and organizing the grocery shopping and being a 'good partner' is less

anxiety provoking than being out there in the adult world making a life for oneself. (Colette qtd. in Hanes 2020, n. pag.)

That is not to say that all women who choose to play the traditional role of a spouse/ mother/ caregiver/ nurturer exhibits Cinderella Complex; many participate in the heteronormative family arrangement with equal decision-making power and autonomy and build a life and a home as the outcome of the choices they make.

The Cinderella complex is not just a manifestation of women's latent fear of independence; it is also a manifestation of the lack of agency that is the root cause of the fear of independence. Social conditioning is a cumulative outcome of the literature one reads, the music one listens to, the movies one watches, the kind of small or deep talks one engages in, the company one keeps, the social media posts one creates or follows. It is an ensemble of anything and everything one is exposed to and absorbs. In this age of technological advancement and an upsurge of information one cannot avoid being exposed to information, but one can always choose the filters of absorption. This filter is agency. When a child protégé is exposed to seemingly innocent children's literature like the fairy tale of Cinderella, they may not be aware of how its effect may snowball into gender stereotypes. The impact of the Cinderella story on the feminine psyche and channelising young girls into the direction of perfect womanly conduct is only one side of the story. By shaping one gender stereotype it also sets another stereotype into motion—the male child is socialised into believing himself to be solely responsible for the well-being of a dependent female. He lives with this burden of masculinity all his life which often takes monstrous proportions manifesting itself in toxic male behaviour. Informed parents should always act as that filter of absorption so that the child does not passively accept the rationale of the story without raising a few important questions, or looking into the choices Cinderella could have made to shape her own destiny.

So, when the little girl from the 90's outgrows her dejection at being denied the role of Cinderella, grows into a thirty something who can see through the textual ploys and patriarchal subtext of pitting one archetype of womanhood against another to perpetuate the third conventional and convincing stereotype of femininity, she fears her progeny, real or imaginary, may fall into the same trap of taking Cinderella as a role model. For those who have chosen to live childfree, this fear of the Cinderella syndrome conjures up imaginary children who need to appreciate the story in complete understanding of the textual politics and the sexual politics going on beneath the seemingly innocent world, where everything is happily concluded. Like Charles Lamb's Elia in *Dream Children: A Reverie*, the childfree mother seats her imaginary children—a boy and a girl, in the most comfortable couch by the fireside and reads *Cinderella* to them with the hope that the children do not take a liking to the characters as they were sketched in the ancient fairy tale. She is as wary of the burden of the perfect woman image of Cinderella as of the gallant saviour image projected by the prince. Keeping her faith in the power of narration, she tries to strike a balance and create a new fairy tale out of her retelling of the age-old Cinderella story. She tutors her Cinderella to say no whenever she is not in the mood for doing the household chores, she paints the stepmother as equally loving and strict to all the children as and when needed. In that balanced world that is born in conscious narration, Cinderella scrubs the floor after finishing her school homework and the sisters help the mother in making dinner in a happy home where women back each other up. Then, on the day of the grand ball, the mother helps Cinderella and her sisters get ready within the limited means they can afford and encourages them to project their real selves and be appreciated for their real worth. This cancels out the need for sneaking into the ball and exiting it on time to avoid being divested of the borrowed glory, because Cinderella is glorious in her own being, comfortable in her own skin. It also makes a fairy godmother redundant as the stepmother adequately takes care of the whole situation. In the ball, Cinderella meets a charming young man with whom she forms a better connection than with the prince—one does not necessarily have to be a prince to be an agreeable choice for a partner or a friend. Cinderella exchanges contact (email, phone number, social media handle) with that new friend and decides to keep in touch. The story ends with Cinderella leaving the town for university education in the quest of building a happily ever after life for herself. By making the love story incidental, the narrator can save both the male and the female child from the repeating pattern of the damsel in distress and the Knight in shining armour coming to her rescue. Cinderella can be turned into a story of love, not a love story, a story of evolving mother-and-daughter relationship instead of a toxic tale of abuse by a step parent by clubbing the two mother figures into one. The essence of it being a success story of the underdog, the major motif of *Cinderella* has to be retained, only this time Cinderella reserves the agency of making her choices and shaping her own destiny. So even if gender is the effect of a set of repetitive performances, as Judith Butler has maintained in *Gender Trouble*, there is always a choice. The choices of performances are regulated, limited and discursive but there is an agency not in the 'what' but in the 'how' of doing a gender role.

Bibliography:

Browning, Robert. 2006. "The Pied Piper of Hamelin", Project Gutenberg. https://www.gutenberg.org/files/18343/18343-h/18343-h.htm. Accessed on 5th November, 2020.

Butler, Judith. 1990. *Gender Trouble*. London: Routledge.

… 1986. "Sex and Gender in Simone de Beauvoir's The Second Sex". *Yale French Studies: Simone de Beauvoir: Witness to a Century*, No. 72: 35-49. JSTOR. Stable URL Link: https://www.jstor.org/stable/pdf/293022 5.pdf?ab_segments=0%2FSYC-6168%2Fcontrol&refreqid=fastly-def ault%3A2c91e790a7235e2db66c19c865618c38. Accessed on 13th November, 2020.

Christie, Agatha. 2015. *Hickory, Dickory, Dock*. London: Harper Collins, 125th Anniversary Edition.

Collodi, Carlo. 2006. *The Adventures of Pinocchio*. Project Gutenberg. http://www.gutenberg.org/files/500/500-h/500-h.htm. Accessed on 11th November, 2020.

Daly, Martin and Margo Wilson. n.d. "The 'Cinderella Effect': Elevated Mistreatment of Stepchildren in Comparison to those Living with Genetic Parents". Semantic Scholar.org. https://www.cep.ucsb.edu/buller/cinderella%20effect%20facts.pdf. Accessed on 3rd November, 2020.

Dowling, Colette. 1981. *The Cinderella Complex: Women's Hidden Fear of Independence*. London: Fontana Paperbacks.

Fielding, Henry.1908. *The History of the Adventures of Joseph Andrews and his Friend Mr. Abraham Adams*. George Bell and Sons. https://www.stmarys-ca.edu/sites/default/files/attachments/files/Joseph_Andrews.pdf. Accessed on 9th November, 2020

Gilbert, Sandra and Gubar, Susan. 2004. "The Madwoman in the Attic". In *Literary Theory: an Anthology*, edited by Julie Rivkin and Michael Ryan, 812-825. Oxford: Blackwell Publishing. 2nd Edition.

Grimm, Jacob & Wilhem Grimm. n.d. *Cinderella*, https://www.pitt.edu/~dash/grimm021.html. Accessed on 19th November, 2020.

Hanes, Elizabeth, RN. 2020."Cinderella Syndrome: Signs you have it and How to Overcome it". Healthgrades. https://www.healthgrades.com/right-care/mental-health-and-behavior/cinderella-syndrome-signs-you-have-it-and-how-to-overcome-it. Accessed on 21st November, 2020.

Keyber, Conny (Henry Fielding). 2010. An Apology for the Life of Mrs. Shamela Andrews. Project Gutenberg. http://www.gutenberg.org/files/30962/30962-h/30962-h.htm. Accessed on 13th November, 2020.

Lamb, Charles.1883. "Dream Children: A Reverie". In *Essays of Elia*, 137-141. Macmillan & Co. https://www.google.co.in/books/edition/The_Essays_of_Elia/Q304AAAAYAAJ?hl=en&gbpv=1&dq=the+essays+of+elia&printsec=frontcover. Accessed on 16th November, 2020.

Levine, Gail Carson. 2017. *Ella Enchanted*. London: Harper Collins.

Milton, John. 2001. *Samson Agonistes*. Global Language Resources Inc., Djvu e-book edition. http://triggs.djvu.org/djvu-editions.com/MILTON/SAMSON/Download.pdf. Accessed on 7th November, 2020.

Pretty Woman. 1990. Directed by Garry Marshall, Performances by Julia Roberts and Richard Gere, Touchstone Pictures, Silver Screens Partners, regency International Pictures.

Richardson, Samuel. 2020. *Pamela or Virtue Rewarded*. Oxford: OUP.

The Cinderella Man. 2020. Directed by Ron Howards, performances by Russell Crowe and Renée Zellweger, Miramax Films.

Wiggin, Kate Douglas & Smith, Nora A. (Eds). 1909. *The Arabian Knights*, Charles Scribner's Sons. http://www.read.gov/books/pageturner/2003juv28132/#page/8/mode/2up. Accessed on 1st November, 2020.

About the Contributors

Arnab Dasgupta is a Ph.D. scholar at the Department of English, Presidency University, West Bengal, India. His Research Interests include Postmodern Fiction, Urban Literature and Children's Literature.

Mitarik Barma is Assistant Professor of English at Basanti Devi College, West Bengal, India. His research interests include Postmodern Fiction and Indian Writing in English

Shirsendu Mondal is Assistant Professor of English at Barasat College, West Bengal, India. His areas of interest include culture and media studies, Eighteenth century Novel and Postcolonial Literature.

Rajadipta Roy is Associate Professor of English at Maynaguri College, West Bengal. His research areas include Postcolonial Studies, modern Indian Literature and studies in visual arts.

Pinaki Roy is Professor of English, Raiganj University, West Bengal, India. He is a distinguished scholar of Detective Fiction and takes interest in War History and Literature.

Mandika Sinha is Assistant Professor of English at Southfield College, Darjeeling, West Bengal, India. Her areas of interest include Detective Fiction and Postcolonial Feminist Studies.

Shubham Dey is a Ph.D. scholar at the Department of English, University of North Bengal, West Bengal, India. He seeks interest in Genre Studies, Postcolonial Literature and Studies in Visual Arts.

Puja Chakraborty is a Faculty Member in the department of English at Malda Women's College, West Bengal, India. Her area of research focuses on Indian Genre Fiction and she takes interest in Gender studies, Postcolonial studies and contemporary Indian writing in English.

Jaya Sarkar is pursuing her Ph.D. in Cultural Studies at BITS Pilani (Hyderabad Campus), India. Her research areas include Posthumanism, Postmodernism, Feminist Studies, Digital Humanities, and Disability Studies.

Goutam Karmakar is Assistant Professor of English at Barabazar Bikram Tudu Memorial College, Sidho-Kanho-Birsha University, West Bengal, India. His areas of interest include Postcolonial Urban studies, Woman writing in Indian English and Diasporic Indian Poetry.

Madhuparna Mitra Guha is Associate Professor of History, University B.T. & Evening College, West Bengal, India. She is an expertise on Modern Indian History and takes interest in Partition studies and nineteenth century cultural history of England and India.

Anisha Ghosh is Assistant Professor of English at Inspiria Knowledge Campus, Siliguri, West Bengal, India. Her research interests include Modernism, Post-Modernism and Feminism.

ibidem.eu